READINGS IN RUSSIAN POLITICAL AND DIPLOMATIC HISTORY

THE DORSEY SERIES IN EUROPEAN HISTORY

EDITOR THEODORE S. HAMEROW *University of Wisconsin*

STROMBERG *A History of Western Civilization*

BLACK *Posture of Europe, 1815–1940: Readings in European Intellectual History*

WHITE *Medieval History: A Source Book*

SENN *Readings in Russian Political and Diplomatic History,* Volumes I and II

READINGS IN
RUSSIAN POLITICAL AND
DIPLOMATIC HISTORY

Volume I
The Tsarist Period

by

Alfred Erich Senn
University of Wisconsin

1966

THE DORSEY PRESS
Homewood, Illinois

For Ann, Eric, and Theresa

Preface

The student of Russian history is faced by a wealth of materials. Since 1945 an enormous literature on the Soviet Union has come into being in this country, consisting in monographs, text books, and anthologies. To be sure, this literature has tended to concentrate on the Soviet period of Russian history, but Russian history has more than a topical significance. American contributions to pre-1917 Russian history are also impressive. Therefore, any new collection of readings obviously has to justify itself as to its purposes and its manner of selection.

The editor's first concern has been to assemble items which are at the same time useful and hard to find. In this vein, he has intentionally ignored recent American writings. These are generally available to college students, and it seems senseless to reproduce them here.

On the other hand, a number of Soviet writings have been included in this collection. For the period before 1917 there are several accounts by Soviet historians. For the post-1917 period, these Soviet selections have a primarily documentary nature. (It may seem anachronistic to some to include readings from Stalin's works, but one must remember that Stalin molded the Soviet Union in his own image for a quarter of a century. His views were the official views of the Soviet government.)

Beyond this, contemporaneous materials have generally been chosen, ranging from Giles Fletcher's account of 16th-century Russia to 20th-century diplomatic dispatches.

As far as the emphases of the readings are concerned, the volume's major innovation is probably its concern for Russian diplomatic history. This has generally been a neglected field, at least for pre-1917 Russian history. Otherwise the readings are oriented toward political and economic history.

A last word on transliteration and spelling: all texts originally in English have been reproduced without change, whether they were written by Chinese, Russians, or 17th-century Englishmen. This of course has resulted in inconsistencies and even contradictions. Nevertheless, in the belief that such confusions are themselves a part of historical study, the decision was made to adhere to the original texts.

AES

Madison, Wisconsin
July, 1966

Table of Contents

CHAPTER 1

The Emergence of Muscovy

POLITICAL UNIFICATION

Modern Russian history begins with the reign of the Muscovite Grand Duke Ivan III, 1462–1505, a contemporary of Louis XII, Henry VII and Ferdinand and Isabella. Up to this time, the land inhabited by the East Slavs was divided into a multitude of principalities, most of them under the nominal suzerainty of the Golden Horde. The reigns of Ivan and of his father, Vasily the Blind, marked the beginning of a new era. Moscow first eclipsed and then subjugated most of the other principalities. The "Mongol yoke" was cast off. The rulers of Lithuania, long a serious rival, alienated themselves from the East Slavs by accepting the Roman Catholic religion. The following excerpt, by a noted Soviet historian, describes the "objective" conditions for Moscow's dramatic emergence. The writing is also notable as a period piece, written in the shadow of Stalin's last years in power.

The political unification of the Russian lands around Moscow constituted the most basic condition for their liberation from foreign rule, for "only a land united into a single centralized government could count on the possibility of a serious cultural-economic growth, on the possibility of establishing its own independence" (Stalin). The victory in the battle of Kulikovo, won by all-Russian forces under the leadership of the Grand Prince of Moscow, clearly showed to all the Russian people that there was only one historical path for the victory of the struggle for liberation—the path of creating a single, centralized state. A whole century, however, still passed before this difficult historic path was completed. Success in the struggle with the Golden Horde was closely tied with the success of the unification policy of the Muscovite grandducal authority. To the time of Ivan III belong the two most important developments: the basic liquidation of feudal disintegra-

Source: K. B. Bazilevich, *Vneshniaia politika russkogo tsentralizovannogo gosudarstva: vtoraia polovina XV veka* (Moscow, 1952), pp. 15–21.

1

tion and the final destruction of the rule of the Golden Horde. ". . . In Russia the subjugation of the appanage princes went hand in hand with the liberation from the Tatar yoke and it was finally established by Ivan III." (Marx and Engels)

The influence of external danger on the development of the Russian centralized political system did not disappear with the disintegration of the Golden Horde and with the full liberation of the Russian lands from their rule and oppression. The young Russian state historically was in a most difficult position. In the second half of the 15th century it was hemmed in by a ring of hostile encirclement: the eastern and southern frontiers were under assault by the Tatar khanates formed after the collapse of the Golden Horde; on the western border, the struggle with the Grand Duchy of Lithuania continued for the old Russian lands; the Livonian Order and Sweden were the source of a constant threat to the northwest Russian territory. The Russian nation, the true master of the great East European plain, was cut off from the seas which washed the shores of Eastern Europe. In such an unfavorable situation no country could count on a normal economic development. The hostile neighbors of Russia were interested in preserving the remains of feudal disintegration there, in creating conditions which would prevent the development of her military-political might. Therefore the struggle for the final unification of the Russian lands into a single state passed beyond the bounds of internal life and, in the 15th and the beginning of the 16th century, were a very important part of the foreign policy of the Moscow government.

The wars with the Kazan and Crimean khanates, the wars with Sweden, with the Livonian Order, and with Poland and Lithuania kept the whole military system of *Rus'* in constant battle readiness, and they were one of the chief sources of the tremendous material strain which lay very heavily on the peasant and urban population in the feudal order. Not to consider the influence of foreign affairs on the internal policy of Ivan III or of Ivan the Terrible is impossible, just as one cannot separate Peter the Great's reform work from the Northern War, although in both instances the regularity of internal socio-economic and political development is the basic factor. Thus the great reforms of Ivan III, which strengthened the centralized system of governmental authority, were enacted in the 1490s, before the war with Alexander Kazimirovich and the Livonian Order, 1500–1503, and the still more significant reforms of the 1550s, directed against the remnants of feudal disintegration, immediately preceded the Livonian war.

The foreign policy of Russia in the 15th–16th centuries was a part of the general process of the formation of the Russian centralized state.

The study of the foreign policy of Ivan III, from this point of view, is one of the tasks of the present study.

With this task is connected another, relating to the area of the international position of Russia and of its diplomatic system. In the course of the whole period of feudal disintegration and of the rule of the Golden Horde, *Rus'* could not have either a foreign policy or a general diplomatic system in the full sense of this word. At the end of the 15th century, the young Russian state entered into the wide area of international life at a very important moment in the history of Europe, when its new political map was being determined, the basic features of which lasted for some two centuries.

With the rise of the great European powers, the character of European conflicts changed sharply. In place of the internal feudal wars, which had continued throughout the Middle Ages, wars began between national states. Their goal was the winning of economic and political advantages. The struggle concerned disputed lands, the gaining of new territories in the interests of the nobility, and the growing bourgeoisie, new markets and the broadening of spheres of political influence. A special characteristic of the beginning of the new period in international relations was the formation of more or less significant coalitions, which broke Europe up into several hostile parts. Together with this, the Turkish danger took an ever greater meaning, really threatening Southern Europe after the taking of Constantinople by Muhammed II in 1453.

The great social and political changes in the life of the European peoples had a strong influence on the development of military affairs. The second half of the 15th century was the time of the rapid dying out of the medieval knightly organizations and the development of the hired infantry (*Landknechte*). Artillery became ever more important, especially after the firepower of the weapons was significantly increased by the use of iron balls. From this time the old knightly castles could not resist the force of artillery fire.

In the international struggle great advantages accrued to those powers who could first end feudal disintegration, and, on the other hand, those countries in which the medieval political system continued and in which the royal power was limited by feudal establishments, found themselves in a dangerous situation.

At the end of the 15th century Russia belonged to that number of states which had achieved great successes in national-political unification.

The power of the Muscovite Grand Duke significantly surpassed the power of his nearest western neighbors—the Grand Duke of Lithuania and the Polish King. Ivan III, after the annexation of Novgorod and Tver, in fact commanded all the forces of the country, and in foreign policy, as in military enterprises, he did not have to rely on the approval of his vassals—neither the "appanage" princes of the Muscovite grandducal family nor the heirs of the princely families who had merged into the old Muscovite nobility (*boiarstvo*). The concentration of power in his own hands made it possible for Ivan III, in the field of foreign policy, to turn to the resolution of the most important political tasks determining the honorable place of Russia in the system of European powers. Although not all Russia's interests, as a growing state, were satisfied, still in Ivan III's reign, there was gradually outlined that program of an active foreign policy which was only finally completed at the end of the 18th century.

That program can be defined in three basic directions: the struggle on the eastern and southern frontiers with the Tatar khanates which had been formed as a result of the disintegration of the Golden Horde; the struggle on the western frontier with Lithuania and Poland with the aim of uniting all the lands of *Rus'* (Russian, Ukrainian, Belorussian); and the struggle in the northwest against the aggressive actions of the Livonian Order and of Sweden, which gradually turned into a struggle for the winning of exits to the Baltic Sea. The priority and immediacy of these tasks changed depending on many circumstances, but on the whole they determined the general character of foreign policy of Russia in the course of some three centuries.

Although with the unification of the Russian lands around Moscow and with the development of the centralized governmental system at the end of the 15th and the beginning of the 16th centuries, the political disintegration of the Russian lands was basically ended, still the economic disintegration, characteristic of a feudal economy, was finally liquidated only in the 17th century in the process of the formation of an all-Russian market. But, although in the formation of the Russian centralized state, founded on a feudal economic base, the struggle with foreign danger had a great significance as a factor which hastened the formation of the centralized political system, the economic development of the Russian lands played a basic role in the matter of their unification under the Muscovite grandducal authority. In answer to the letter of Comrades Tsvetkov and Alypov, Comrade Stalin wrote: "Neither in my report nor in the theses, was anything said about the formation of the centralized state in Russia being '*not* a result of economic development *but rather* a result of the struggle with the Mongols and the other peoples of the East.' You must answer for this contrast, not I. I only said that the process of the formation of centralized states in the East of Europe, because of the necessity of defense, went *faster* than the process of the merging of the peoples into nations, as a result of which multi-national states were formed here before the liquidation of feudalism."

It is completely understandable that not one major question relating to the problem of the formation of the Russian centralized state, not only in the field of internal development, but also in foreign relations, can be separated from the socio-economic character of the land, from the class antagonisms and the class struggle. "One of the *characteristics* of production is that it never remains at one point for a long period and is always in a state of change and development, whereby changes in the means of production unavoidably bring change of the whole social structure, of social ideas, of political views, of political institutions—they call forth a reorganization of the whole social and political structure" (*History of the CPSU: Short Course*).

The rise in productive forces, which was already clearly expressed by the end of the 14th century, promoted the success of the unification policy of Moscow, and in turn the formation of the single Russian state produced propitious conditions for its economic development. The ending of feudal wars and hostile incursions, which were extremely ruinous to the population, had tremendous significance. After the attack on Moscow in 1451 by the Tsarevich Mazovshi, the Tatars did not come north of the Oka River until 1521, when the Crimean khan Muhammed-Firei and the Kazan khan Saip Girei succeeded in reaching the environs of the capital. This peaceful condition, continuing for seventy years, was not again repeated until the liquidation of the intervention in the first quarter of the 17th century. Therefore it is completely understandable that just in this period, the second half of the 15th century and the beginning of the 16th century, there occurred the intensive settling of the Muscovite center. . . . Above all one must note the significant successes in the area of artisan production, possible only on the basis of the social division of labor. Although we cannot, on the basis of the courses, draw up a more or less complete list of artisan specialties at the end of the 15th or at the beginning of the 16th centuries, still the rapid development in this period of artisan industry, especially in the cities, is not open to doubt.

According to the research of B. A. Rybakov, a new period in the development of the productive forces of the Russian village and estates begins with the middle of the 15th century. This is true even to a greater degree in the city. The great stone construction in the cities, far surpassing anything of this sort done in the period from the mid 14th to the mid 15th centuries, itself is a sure indicator of great successes achieved in construction and in a number of subsidiary specialties. The work of the blacksmiths and of the foundries also underwent a significant development, a number of relics being left of a high technical and artistic accomplishment. Among these are bells, cannon, weapons, church and every day utensils. There is every reason to assume that the demand for weapons, many times heightened because of the development of armed forces and of the great wars at the end of the 15th and the beginning of the 16th centuries, was completely satisfied by internal production. We cannot find one instance where Ivan III, in calling for foreign masters, invited specialists in the preparation of armor or of hand weapons. At the same time, such requests directed to the Grand Duke are often to be found in the relations with the Crimea.

CONSOLIDATION

The speed of Moscow's growth at the turn of the 15th to the 16th centuries necessitated great innovations at the Tsar's court. Soviet historians have defined these changes in sharp class terms.

The Grand Duke gradually tightened all the threads of administration of the united Russian lands around himself in Moscow. The centralization of the administration was achieved first by a mechanical unification of the governmental organs of the united duchies. Alongside the Muscovite servitor, managing the economy and land fund of the Muscovite duchy, there appeared the Tver, Nizhegorod, Ryazan, and Novgorod *dvoriane* (literally "courtiers"). Gradually central governmental agencies were organized. Thus, at the end of the fifteenth century the post of treasurer arose to direct the Grand Duke's treasury and relations with foreign states.

But it is still difficult to speak of any complete system of central administration at that time. It is enough to say that there was not even a special agency to direct such an important branch of governmental administration as foreign policy. The reception of foreign emissaries and the concern for their care devolved on the treasurers, the negotiations on clerks designated specially each time by the Grand Duke, who often talked with the envoys personally.

The organization of the military forces of the new state was a very difficult and important question. The basic nucleus of the Muscovite army was the "court" of the Grand Duke, i.e., the *dvoriane* who received parcels of land (*pomestie*) with peasants from the state on the condition of service. As the previously independent duchies were added to the Muscovite Grand Duchy, the appanage forces of the dukes who now lost their independence were added to the Grand Duke's forces and they were united under the general command of the Grand Duke.

Local administration, as before, was carried on by naming lieutenants (*namestniki*) and district leaders (*volosteli*) in the cities and regions, who took part of the income for themselves and thus "fed" themselves at the

---

Source: S. V. Bakhrushin, *Nauchnye trudy* (Moscow, 1954), II, 258–60, 261.

cost of the population. Under Ivan III only the first steps were taken to limit this system of "feeding" (*kormlenie*) which was difficult for the population and unprofitable for the Grand Duke's treasury. The government began to give the cities and regions special "regulatory deeds" which defined exactly the obligations to the tax collector.

Finally in 1497 a very important measure was introduced, strengthening the process of centralization. The *Sudebnik* was published which established order to judicial procedures throughout the state and which established a control over the tax collector. A special article was also put in the *Sudebnik* introducing a single time and special conditions for the "departure" of peasants, the so-called law of St. George's day. This law testifies to the success of centralization, but on the other hand, it clearly shows whose interests this centralization served. Such a law was necessary for the weaker feudal lords who could not keep the dependent peasants on their lands without the help of the central authority. . . .

Despite these steps toward centralization, the state which developed at the turn of the century, still cannot be considered centralized in the full sense of the word. Many traces of the earlier feudal disintegration still lived on. Yesterday's appanage dukes, subjected to the Muscovite Grand Duke, maintained their inherited lands, *vochinny*, and, passing into the role of vassals, they continued to exercise many sovereign rights. Besides the enserfed peasants, they had their own vassals and military servants, whose service they rewarded with land just as the Muscovite ruler rewarded his courtiers.

*   *   *   *   *

These powerful feudal lords continued to look upon their service to the Grand Duke not as an obligation of subjects but as a voluntary agreement of a vassal with a *seigneur*. When dissatisfied, therefore, they considered themselves justified in "refusing" service, in passing over to another ruler, even to an enemy of the Grand Duke. They did not consider such a step the treason it actually was; in their opinion, they were only asserting the right of "free servitors."

The service of the feudal nobility, as established by the formation of the unified state, was based on the system of *mestnichestvo*, which assured the better posts of administration to the high-born vassals of the Muscovite ruler. In summoning nobles to military service, to tax collecting, in seating them at the table, always and everywhere, the ruler had to observe considerations of birth and of governmental service. The greatest vassals of the Grand Duke made up a permanent council (*Duma*), into which automatically entered the princes who had lost their independence and also representatives of the more important boyar families. In the company of the powerful feudal lords who made up the Council, the Grand Duke remained "the first among equals." He could not decide one important matter without "consultation" with them. . . . Thus sharing power with his vassals at the center, the Grand Duke, faced by the weakness of his own governmental apparatus, also had to compromise with the system of tax farming, which in fact delivered all the local administration into the hands of the feudal nobility.

THE TSAR'S AUTHORITY

A service state such as Moscow was required a strong leader, but in the 16th century the ruling dynasty was in fact plagued by the chances of human mortality. When Vasily III died in 1533, his heir, Ivan, was yet a small child. A regency took office, replete with boyar intrigues aimed at regaining some semblance of their former powers. When Ivan IV, the Terrible finally took the reins of government for himself, he had first to reestablish the sovereignty of the Grand Duke. The following piece, also by Bakhrushin, offers an interpretation of Ivan's actions as reflecting Moscow's class antagonisms.

The Muscovite rising [of 1547] was the result of the deep discontent of the popular masses with the situation brought about as a result of the boyars' administration, which sought to revive the former feudal disintegration. Not only the peasant and urban masses, but also the broad strata of feudal lords, suffered from these practices. The boyars did not constitute the basic mass of feudal lords. The majority of the lords were courtiers (*dvoriane*) or, as they were called in the 16th century, the boyars' children (*deti boiarskie*), the comparatively weak landholding servitors who received their land, together with peasants, from the Tsar for their service. Under the boyars' administration they suffered greatly from the arbitrary rule of the great lords, who took their land and peasants and often even converted them into their own vassals. Without the support of Tsarist authority they could not defend themselves from the great lords nor compel the peasants to obedience. Therefore the *dvoriane* demanded that the boyars be excluded from the administration and that all power be concentrated in the hands of the Tsar.

The *dvorianin* Ivan Peresvetov expressed such thoughts with great passion and vigor in notes which he handed directly to the Tsar. Peresvetov's

Source: *Ibid.*, II, 267–69, 274–75.

political ideal was absolutism. Pointing to the example of Sultan Makhmud (the conqueror of Constantinople), Peresvetov demanded an end to tax farming, the concentration of all governmental incomes in the Tsarist treasury, the replacement of the tax collectors' courts by state courts and the promulgation of a new "Sudebnik." To support the Tsar and to protect the froniters, he recommended the introduction of a regular force of young men, modelled after the Turkish Janissaries, "well trained in the use of guns." All these measures were to be directed against the great lords. . . . Peresvetov knew well that the reforms which he proposed must meet with strong opposition from the boyars; he called on the Tsar to suppress this resistance by terror, since "the Tsar cannot rule without terror." He counterposed the *dvoriane* to the boyars. . . . Peresvetov advised the naming of persons to higher posts on the basis of service, "even though of lower stock," in other words the elimination of *mestnichestvo*.

*   *   *   *   *

Around the [Tsar's] two favorites, Silvester and Adashev, a strong and influential party, "advisors," formed a circle known as the "select council." This Polish name [*izbrannaia rada*] apparently designated a "privy council," which in fact began to administer the country in the name of the Tsar. . . . Before the Select Council stood two closely connected tasks: the consolidation of power and the enactment of reforms desired by the *dvoriane*.

*   *   *   *   *

Thus very great and responsible tasks fell on the Russian government in the field of foreign policy. Three basic problems stood before it, problems only finally resolved in the 18th century: the Tatars, the Baltic and the Belorussian-Ukrainian questions. First stood the Tatar problem, for without its even partial resolution, it was impossible to act positively in the west.

Those circles of feudal lords on which the government based itself demanded decisive action against the Tatars. The *dvoriane* was interested in the expansion onto the Volga region of its land fund. Through the lips of Peter Volorsky, Ivan Peresvetov, in a pamphlet written no later than in 1549, called on Tsar Ivan to conquer Kazan. . . .

But not only the narrow class interests of the *dvoriane* pressed Moscow into war with Kazan. The Kazan Khanate was a continued obstacle to the economic development of the Russian lands. The Kazan Tatars annually conducted devastating raids on bordering Russian lands, at times penetrating deeply in the land up to Kostroma and Usting. Besides the destruction which these raids brought, the Tatars took a great number of people prisoner. In 1551, according to moderate figures, 60,000 persons of Russian descent were in Kazan, not to mention the Russian prisoners sold en masse in Asiatic markets. Trade interests also militated for the liquidation of the Tatar Khanate, since Kazan controlled the Volga route connecting Eastern Europe, through the Caspian Sea, with the market of Azerbaidzhan and Persia. . . .

TECHNICAL ASSISTANCE

Despite assertions of Moscow's self-sufficiency, such as that made by Bazilevich in the work cited, the Muscovite state of the 16th century had great need of western technicians. Moscow's western neighbors, in turn, protested that the Grand Duchy must not be allowed to import specialists from abroad. The result was an embargo on strategic goods to Russia, imposed by the Holy Roman Emperor. Nevertheless Moscow found ways and means of obtaining what it wanted. The following is an account of one man's misadventures in recruiting.

If we accept the thought that Moscow, already from the 15th century, was familiar with foreigners, that it carried on relations with European governments, that it admitted to its markets (in Novgorod and Moscow) foreign merchants, that it accepted foreign masters and technicians into its service—then there should be no surprise for us in the role which a rather well known adventurer of the mid-16th century, Hans Schlitte, took for himself. He had lived in Moscow in the years of the adolescence and youth of Ivan the Terrible, and had engaged in commerce, learned the Russian language, and, like many foreigners of that epoch, he became an agent of the Muscovite government in its relations with the West. He was commissioned to recruit abroad experienced persons of all sorts and to bring them to Moscow. Schlitte went to Germany on this matter and carried it out with unusual attributes. He presented himself to the Emperor as the envoy of the Muscovite ruler, having a diplomatic mission. In the name of Ivan the Terrible, he proposed to Charles V to begin talks on the union of the Orthodox Church with the Catholic. Actually there was no mention of union of the churches in the Terrible's commission; the commission contained only a request to allow the passage to Moscow of masters and of learned persons. But for Schlitte, it was important to give the matter just such a religious

Source: S. F. Platonov, *Moskva i zapad* (Berlin, 1926), pp. 9–12.

coloring. There is no need to consider him utopian or a fantast. He apparently made a purely practical evaluation of the personal characteristics of Emperor Charles V and of the conditions of that political moment. Schlitte came before the Emperor in Augsburg, at the time of the greatest victory of Charles the Catholic over the Protestant princes of Germany. Coming himself from Goslar, a Protestant city, Schlitte had to demonstrate his Orthodoxy before Charles for the success of his work. He did this very skillfully presenting to the Catholic monarch the possibility of victory not only over the Protestants of Germany but also over Orthodoxy in Moscow. The flattering approach succeeded; the Emperor gave Schlitte permission to invite the necessary people on the condition that none of them go to the Turks, the Tatars, or generally to any non-Christian land. Schlitte selected 123 persons—according to a contemporary account, "doctors, masters, and other learned persons, casters, masters of bell casting, mining, and goldsmithing, architects, lapidaries, hydraulic engineers, papermakers, doctors, typographers, and other such artisans." They were all taken to Lubeck for further transport to *Rus'*, but here they were detained. Schlitte himself was even arrested as a debtor of the city of Lubeck and was thrown into prison. By the time he was freed, the people he had collected had dispersed. The enterprise was thus upset.

The reason for this lay, naturally, in no fault of Schlitte's. The selection of masters and learned persons for Moscow, being carried out in Germany, quickly became widely known. The Hanseatic ruling circles, well acquainted with Muscovite affairs, did not believe that Moscow was ready to unite the churches and they studied the possible consequences of the free exchange of persons between Moscow and the West. From Revel they wrote officially to Lubeck, to the center of the Hanseatic League, asking not to permit Schlitte to proceed to Moscow so as to avert all those horrible troubles which would follow not only for Livonia but also for the German nation if the Muscovites mastered for themselves the art of war and generally the technology of the West. This fear of Moscow ruled not only the Revel council, but also the other neighbors of Moscow. When fleeing from Lubeck, Schlitte renewed his intrigue on Moscow's behalf not only in Germany, but also in Rome, always playing on the idea of church union. Then the Polish government also came out against him. In 1553 it sent to the Emperor and the Pope a special embassy to explain all the vanity of hopes for a rapprochement with Moscow. With complete justice the Poles pointed to the hostile relation of the Russians to the Pope and to Catholicism and to the chimera of union and alliance with Moscow against the Turks. Just as the Hanseatics did, the Poles feared the military strengthening of Moscow and they revealed to the Pope the dangers which would threaten Europe in the event of an excessive strengthening of the Muscovite Grand Duke. Thus, thanks to the intrigues of Schlitte, the question of the "Russian danger" and of the necessity of carrying on a policy of isolation and repression toward Moscow arose for the first time before Europe in a concrete fashion. Both the Emperor and the Pope were now on their guard, and to all proposals of union and close rapprochement, which Schlitte had made falsely in the name of the Tsar, they answered either evasively or with a direct rejection. The Hanseatic and Livonian cities strictly refused to allow over the Muscovite frontier either persons who might "civilize" Moscow or goods which might strengthen the military might of the Muscovite ruler. Moscow protested against this policy of the Livonian authorities. In 1551 it even threatened war if they limited Russian trade at the frontiers and held up foreigners travelling to Moscow. Under such conditions it remained for the Russians to obtain the necessary technicians by public and official channels, and the most convenient roundabout way was apparently Denmark, under whose flag it was possible to transport the necessary persons and goods with the least risk. In this regard, there occurred one curious incident when Moscow received an essential specialist from Denmark. In 1535, during a war with Livonia, Moscow for the first time learned the method of storming a fortress with the use of sappers, mines. The Lithuanian forces took the city of Starodub from Moscow with the use of "mines underground to the city." The Muscovite garrison of Starodub perished because "they knew not such cunning of sapping, up to then there was no sapping in our land."

In Moscow they decided to imitate and master the "cunning of sapping" and at the time of the taking of Kazan (1552) they already had in their forces "a sly German trained in city destruction," who already had students building mines up to Kazan together with the teacher. From the name of this teacher, Rasmussen, we conclude that he was a Dane, brought by Moscow from Denmark.

A EUROPEAN'S VIEW

The westerners who visited Moscow in this period later wrote some of our most valuable accounts for the study of that period. They are especially useful because they often contrast Russian conditions to those in western Europe and thereby point up details which a Russian chronicler might not have thought worth recording.

Source: *Hakluyt's Voyages* (London, 1907), I, 279–82.

Of Mosco the chiefe Citie of the kingdome, and of the Emperour thereof.

The Empire and government of the king is very large, and his wealth at this time exceeding great. And because the citie of Mosco is the chiefest of al the rest, it seemeth of it selfe to challenge the first place in this discourse. Our men say, that in bignesse it is as great as the Citie of London, with the suburbes thereof. There are many and great buildings in it, but for beautie and fairenesse, nothing comparable to ours. There are many Townes and Villages also, but built out of order and with no hansomnesse: their streetes and wayes are not paved with stone as ours are: the walles of their houses are of wood: the roofes for the most part are covered with shingle boords. There is hard by the Citie a very faire Castle, strong, and furnished with artillerie, whereunto the Citie is joyned directly towards the North, with a bricke wall: the walles also of the Castle are built with bricke, and are in breadth or thickenesse eighteene foote. This Castle hath on the one side a drie ditch, on the other side the river Moscua, whereby it is made almost impregnable. The same Moscua trending towards the East doth admit into it the companie of the river Occa.

In the Castle aforesaide, there are in number nine Churches, or Chappels, not altogether unhansome, which are used and kept by certaine religious men, over whom there is after a sort, a Patriarke, or Governour, and with him other reverend Fathers, all which for the greater part, dwell within the Castle. As for the kings Court and Palace, it is not of the neatest, onely in forme it is foure square, and of lowe building, much surpassed and excelled by the beautie and elegancie of the houses of the kings of England. The windows are very narrowly built, and some of them by glasse, some other by lettisses admit the light: and whereas the Palaces of our Princes are decked, and adorned with hangings of cloth of gold, there is none such there: they build and joyne to all their wals benches, and that not onely in the Court of the Emperour, but in all private mens houses. . . .

* * * * *

[The Emperor's] seate was aloft, in a very royall throne, having on his head a Diademe, or Crowne of golde, apparelled with a robe all of Goldsmiths worke, and in his hand hee held a Scepter garnished, and beset with precious stones: and besides all other notes and apparances of honour, there was a Majestie in his countenance proportionable with the excellencie of his estate: on the one side stood his chiefe Secretarie, on the other side, the great Commander of silence, both of them arayed also in cloth of gold: and then there sate the Counsel of one hundred and fiftie in number, all in like sort arayed, and of great state. This so honorable an assemblie, so great a Majestie of the Emperour, and of the place might very well have amazed our men, and have dasht them out of countenance: but notwithstanding Master Chanceler being therewithall nothing dismaied saluted, and did his duetie to the Emperour, after the maner of England, and withall, delivered unto him the letters of our king, Edward the sixt.

*   *   *   *   *

. . . and being conducted into the golden Court, (for so they call it, although not very faire) they finde the Emperour sitting upon an high and stately seate, apparelled with a robe of silver, and with another Diademe on his head: our men being placed over against him, sit downe: in the middes of the roome stoode a mightie Cupboord upon a square foote, whereupon stoode also a round boord, in manner of a Diamond, broade beneath, and towardes the toppe narrowe, and every steppe rose up more narrowe then another. Upon this Cupboorde was placed the Emperours plate, which was so much, that the very Cupboord it selfe was scant able to sustaine the waight of it: the better part of all the vessels, and goblets, was made of very fine gold: and amongst the rest, there were foure pots of very large bignesse, which did adorne the rest of the plate in great measure: for they were so high, that they thought them at the least five foote long. There were also upon this Cupbord certaine silver caskes, not much differing from the quantitie of our Fyrkins, wherein was reserved the Emperours drinke: on each side of the Hall stood foure Tables, each of them layde and covered with very cleane table clothes, whereunto the company ascended by three steps or degrees: all which were filled with the assemblie present; the ghests were all apparelled with linnen without, and with rich skinnes within, and so did notably set out this royall feast. The Emperour, when hee takes any bread or knife in his hand, doth first of all crosse himselfe upon his forehead: they that are in speciall favour with the Emperour sit upon the same bench with him, but somewhat farre from him: and before the comming in of the meate, the Emperour himselfe, according to an ancient custome of the kings of Moscovy, doth first bestow a piece of bread upon every one of his ghests, with a loud pronunciation of his title, and honour, in this manner: The great Duke of Moscovie, and chiefe Emperour of Russia, John Basiliwich (& then the officer nameth the ghest) doth give thee bread. Whereupon al the ghests rise up, and by & by sit downe againe. This done, the Gentleman Usher of the Hall comes in, with a notable company of servants, carying the dishes, and having done his reverence to the Emperour, puts a yong Swanne in a golden platter upon the table, and immediatly takes it thence againe, delivering it to the Carver, and seven other of his fellowes, to be cut up: which being perfourmed, the meate is then distributed to the ghests, with the like pompe, and ceremonies. In the meane time, the Gentleman Usher receives his bread, and tasteth to the Emperour, and afterward, having done his reverence, he departeth. Touching the rest of the dishes, because they were brought in out of order, our men can report no certaintie: but this is true, that all the furniture of dishes, and drinking vessels, which were then for the use of a hundred geests, was all of pure golde, and the tables were so laden with vessels of gold, that there was no roome for some to stand upon them.

A BANQUET

The westerners, however, did not always enjoy their contact with Moscow.

So one sat for more than three long hours at these banquets. One ate little, but drank with great noise, and many boyars were completely drunk. When the servants came to clear the food and the utensils, everyone hurried to leave his place. The Grand Duke, however, remained on his seat, called the ambassadors before him, and with his own hand extended to each of them a goblet of wine. The foreigners, who had been instructed about the customs of the land by the interpreters, took the goblets with caps in hand. Then they turned, took five or six steps, turned back again to the Grand Duke, bowed deeply, with head down in the Turkish fashion, drank all or part— as they wished—and then immediately departed. After the ambassadors had left, the Grand Duke likewise summoned me and handed me, as he had the others, a goblet of wine, and I did everything which I had been taught and as the others had done. I was then, just as the others, also directed out. The publicans and the pharisees, I believe, left the temple no faster than we did that hall. We hurried through the rooms, past the noisy drunken courtiers, and came to the steps of the palace without any light. There, about twenty steps away, a great number of servants waited with horses. In order, how-ever, to get from the steps to the horses, one had to wade, in the dark of night, in filth over the knees. So we went a good way before we could mount our horses, for it is a custom with them that one can neither mount nor dismount by the palace.

RUSSIAN LIFE

Most western visitors were highly critical of conditions in Russia, and the Tsarist government sometimes protested against their comments. Such

Source: An account by Rafael Barberino, written in 1565, in Friedrich v. Adelung, *Kritische-literarische Übersicht der Reisenden in Russland bis 1700, deren Berichte bekannt sind* (St. Petersburg, 1846), I, 236–37.

was the case with Giles Fletcher's account, Of the Russe Common Wealth,
*first published in 1591. The Russian government objected not only to
Fletcher's criticisms but also to his having revealed matters which it thought
should have remained secret.*

The manner of their government is much after the Turkish fashion: which
they seeme to imitate as neare as the countrie, and reach of their capacities
in pollitique affayres, will give them leave to doo.

The state and forme of their government is plaine tyrannicall, as applying
all to the behoofe of the prince, and that after a most open and barbarous
manner: as may appeare by the *sophismata* or secretes of their government
afterwards set downe, as well for the keeping of the nobilitie and commons
in an under proportion, and far uneven balance in their severall degrees, as
also in their impositions and exactions, wherein they exceede all just measure, without any regard of nobilitie or people: farther then it giveth the
nobilitie a kinde of injust and unmeasured libertie to commaund and exact
upon the commons and baser sort of people in all partes of the realme where
so ever they come, specially in the place where their landes lye, or where
they are appoynted by the emperour to governe under him; also to the
commons some small contentment, in that they passe over their landes by
discent of inheritance to whither sonne they will; which commonly they doo
after our gavillkinde; and dispose of their goods by gifte or testament without any controlment. Wherein notwithstanding both nobilitie and commons
are but storers for the prince, all running in the ende into the emperours
coffers: as may appeare by the practise of enriching his treasurie, and the
manner of exactions set downe in the title of his customes and revenues.

Concerning the principall pointes and matters of state, wherein the soveraintie consisteth (as the making and annulling of publike lawes, the making
of magistrates, power to make warre or league with any forraine state, to
execute or to pardon life, with the right of appeale in all matters, both civill
and criminall) they doo so wholy and absolutely pertaine to the emperour,
and his counsell under him, as that hee may be saide to be both the soveraine
commaunder, and the executioner of all these. For as touching any lawe or
publique order of the realme, it is ever determined of before any publique
assemblie or parliament bee summoned. Where, besides his councell, hee
hath none other to consult with him of such matters as are concluded before
hand, but onely a fewe bishops, abbots, and friers: to no other end then to
make advantage of the peoples superstitions, even against themselves, which
thinke all to bee holy and just, that passeth with consent of their bishops
and cleargie men, whatsoever it be. For which purpose the emperours are

Source: *Russia at the Close of the Sixteenth Century,* Works Issued by the
Hakluyt Society, XX (London, 1856), 26–29, 59–64, 146–52.

content to make much of the corrupt state of the Church, as now it is among them, and to nourish the same by extraordinarie favours, and immunities to the bishops seas, abbeies, and frieries: as knowing superstition and false religion best to agree with a tyrannicall state, and to be a speciall meanes to uphold and mainteyne the same.

Secondly, as touching the publike offices and magistracies of the realme, there is none hereditarie, neither any so great nor so litle in that countrie, but the bestowing of it is done immediatly by the emperour himself. Insomuch that the very diacks or clearkes in every head towne, are for the most part assigned by himselfe. Notwithstanding, the emperour that now is (the better to entend his devotions) referreth al such matters perteyning to the state, wholly to the ordering of his wives brother the Lord Borris Federowich Godonoe.

Thirdly, the like is to be said of the jurisdiction concerning matters judiciall, specially such as concerne life and death. Wherein there is none that hath anie authoritie or publike jurisdiction that goeth by discent, or is held by charter, but all at the appoyntment and pleasure of the emperour, and the same practised by the judges with such awe and restraint, as that they dare not determine upon anie speciall matter, but must referre the same wholly up to the Mosko to the emperours councell. To shewe his soveraintie over the lives of his subjects, the late emperour Ivan Vasilowich, in his walkes or progresses, if hee had misliked the face or person of any man whom hee met by the way, or that looked upon him, would command his head to be strook off. Which was presently done, and the head cast before him.

Fourthly, for the soveraigne appeale, and giving of pardons in criminall matters to such as are convicted, it is wholly at the pleasure and grace of the emperour. Wherein also the empresse that nowe is, being a woman of great clemencie, and withall delighting to deale in publike affairs of the realme (the rather to supply the defect of her husband), doeth behave her selfe after an absolute manner, giving out pardon (specially on his byrth day and other solemne times) in her owne name, by open proclamation, without any mention at all of the emperour. Some there have beene of late of the auncient nobilitie, that have held divers provinces by right of inheritaunce, with an absolute authoritie and jurisdiction over them, to order and determine all matters within their owne precinct without all appeale or controlement of the emperour. But this was all annulled and wrung cleane from them by Ivan Vasilowich, father to this emperour.

*   *   *   *   *

The condition of the commons and vulgar sort of people, may partly be understood by that which already hath bin said concerning the manner of their government and the state of the nobilitie, with the ordering of their provinces and chiefe townes of the land. And first, touching their libertie, how it standeth with them, it may appeare by this: that they are reckoned in no degree at all, nor have any suffrage nor place in their zabore or high court of parliament, where their lawes and publique orders are concluded upon. Which commonly tend to the oppression of the commons. For the other two degrees, viz., of the nobilitie and cleargie, which have a vote in the parliaments (though farre from that libertie that ought to bee in common consultations for the publique benefits, according to the measure and proportion of their degrees) are well contented that the whole burden shall light upon the commons, so they may ease their owne shoulders by laying all upon them. Againe, into what servile condition their libertie is brought, not onely to the prince, but to the nobles and gentlemen of the countrie (who themselves also are but servile, specially of late years), it may farther appeare by their owne acknowledgements in their supplications and other writings to any of the nobles or chiefe officers of the emperours. Wherein they name and subscribe themselves *kolophey*, that is, their villaines or bondslaves: as they of the nobilitie doo unto the emperour. This may truly be saide of them, that there is no servant nor bondslave more awed by his master, nor kept downe in a more servile subjection, then the poore people are, and that universally, not only by the emperour, but by his nobilitie, chief officers, and souldiers. So that when a poore *mousick* meeteth with any of them upon the high way, he must turne himselfe about, as not daring to looke him on the face, and fall down with knocking of his head to the very ground, as he doth unto his idoll.

Secondly, concerning the landes, goods, and other possessions of the commons, they answere the name and lie common indeed without any fense against the rapine and spoile, not onely of the highest, but of his nobilitie, officers, and souldiers. Besides the taxes, customes, seazures, and other publique exactions done upon them by the emperour, they are so racked and pulled by the nobles, officers, and messengers sent abroad by the emperour in his publique affaires, specially in the *yammes* (as they call them) and through faire townes, that you shall have many villages and townes of halfe a mile and a mile long, stande all unhabited: the people being fled all into other places, by reason of the extreame usage and exactions done upon them. So that in the way towards Mosko, betwixt Vologda and Yaruslaveley (which is two nineties after their reckoning, litle more then an hundredth miles English) there are in sigt fiftie villages at the least, some halfe a mile, some a mile long, that stand vacant and desolate without any inhabitant. The like is in all other places of the realme (as is said by those that have better travelled the countrie than my selfe had time or occasion to doo).

The great oppression over the poore commons, maketh them to have no courage in following their trades: for that the more they have the more daunger they are in, not only of their goods but of their lives also. And if they have any thing, they conceale it all they can, sometimes conveying it into monasteries, sometimes hiding it under the ground and in woods, as men are woont to doo where they are in feare of forreine invasion. In so much that many times you shall see them afraid to be knowen to any gentleman of such commodities as they have to sell. I have seene them sometimes when they have layed open their commodities for a liking (as their principall furres and such like) to looke still behind them and towards every doore: as men in some fear, that looked to be set upon and surprised by some enimie. Whereof asking the cause, I found it to be this, that they have doubted least some nobleman of the emperour had bene in companie, and so layed a traine for them to pray upon their commodities perforce.

This maketh the people (though otherwise hardened to beare any toile) to give themselves much to idlenes and drinking: as passing for no more then from hand to mouth. And hereof it commeth that the commodities of Russia (as was said before) as tallow, wax, hydes, flaxe, hempe, etc., grow and goe abroad in farre lesse plentie then they were woont to doo: because the people, being oppressed and spoiled of their gettings, are discouraged from their laboures. Yet this one thing is much to be noted, that in all this oppression there were three brethren marchants of late, that traded together with one stocke in common, that were found to be worth 300,000 rubbels in money, besides landes, cattels, and other commodities. Which may partly be imputed to their dwellings far of from the eye of the court, vz., in Wichida, a 1000 miles from Mosko and more. The same are said by those that knew them to have set on worke all the yeare long ten thousand men in making of salt, carriages by cart and boat, hewing of wood, and such like: besides 5,000 bondslaves at the least, to inhabite and till their land.

They also had their physitions, surgeons, apothecaries, and all manner of artificers, of Doutches [Germans], and others, belonging unto them. They are said to have paied to the emperour for custome to the sume of 23,000 rubbles a yeare (for which cause they were suffered to enjoy their trade) besides mainteining of certeine garrisons on the borders of Siberia, the which were neare unto them. Wherin the emperour was content to use their purse, till such time as they had got ground in Siberia and made it habitable, by burning and cutting downe woods from Wichida to Perm, above a 1,000 verst, and then tooke it all away from them perforce.

But this in the end beying envied and disdained, as a matter not standing with their pollicie to have any so great, specially a *mousick*, the emperour began first to pull from them by pieces, sometimes 20,000 rubbels at a time, sometime more: till in the end their sonnes that now are, are well eased of their stocke, and have but small parte of their fathers substance: the rest being drawen all into the emperours treasurie. Their names were Jacove, Gregorie, and Simon, the sonnes of Onyka.

For the qualitie of their people otherwise, though there seemeth to be in them some aptnesse to receyve any art (as appeareth by the naturall wittes in the men, and very children) yet they excell in no kinde of common arte, much lesse in any learning or litterall kinde of knowledge: which they are kept from of purpose, as they are also from all militarie practise: that they may be fitter for the servile condition wherein now they are, and have neyther reason nor valure to attempt innovation. For this purpose also they are kept from traveling, that they may learne nothing, nor see the fashions of other countries abroad. You shall seldome see a Russe a traveller, except he be with some ambassadour, or that he make a scape out of his countrie. Which hardly he can doo, by reason of the borders that are watched so narrowly, and the punishment for any such attempt, which is death if he be taken, and all his goods confiscate. Onely they learne to write and to read, and that very few of them. Neither doo they suffer any straunger willingly to come into their realme out of any civill countrie for the same cause, farther then necessitie of uttering their commodities and taking in of forreine doth enforce them to doo.

And therefore this yeare 1589 they consulted about the removing of all marchants straungers to the border townes, to abide and have their residencie there, and to bee more wary in admitting other straungers hereafter into the inland parts of the realm, for feare of infection with better manners and qualities then they have of their owne. For the same purpose also they are kept within the boundes of their degree by the lawes of their countrie: so that the sonne of a *mousick*, artificer, or husbandman, is ever a *mousick*, artificer, etc.: and hath no means to aspire any higher: except, having learned to write and read, he attaine to the preferment of a priest or dyack. . . .

Concerning their trades, diet, apparell, and such like, it is to be noted in a severall chapter of their private behaviour. This order that bindeth every man to keepe his rancke and severall degree, wherein his forefathers lived before him, is more meet to keepe the subjects in a servile subjection, and so apt for this and like common-wealths, then to advaunce any vertue, or to breed any rare or excellent qualitie in nobilitie or commons: as having no farther rewarde nor preferment whereunto they may bend their endevours and imploy themselves to advaunce their estate, but rather procuring more danger to themselves the more they excell in any noble or principall qualitie.

* * * * *

The private behaviours and qualitie of the Russe people, may partly be understood by that whiche hath beene said concerning the publique state and usage of the countrie. As touching the naturall habite of their bodies, they are for the most parte of a large sise and of very fleshly bodies, accounting it a grace to bee somewhat grosse and burley, and therefore they nourish and spread their beardes to have them long and broad. But, for the most part, they are very unweldy and unactive withall. Which may bee thought to come partly of the climate, and the numbnes which they get by the cold in winter, and partly of their diet, that standeth most of rootes, onions, garlike, cabbage, and such like things that breed grosse humors, which they use to eate alone and with their other meates.

Their diet is rather much then curious. At their meales they beginne commonly with a *chark*, or small cuppe, of *aqua vitae* (which they call Russe wine) and then drinke not till towardes the ende of their meales, taking it in largely and all together, with kissing one another at every pledge. And therefore after dinner there is no talking with them, but every man goeth to his bench to take his afternoones sleepe, which is as ordinary with them as their nightes reste. When they exceede and have varietie of dishes, the first are their baked meates (for roste meates they use little) and then their broathes or pottage. To drinke drunke, is an ordinary matter with them every day in the weeke. Their common drinke is mead; the poorer sort use water, and thinne drink called quasse, which is nothing els (as wee say) but water turned out of his wittes, with a little branne meashed with it.

This diet would breede in them many diseases, but that they use bath-stoves or hote houses in steede of all phisicke, commonly twise or thrise every weeke. All the winter time, and almost the whole sommer, they heat their *peaches*, which are made lyke the Germane bathstoaves, and their *potlads*, like ovens, that so warme the house, that a straunger at the first shall hardly like of it. These two extremities, specially in the winter, of heat within their houses and of extreame colde without, together with their diet, maketh them of a darke and sallow complexion, their skinnes beying tanned and parched both with colde and with heate, specially the women, that for the greater parte are of farre worse complexions then the men. Whereof the cause I take to bee, their keeping within the hote houses, and busying them-selves about the heating and using of their bathstoves and peaches.

The Russe, because that hee is used to both these extremities of heat and of cold, can beare them both a great deale more patiently then straungers can doo. You shal see them sometimes (to season their bodies) come out of their bathstoves all on a froth, and fuming as hote almost as a pigge at a spitte, and presently to leape into the river starke naked, or to poure colde water all over their bodies, and that in the coldest of all the winter time. The women, to mende the bad hue of their skinnes, use to paint their faces with white and redde colours, so visibly that every man may perceyve it. Which is made no matter, because it is common and liked well by their husbandes, who make their wives and daughters an ordinarie allowance to buy them colours to paint their faces withall, and delight themselves much to see them of fowle women to become such faire images. This parcheth the skinne, and helpeth to deforme them when their painting is of.

They apparell themselves after the Greeke manner. The noblemans attire is on this fashion. First, a *taffia*, or little night cappe, on his head, that covereth little more then his crowne, commonlie verie riche wrought of silke and gold thread, and set with pearle and pretious stone. His head he keepeth shaven close to the very skin, except he be in some displeasure with the emperour. Then hee suffereth his haire to growe and hang downe upon his shoulders, covering his face as ugly and deformedly as he can. Over the *taffia* he weareth a wide cap of black foxe (which they account for the best furre) with a tiara or long bonnet put within it, standing up like a Persian or Babilonian hat. About his neck (which is seene al bare) is a coller set with pearle and pretious stone, about three or foure fingers broad. Next over his shirt (which is curiously wrought, because he strippeth himself into it in the sommer time while he is within the house) is a *shepon*, or light garment of silke, made downe to the knees, buttoned before; and then a *caftan*, or a close coat buttoned, and girt to him with a Persian girdle, whereat he hanges his knives and spoone. This commonly is of cloth of gold, and hangeth downe as low as his ankles. Over that he weareth a lose garment of some rich silke furred and faced about with some gold lace, called a *ferris*. An other over that of chamlet and like stuffe, called an *alkaben*, sleeved and hanging low, and the cape commonly brooched and set all with pearle. When hee goeth abroad he casteth over all these (which are but sleight, though they seeme to be many) an other garment, called an *honoratkey*, like to the *alkaben*, save that is made without a coller for the neck. And this is commonly of fine cloth or camels haire. His buskins (which he weareth in stead of hose, with linnen folles under them instead of boot hose) are made of a Persian leather called *saphian*, embroidered with pearle. His upper stockes are commonly of cloth of gold. When he goeth abroad he mounteth on horse-backe, though it be but to the next doore, which is the manner also of the *boiarskey* or gentlemen.

The *boiarskey* or gentlemans attire is of the same fashion, but differeth in stuffe; and yet he will have his *caftan* or undercoat sometimes of cloth of gold, the rest of cloth or silke.

The noble woman weareth on hir head, first, a caull of some soft silke (which is commonly redde) and over it a fruntlet, of white colour. Over that, hir cap (made after the coife fashion of cloth of gold), edged with some riche furre, and set with pearle and stone. Though they have of late begonne to disdaine embrodering with pearle about their cappes, because the diacks and some marchants wives have taken up the fashion. In their eares they weare earerings of two inches or more compasse, the matter of gold, set with rubies, or saphires, or some like pretious stone. In sommer, they goe often with kerchieffes of fine white lawn or cambricke fastned under the chinne, with two long tassels pendent. The kerchiefe spotted and set thicke with rich pearle. When they ride or goe abroad in raynie weather, they weare white hattes with coloured bands. About their necks they weare collers of three or foure fingers broad, set with riche pearle and pretious stone. Their upper garment is a loose gowne, commonly of skarlet, with wide loose sleeves hanging downe to the ground, buttoned before with great gold buttons, or at least, silver and guilt, nigh as bigge as a walnut. Which hath hanging over it, fastned under the cappe, a large broad cape of some rich furre, that hangeth downe almost to the middes of their backes. Next under the *oposken* or upper garment they weare another, called a *leitnick*, that is made close before with great wide sleeves, the cuffe or half sleeve up to the elbowes, commonly of cloth of gold; and under that a *ferris zemskoy*, which hangeth loose, buttoned throughout to the very foote. On the hand wrests they weare very faire braselets, about two fingers broad, of pearle and pretious stone. They go all in buskins of white, yellow, blew, or some other coloured leather, embrodered with pearle. This is the attire of the noblewoman of Russia, when shee maketh the best shew of hir selfe. The gentlewomans apparell may differ in the stuffe, but is all one for the making or fashion.

As for the poore *mousick* and his wife, they go poorely cladde. The man, with his *odnoratkey*, or loose gowne, to the small of the legge, tyed together with a lace before, of coarse white or blew cloth, with some *shube*, or long wastcoat, of furre or of sheepskinne under it, and his furred cappe and buskins. The poorer sort of them have their *odnoratkey* or upper garment, made of kowes haire. This is their winter habite. In the sommer time, commonly they wear nothing but their shirts on their backes and buskins on their legges. The woman goeth in a redde or blew gowne when she maketh the best shew, and with some warme *shube* of furre under it in the winter time. But in the sommer nothing but her two shirts (for so they call them) one over the other, whether they be within doores or without. On their heades they weare caps of some coloured stuffe, many of velvet or of cloth or golde; but for the most part kerchiefes. Without earings of silver or some other mettall, and her crosse about her necke, you shal see no Russe woman, be shee wife or maide.

As touching their behaviour and quality otherwise, they are of reasonable capacities, if they had those means that some other nations have to traine up their wittes in good nurture and learning. Which they might borrowe of the Polonians and other their neighbours, but that they refuse it of a very self pride, as accounting their owne fashions to be far the best. Partly also (as I said before) for that their manner of bringing up (voide of all good learning and civill behaviour) is thought by their governours most agreeable to that state and their manner of government. Which the people would hardly beare, if they were once civilled and brought to more understanding of God and good policie. This causeth the emperours to keep out al meanes of making it better, and to be very warie for excluding of all peregrinitie that might alter their fashions. Which were lesse to bee disliked if it set not a print into the very mindes of his people. For as themselves are verie hardlie and cruellie dealte withall by their chiefe magistrates and other superiours, so are they as cruell one against an other, specially over their inferiours and such as are under them. So that the basest and wretchedest *Christianoe* (as they call him) that stoupeth and croucheth like a dogge to the gentleman, and licketh up the dust that lieth at his feete, is an intollerable tyrant where he hath the advantage. By this meanes the whole countrie is filled with rapine and murder. They make no account of the life of a man. You shall have a man robbed sometime in the very streats of their townes if hee goe late in the evening, and yet no man to come forth out of his doores to rescue him, though hee heare him crie out. I will not speake of the straungenesse of the murders and other cruelties committed among them, that would scarsly bee beleeved to bee done among men, specially such as professe themselves Christians.

The number of their vagrant and begging poore is almost infinite, that are so pinched with famine and extreame neede, as that they begge after a violent and desperate manner, with "give mee and cut mee, give mee and kill me," and such like phrases. Whereby it may bee gheassed what they are towardes straungers, that are so unnaturall and cruell towardes their owne. And yet it may bee doubted whither is the greater, the crueltie or intemperancie that is used in that countrie. I will not speake of it, because it is so foule and not to bee named. The whole countrie overfloweth with all sinne of that kinde. And no marveile, as having no lawe to restraine whoredomes, adulteries and like uncleannesse of life.

As for the truth of his word, the Russe for the most part maketh small regard of it, so he may gaine by a lie and breache of his promise. And it may be saide truely (as they know best that have traded most with them) that from the great to the small (except some fewe that will scarcely be founde) the Russe neither beleeveth any thing that an other man speaketh, nor speaketh any thing himselfe worthie to be beleeved. These qualities make them very odious to all their neighbours, specially to the Tartars, that account themselves to be honest and just in comparison of the Russe. It is supposed by some that doo well consider of the state of both countries, that the offence they take at the Russe government and their manner of behaviour, hath beene a great cause to keepe the Tartar still heathenish, and to mislike (as he doeth) of the Christian profession.

CHAPTER 2

The Seventeenth Century

STRUGGLE FOR THE THRONE

At the end of the 16th century, Russia underwent serious internal tur-moil, as the Muscovite royal line came to an end. Ivan the Terrible (Grozny) killed one son in a fit of anger, and the son who succeeded him, Fedor Ivanovich, was an incompetent who had no heirs of his own. At Fedor's death, struggle for the throne ensued, and the Grand Duchy of Moscow was almost destroyed. Before its end, the "time of troubles" tested both the Mus-covite state's inner cohesion and its ability to defend itself against its neigh-bors. In the eyes of the historian S. F. Platonov, the "time of troubles" was a greater watershed in Russian history than was the reign of Peter I.

In the territorial make-up of the Muscovite state at the end of the XVI century, we have distinguished five regions with distinctive characteristics in their social structure: the Muscovite center or *Zamoskovie*, the Novgorod quarters, *Pomorie, Niz,* and *Polie.* The first two regions were the basic parts of the state and they were experiencing a severe crisis. Politically the *oprich-nina* raged, and economically they were experiencing the greatest destruc-tion and desolation. The upper strata of the population fell victim to the executions and deportations of the sovereign, and the lower strata fell into bondage to the landlords, the *pomeshchiki* placed over the peasant volosts. The top of society was dispersed by the wrathful Tsar, and the lower parts themselves fled, unable to suffer their troubles. In these regions, one can say, agriculture died, and commerce was paralyzed along the whole western boundary because of war and internal disorders. The crisis did not touch *Pomorie,* being a region of free peasantry after the withdrawal from it of the Novgorod boyars. Its population in the XVI century had not yet divided itself into mutually antagonistic groups, and it knew no other authorities than its own elected administration and organs of governmental supervision.

Source: S. F. Platonov, *Smutnoe vremia* (Prague, 1924), pp. 60–66.

With the beginning of the White Sea trade, *Pomorie* revived and began to prosper from participation in commerce and transit between the capital and the ports (Kola and Arkhangel). Trade centers and routes grew in *Pomorie,* and ties were strengthened between the volosts and the once isolated "lands" into which the region was divided. In contrast to the center, for *Pomorie* the XVI century was a "golden age" of flowering of its social forces and their activity. The *Niz* presented a special picture, a foreign land, just conquered, pacified and colonized by Russians. On the basis of the heterogeneous life and work the regular forms of Muscovite public life grew there. The sharp contradictions between Muscovite authority and the nobility, between the Muscovite *pomeshchik* and the peasant, had yet to express itself, but a distinctive crisis arose there—a struggle for land between the aborigines and the newcomers, who were imperiously seizing the agricultural wealth of the heterogeneous land. *Polie* also presented a special picture to which, in great mass, the victims of crisis had fled the state: unfortunate people seeking freedom and happiness in those places where serfdom had not yet come. Muscovite authority came to the *Polie* after the refugees, furnished the land with cities, and, instead of bondage, created there a service dependence—military and agricultural. Only those remained free in the *Polie* who did not become serving people and who went south beyond the state's fortified frontier.

In the conditions of Muscovite life, described above, observant contemporaries saw a threat of open trouble. They understood that the destruction which was overtaking the state center, complicated by the prolonged war and governmental terror, could not pass without a shock. The Englishman G. Fletcher, in his book on Russia, *Of the Russe Common Wealth*, printed in 1591 in London, definitely predicted trouble in the Muscovite state—revolution and civil strife, as the consequence of the terror of *Grozny*, which had aroused grumbling and irreconcilable hatred. He linked the beginning of the trouble with the end of the Muscovite dynasty, which he expected at the death of Tsar Fedor Ivanovich. As to the result of the trouble, he said that the decisive role—and therefore the victory—would belong not to the nobility or to the popular mass, but to the social middle, "the military forces." Such perspicacity was not distinctive of the Russian people of the XVI century. But they foresaw trouble. They even predicted shocks, but only in the form of unclear implications and threats. Nevertheless one of the anonymous writers of that period displayed remarkable foresight when he said that in *Rus'*, in the near future, the volosts and villages would be devastated. . . .

*   *   *   *   *

In a word it was clear to observant people that there would be no peace and well being in a country where whole regions were destroyed, where hereditary nobility were oppressed and burning with hatred for the dynasty and its court favorites, where the serving class was deprived of the possibility to serve and to administer, where the lower classes fled from dependent and ruinous conditions of labor, and where, finally, the government had to rule in the absence of income and an army, in the presence of general discontent and grumbling. It is understandable with what fear the Muscovite people, in the last years of the reign of the childless Tsar Fedor, awaited his death. With him would end his line; the "root" of the Muscovite sovereigns would stop, and the trouble would begin.

This fear was well founded: with the death of Tsar Fedor the trouble began. The coincidence of the governmental disorder with the end of the dynasty was the main reason for the arising of open trouble. A strong governmen could have dealt with the social movement and sought some way out of the difficulties. But the administration of the irresponsible Tsar Fedor was hardly capable of this. The great political talent in this administration was Boris Godunov, but he had to work in an atmosphere of constant intrigues and extraordinary complications. The trouble was stronger than Boris. It attended the beginning of his career, and it was the reason for his premature death and the destruction of his family.

* * * * *

Thus open trouble in the Muscovite state began with the death of the childless Tsar Fedor Ivanovich (1598). It is commonly thought to end with the accession to the throne of Tsar Michael Fedorovich (1613). In this interval of time Muscovite life was filled with the struggle of different social and political forces. Looking at the course of this struggle, we note that from the beginning its object was the Muscovite throne. Various "seekers of power" struggled for its possession; the Romanovs with the Godunovs, the Godunovs with the self-styled Tsarevich Dmitri Ivanovich, and finally, the impostor having been killed, a Prince of the descendants of Rurik, Vasily Ivanovich Shuiskii, ruled the throne. This period (1598–1605) was the period of the dynastic trouble. Soon after the crowning of Shuisky there begins a number of risings against Tsar Vasily and against the "evil boyars" around him. Although the rebels also used the name of Tsar Dmitri, whom they did not believe to have been killed, nevertheless it is clear that the movement was directed no longer by dynastic motives but by motives of class enmity. Against the slave-holding top of society rise the social lower classes—the Cossacks—with the hope of political and social revolution. This open civil struggle lasts from 1606 to 1610 and can be called the time of social struggle. Into the Muscovite civil strife, soon after its beginning, all sorts of foreigners begin to interfere, seeking to exploit Moscow's weakness for their own personal interests or for the benefit of their states— Sweden and Poland. This intervention leads to the passage of Novgorod and Smolensk under the authority of the Swedes and the Poles, and in Moscow itself, after the deposition of Tsar Vasily from the Muscovite throne, a Polish-Lithuanian garrison settles. Thus the social trouble leads to the dislocation of the social order in the Muscovite state and to the fall of national political independence. The foreigners' intervention and their triumph over Moscow aroused in the Russians a national feeling and turned all elements of the Muscovite population against the foreign enemies. In 1611 the efforts to throw off the foreign rule begin. But they cannot succeed so long as they are hindered by the blind irreconcilability of the social classes. But when, in 1612, a military organization was formed in Yaroslavl, uniting the middle classes of Muscovite society, the matter took a new turn. The Yaroslavl provisional government succeeded, both by suggestion and by force, in so influencing the Cossack masses that it achieved the unification of all national forces, and it reconstructed Tsarist authority and a united government in the land. This period of the struggle, 1611–1613, can be called the period of the struggle for nationality.

SERFDOM

The peasantry comprised the majority of the Russian people on into the middle of the 20th century. As such, it played a major role, either actively or passively, in almost every crisis of the Russian state, and major peasant rebellions periodically threatened the very existence of the state. It was in the 17th century that the peasants were subjugated by serf law.

Next we turn to one of the most important and one of the most difficult questions in our historiography—the question of when and how serfdom arose. In describing the results of the *pomestie* system I said that it led to a basic change in the peasantry's fortunes. This change is usually outlined as follows. Up to the end of the 16th century the peasant was a free agriculturalist who had the right of free movement from one plot to another, and from one landlord to another. But this removal gave rise to great inconveniences for both the social order and for the state economy, and especially for the smaller landowners, who saw their peasantry attracted away from them to the estates of the richer *ochinniki* and *pomeshchiki* and themselves left without the labor which was needed to perform their service to the state. As a result of these difficulties, the government of Tsar Fedor pub-

Source: V. Kliuchevskii, *Kurs russkoi istorii*, 2d ed. (Moscow, 1937), II, 330–38.

lished an *ukaz* which took away the peasant's right of removal—i.e. of leaving the land which he had occupied. All the unfortunate results of serfdom which later manifested themselves came from this attachment to the soil. Since the original *ukaz* abolishing the peasant's right of removal was promulgated while Boris Godunov governed in Fedor's name, it is upon Boris that the responsibility for these results must fall. It was he who originated serf right and laid the foundations of serfdom. In this view of the development of serf right one can distinguish two main theses: (1) at the end of the 16th century the Government altered the juridical status of the peasants by one legal act, depriving them of the right of removal and tying them to the soil, and (2) as a result of this act the peasantry became prisoners of the landowners.

In this representation of the situation however, not everything is clear and precise. Firstly, it makes it appear as though one and the same legislative act established both agrarian attachment and serf right. But these two conditions are not only different in character and origin, but also even exclusive of one another in many respects. Agrarian attachment means the tying of the peasantry to the soil by a state measure, independently from the peasant's personal relation to the landowner, or, more precisely, it means that that relation is subordinated to the agrarian attachment. By serf right is meant that right of a man against the person of another man which, at its inception, was founded upon a *private* juridical act, namely, upon the act of binding into forced service, independently of the relation of the serf to the soil, this right, according to our Code of Laws, delivered the serf over "into the privy power and dominion" of his master. Consequently the interpretation which we have described combines two acts dissimilar to each other, attachment to the soil and personal enserfment. This is my first objection. Secondly, not only is the text of this *ukaz*, whereby peasant removal is alleged to have been abolished, not available to us but of all the acts of the state that have come down to us not one gives any indication that such an act was ever published. The first act in which one finds indications of an agrarian attachment to the land, as a general measure, is an *ukaz* dated November 24, 1597. But in this *ukaz* there is nothing to justify these tales concerning a general agrarian attachment to the land at the end of the 16th century. From this *ukaz* we know only that if any peasant ran away from his landlord at a date no earlier than five years previous to September 1 (then New Year's day), 1597, and if the landlord had entered suit against him, then the peasant was to be returned to the landlord, "where he had lived," together with his family and property. If the peasant had run away more than five years before, and if the landlord had not instituted a search before September 1, 1592, then he was to be immune from arrest and no petitions for his arrest would be accepted. More than this the Tsar's *ukaz* and the boyars' agreement of November 24 says no more than this. The *ukaz*, obviously, spoke only of runaway peasants who had left their landlords "not according to term and without surrender," i.e. not on St. George's Day and without giving legal notice to, or settling accounts with, their landlords. This *ukaz* set a time limit for the return of peasants which was retroactive in its action and fixed no deadline for the future. Such a measure, Speransky explained was adopted to put an end to the troubles and disorders which had arisen in judicial practice through the multitude and tardiness of suits dealing with runaway peasants. The *ukaz* brought nothing new into the law, but only tried to regulate legal procedures in respect to such peasants. Even in the 15th century the appanage princes had adopted measures to deal with runaway peasants who had not settled accounts with them. The conclusion was drawn, however, from the *ukaz* of November 24 that five years earlier in 1592 there had been legislation depriving the peasantry of their right of removal and attaching them to the soil. Pogodin, and after him also Beliaev, had shown that the *ukaz* of November 24th does not give grounds for supporting the supposition that such a general enactment was passed five years before 1597. But Pogodin vaguely saw in this *ukaz* of November 24th the establishment also of a five years time-limit in the future for suits against runaway peasants. Beliaev thought that if no general act eliminating the peasant's right of removal was made precisely in that year (1592), such an act was undoubtedly made at a date not before 1590, since an act of that year has come down to us which indicated that the peasants still had the right of removal. Consequently, said Beliaev, it is to be hoped that in time such a contemporary *ukaz* will be found in our archives. It can be declared with certainty that no such *ukaz*, either from 1590 or 1592, will ever be found, because none was ever published. Some people have even said that the *ukaz* of November 24th 1597 was the real law which bound the peasantry to the soil, albeit not directly; without any previous interdiction the government declared all peasant removals which had taken place in the preceding five years illegal and called upon such peasants who had left their plots to return to them. Pogodin did not accept the idea that any special law was made attaching the peasants during the reign of Fedor, but he thought that the serf right was established sometime later, and gradually, and that it arose of itself, not juridically. Let us therefore examine the land acts of the 16th and early 17th centuries, in order to see for ourselves what really happened to the peasantry during that period.

Many peasant-tenancy agreements have come down to us from this period —documents recording the peasants' bargains with the landlords before settling on their estates. These agreements date from the middle of the 16th century to the middle of the 17th century and even farther. If, while going through these contracts, one should forget the story of the alleged general attachment of the peasantry during the reign of Fedor, they will do nothing to remind you about it. The peasants at the beginning of the 17th century reached agreements with the landowners the same way as they had done in the second half of the 16th century. The peasant bound himself, in case he left, to pay quit rent for the use of his cottage, to return the loan, and to compensate the landowner for any exemptions which he had enjoyed. It was presumed to be the right of the peasant to leave the landlord whenever he wished. The assumption that at the end of the 16th century the peasant was deprived of that right and bound to the soil renders the whole series of tenancy-agreements meaningless. Thus one monastry, in 1599, while transferring some of its peasants from one estate to another, made new contracts with them and reached agreements with them as they would with free lease-holders. Another act of that same year says that the monastry had long sought one of its own peasants who had run away without payment, and finally, having found him on the estate of a certain servitor of the state, had demanded his return. The widow of the servitor gave up the fugitive. During the period of "Russkaia Pravda" the peasant would have been enslaved for such an offense. Now, after the alleged agrarian attachment of the peasantry to the land, the monastery not only did not punish the peasant at all, but even concluded a new contract with him and gave him a new loan and an exemption for his restocking. Similar occurrences can be observed during the reign of Michael. According to an agreement in 1630 one peasant settled on the land of the Tikhvin monastry and was accorded a loan and an exemption. He was relieved for one year of both fiscal taxes and estate dues and also received from the monastery 10 rubles (more than 100 rubles in our money) for the stocking of his farm as well as 10 *chetverti* of grain. In the agreement stands this condition: "If I do not live at the monastery, on my plot, according to this agreement, or if I begin to negotiate separately with other peasants, then the monastery shall take the 30 rubles which it has given me in money and grain and exemption under this agreement"—and that is all. The agreement does not even indicate that it would be illegal for the peasant to leave the plot which he was to rent from the monastery; the peasant is bound only to pay a forfeit for the monastery's expenses. Therefore peasant tenancy agreements do not show any general attachment of the peasantry to the soil in the first half of the 17th century, at least not in the reign of Michael. On the other hand, some peasants seemed to have been bound to the soil and deprived of the right of removal already long before the supposed law of general attachment. In the year 1552 the state peasants of the Viazma region were granted an imperial charter which gave the rural communes of that region the right to recover their former members which had moved to mon-asterial estates at other than the legal term and to resettle them on the plots which they had left, though at the same time they were given the right to invite peasantry from elsewhere. This dispensation related to the state peasants. But at the same time all of the tax paying peasantry seemed to have become tied to the soil, or to the dues payable thereupon. In the 1560's the rich Stroganov family were granted extensive vacant lands along the rivers Kama and Tchusova, together with the right to settle anyone they could bring there. The Stroganovs were not to take any peasants "who paid taxes and were inscribed", i.e., those who were already settled on tax paying lands and had their names in the agrarian registers. Such people the Stroganovs were to surrender immediately, together with families and all their goods, upon demand of local authorities. Thus, the theory about an *ukaz* abolishing peasant removal and binding the peasantry to the soil at the end of the 16th century is supported neither by previous nor subsequent events.

In order to understand this matter, we must first ask ourselves the question whether there was anything to be abolished at the end of the 16th century. Careful study of the agrarian contracts of the period yields examples of "refusal", i.e., of the peasant's moving freely and legally from one landlord to another, but it is easy to see that such instances were extremely rare. Tenancy agreements in which such a right of removal was directly mentioned or tacitly postulated were an exceptional phenomena at this time. Such agreements were possible only for those few who could settle with their landlord or who had been free men when they had first settled as tax paying peasants. The great majority of the tenancy agreements known to us were signed by such free men. The great mass of tax paying peasants lost their right of removal not because that right had been eliminated by any general law, but because the peasants themselves had either surrendered or lost the *power* to enjoy this right. This loss was a continuous and complicated process involving the fundamental conditions of serf right. Let me present this process in the most general outline. Approximately from the end of the 16th to the beginning of the 17th century a ceaseless migration continued among the peasantry of the Oka-Volga region, at first in one direction only—to the north and beyond the Upper Volga—and then, in the second half of the 16th century, also south-eastward toward Astrakhan and Kazan along the Don and along the Middle and Lower Volga. During this movement two strata emerged among the peasantry—the "old dwellers" and the new comers. These two met with differing fortunes on state and court lands, with very little difference between the two, and on service, private, and church lands. The term "old dwellers" denoted length of residence or of membership in a rural or urban community, but it was not originally defined by any exact qualifying term. Peasants were called "old dwellers" if they had occupied their plots for five years, as were peasants whose lands were held by their fathers before them. In itself the term had no juridical significance in limiting the personal freedom of the old dwellers; but it took on such a significance through its connection with another bond, i.e., the joint guarantee of taxes which existed in all communes on state and court lands. The old dwellers in such communes formed the basic nucleus upon which the tax solvency of the unit was preserved, and the departure of any old members put an extra burden on the remaining members. Therefore it was necessary for these communes to prevent their old dwellers from leaving for more privileged lands—especially monasterial lands. This was done by means of a very large quit-rent which was calculated on the number of years the old dweller had spent on his holding. (The calculation was impossible if the father and son had spent decades living on the same property.) The government also came to the aid of the state and court communes by binding individuals to their status in order to assure for itself a permanent contingent of tax payers and servitors. Because of these two factors, by the beginning of the 17th century, private and temporary measures had led to a general attachment of the old dwellers, not only to their status but also to their residence. In one act of 1568 we see that the general rule was to return all peasants who had left court lands upon which they had been old dwellers. By the close of the 16th century the term "old dweller" apparently connoted a specific period of time. A charter granted to the town of Toropetz in 1591 speaks about "forbidden years" in which the townsmen might at any time recover and resettle former tax payers who had left the settlement. If these "forbidden years" represent the period of time required to convert a tax payer into an old dweller, then one can expect this to be openly stated in a later document. In 1626 the Spasski Monastery received an order to list for tax purposes all peasants settled on the monastery's lands in Yaroslavl. In 1624 the government, while canvassing the persons living on the lands of the monastery, had ordered that those who were found to be free or old-established tenants of the monastery's (i.e., not state taxpayers), or who, though they were formerly taxpayers of the state, had "come from under the tsar more than 10 years ago or had left tax payers there as their replacements", were to be inscribed to the monastery and not to the city of Yaroslavl. Furthermore, all inhabitants of Yaroslavl who had left their settlement should be traced so as to find out when and where they had moved, and, if they had departed "not more than 10 years ago" they should be returned to Yaroslavl and settled in the places they had left. The principle of replacement, made here equivalent to "old dwelling," points directly to the joint guarantee as the source of the agrarian attachment of the old dwellers. Finally all taxpaying and registered peasantry on state lands were considered bound either to their holdings or to their communes, just as the old dwellers had previously been. We find a clear expression of this attachment in an edict issued in 1610 to Levshin, prefect of the town and region of Chukhloma. The source of the attachment is here indicated: the desire of the state both to maintain the tax solvency of the peasantry and to arrest the shrinkage of tax paying land. Levshin was never to permit any peasants to quit their state lands in his district and never to admit any peasants from other regions, since "some poor and noisy peasants have reduced their holdings, living on a half or a third of it, so as to avoid paying state taxes, and they have turned their land over to younger men, while they themselves work unoccupied land." Levshin was to investigate this and to see that the peasants cultivated their own plots and that they did not reduce their taxable holdings. He was to ensure that the peasants paid according to their stock and work. In this way the peasantry on state and court lands were bound to the soil and formed a distinct class; they were kept from leaving their estates for other private estates, and they were not allowed to bring in peasants from private lands. This was designed to strengthen the joint guarantee for the tax-solvency of the rural communes. This attachment to the soil and serf law had nothing in common. This was purely a police measure.

CRISIS IN THE CHURCH

Efforts to reform Russia along western lines long predated the radical methods of Peter I. Some unhappy Russians in the 16th century labeled Ivan IV the "English Tsar." The experiences of the "time of troubles" stimulated further efforts by the government to modernize itself. At times, these attempts bit deeply into the Russian way of life and they aroused great hostility. One particularly notable crisis came in the middle of the 17th century when the Patriarch Nikon sought to revise the ritual of the Russian church.

On July 13 the relics of St. Philip were brought into Moscow and laid with great pomp in the Uspensky Cathedral. Towards the end of the same month, at a synod assembled at Moscow for the election of a new patriarch, Nikon, who was known to be the Tsar's candidate, was duly chosen. When all the necessary ceremonies had been accomplished, the Tsar summoned to his presence the newly elected patriarch, but Nikon obstinately refused to occupy the patriarchal throne. This was not affectation, but the wise determination of a would-be reformer, conscious of the difficulty of the task before him, to secure a free hand by being elected on his own terms. Again and again the Tsar sent prelates and patricians to persuade Nikon, but he

Source: R. Nisbet Bain, *The First Romanovs (1613–1725)* (London, 1905), pp. 130–39.

remained immovable. At last the Tsar ordered him to be brought to the cathedral by force, and they brought him. Then the Gosudar, the boyars, and the prelates implored Nikon to accept the patriarchate. He persisted in his refusal till the Tsar, and all who were present in the cathedral, fell at his feet and besought him, with tears, to yield to the prayers of the whole community. Nikon, deeply moved, himself began to weep, and, turning to the Tsar and the congregation, uttered these memorable words: "Ye know that in the beginning we received the Holy Gospels, the traditions of the Holy Apostles, the canons of the Holy Fathers, and the imperial laws from orthodox Greece, and thereafter were called Christians. But of a truth we have followed neither the evangelic precepts nor the canons of the Holy Apostles and the Holy Fathers, nor the laws as to religion of the Greek Tsars. . . . If it seem good to you that I should be your patriarch, give me your word, and make a vow in this cathedral church before God our Saviour and His Most Pure Mother, and before the angels and all the saints, that ye will keep the evangelic dogmas and observe the canons of the Holy Apostles and the Holy Fathers, and the laws of the pious Emperors. And if ye promise to obey me also as your chief archpastor and father in every-thing which I shall teach you concerning the divine dogmas and the canons—then will I, according to your wish and supplication, no longer reject this great archpastorate." The Tsar, the boyars, and all the members of the synod, thereupon swore unanimously upon the holy Gospels, and before the holy thaumaturgical ikons, that they would do all that Nikon commanded them, "honour him as their archpastor and father, and assist him to edify the Church." Thus, on August 1, 1652, was Nikon elected. Three days later he was solemnly consecrated and enthroned as the sixth Patriarch of Moscow.

Even before Nikon appeared upon the scene, the necessity of ecclesiastical reform had been admitted in the highest circles, and had found advocates in the immediate *entourage* of the young Tsar, who was keenly interested in all theological questions, and very willing to learn. Among the Tsar's chief advisers at this time was his confessor, Stephen Vonafitev, a relatively learned man, generally beloved for his mild and gentle disposition which made him averse to all harsh measures, though, personally, he led a life of extreme austerity, and was largely responsible for the puritanism of the Court. Vona-fitev was a friend of the excellent Rtishchev, and approved of the introduc-tion of oral preaching and the reform of church music, two questions largely occupying the ecclesiastics of those days. Another leading man at Court was Ivan Neronov, a stern zealot, who regarded even Christmas festivities as "devilish," and who, as a parish priest, had often been nearly beaten to death by his flock for interfering with their juggling, dancing bears, and other pastimes. In his youth Neronov had suffered much from a singularly sluggish brain. His teachers had wept over him in despair, and frequently took his alphabet away from him lest he should read himself blind. But he doggedly persevered, "praying God the while for wisdom," and the famous archimandrite Dionysy finally took him in hand and made a scholar of him. As the pastor of the church of the Resurrection at Nizhny Novgorod, Neronov became very famous as a street preacher, and his reputation for holiness finally procured him, at the suggestion of Vonafitev, the dignity of *protopop*, or dean, of the Kazan Cathedral at Moscow. To the same group belonged the protopop Daniel of Kostroma, and the protopop Login of Murom, both of them men of burning zeal and austere virtue. Presently the Party of the Protopops, the name generally given to this reforming group, was reinforced and overshadowed by a new ally, the priest Avvakum. This perversely heroic creature, the proto-martyr of Russian dissent, and one of the most striking personalities of his age, was born at the village of Gregorovo, near Nizhny Novgorod, fifteen miles from the place where Nikon was born fifteen years before, in 1619 or 1620. The son of a drunken priest, he owed everything to the care of a pious and devoted mother, who educated him, found him an excellent wife, Nastasia Markovna, the orphan daughter of a poor blacksmith, and started him in life as a parish priest (1643). Absolute fearlessness, sublime austerity, and a perfect fidelity to his religious convictions, were to characterise the young priest through life. In his first cure he had the courage, unheard of in those days, to denounce the governor of the place for abducting a poor widow's daughter, and insist on instant and complete restitution. The high-placed ruffian, infuriated at the boldness of a common priest, broke in upon him during divine service with an armed band, dragged him about the church in his vestments, and, after horrible ill-usage, left him for dead on the floor. This is only a specimen of what Avvakum had to endure for endeavouring to do his duty as he understood it. Nothing in the world would ever make him condone wickedness or truckle to the mighty. The following anecdote, recorded in his autobiography, illustrates the moral heroism of the man: On one occasion a woman, who was a grievous sinner, came to confess to him, and, during the narration of her abominable misdeeds, says Avvakum, "the burning of an unchaste desire suddenly gat hold upon me. Now, at that same hour, three lights were burning beside me, and, leaning back against the reading desk, I placed my hand in the flame and held it there till the evil prompting within me died away." Naturally, those who did not regard such a man as a nuisance to be suppressed at any cost, venerated him as a confessor, but saints and sinners were alike subdued by his rare gift of oratory. No other Moscovite ecclesiastic of the seventeenth century could compare with Avvakum as a preacher. He was no imitator of classical models like the Court preacher Polotsky. He spoke to the people in the language of the people, straight from the heart, in a way which made the rudest feel and tremble. His style is always simple, lucid, vigorous, garnished with racy proverbs, full of quaint and vivid touches, and rising at times to flights of irresistible eloquence. For there was as much of the poet as of the preacher in Avvakum; he had imagination as well as humour. His autobiography, one of the most engrossing and pathetic histories ever penned, is, in point of composition, not so much superior to as centuries ahead of what passed for style in his days, an unconscious literary masterpiece as well as a historical document of the highest value. Unfortunately, this great and heroic nature was also one of the most narrow-minded of men, standing far below the intellectual level of a Rtishchev, an Orduin, or even a Nikon. Still more unfortunately, his narrowness was so absolutely conscientious as to be quite incurable, and, as we shall see, it involved him in endless controversies, to his own undoing and to the infinite damage of the Russian Church. Such a champion of orthodoxy was gladly welcomed by the party of Vonafitev, and in 1648 we find Avvakum established in the capital as protopop in one of the Moscow churches.

Before his elevation to the patriarchate, Nikon and the protopops had been induced to co-operate for the good of the Church. Anyhow, there had been no hostility between them, and even Avvakum, in his correspondence, frequently alludes to the archbishop as "our friend." But it is plain that the protopops were apprehensive of what so independent and energetic an archpastor as Nikon might do, for, on the death of the old patriarch Joasaf, after fasting and praying for a whole week, "that God might give his Church a pastor for the salvation of souls," they presented the name of their leader, the gentle and pliant Stephen Vonafitev to the Tsar as a candidate for the vacant patriarchal throne. But Vonafitev, being neither a prelate nor a monk, had little chance against a competitor who was at the same time the highest of the Moscovite metropolitans and the favourite of the Tsar. But in any case the protopops were not the sort of men to undertake even such modest ecclesiastical reforms as were possible in Moscovy in the seventeenth century. Their point of view was erroneous, because they were not sufficiently enlightened to be able to pierce to the root of matters themselves, and nevertheless shrank from the assistance of their natural teachers, the clergy of Kiev and Constantinople, because they suspected the former of being crypto-Catholics, and knew many of the latter to be scoundrels and impostors. They were therefore, thrown back upon Moscovite tradition, as represented by the *Stoglav*, or Reforming Council of Moscow of 1551, a council unrecognised outside of Moscovy, and of questionable authority, inasmuch as its members, while professing to follow Greek precedents, had been notoriously ignorant of the Greek language, the very key of orthodox interpretation. Thus the antiquity to which the protopops were never tired of appealing, was barely a century old, and the canonicity of the *Stoglav*, their ultimate court of appeal, was, at the best, highly problematical. Yet they had pinned their faith implicitly to this purely national synod, and cut off all possibility of a dignified retreat from an impossible position by accepting the responsibility for the revision of the Church service-books inaugurated by the late patriarch Joasaf. This was really no revision at all, but a clumsy attempt to apply the hitherto unexecuted canons of the *Stoglav* to the bettering of the liturgies, which resulted in the interpolation of various schismatical prescriptions into five or six of the thirty-eight books so revised; such, for instance, as the *dvuperstia*, or making the sign of the cross with two fingers, and the *sugubaya alleluya*, or two-fold alleluia, to which the Moscovite Church was consequently committed.

Nikon, as a reformer, was much more liberal. He shared the protopops' distrust of the Greek priests and prelates. He was well aware that the bishops without sees, and the archimandrites without monasteries, who appeared, from time to time, at Moscow with forged letters of recommendation from the Eastern patriarchs, were at best place-seekers and relic-mongers, who, in the words of Krijanic, "sell us Christ a thousand times over, whereas Judas only sold Him once." But he also recognised the fact that if the morals of these vagabond pastors were detestable, their scholarship was far superior to what passed for learning in Moscovy, and he did not see why he should not sift the gold from the dross.

A typical instance of these problematical prelates was Paisios, Patriarch of Jerusalem, who visited Moscow in 1649, with an imposing suite, which included "a number of lewd fellows whom he called archimandrites and archons, so as to obtain a larger alms, inasmuch as all the gratifications received by the members of the patriarchal suite were from first to last appropriated by the patriarch himself." Amongst the patriarch's followers was a Greek monk, Arsenios by name, whose orthodoxy was of so elastic and accommodating a description that the patriarch himself had his doubts about it. Educated at Rome by the Jesuits, Arsenios is next heard of at Stambul, where he professed alternately the orthodox and the Mussulman faith, ultimately resuming orthodoxy in Moldavia, and turning Uniate when adverse circumstances drove him into Lithuania. In Moscovy, on the other hand, he made friends by praising the *Stoglav*. Both Paisios and Arsenios were learned men, however, and their visit to Moscow profoundly affected the fortunes of the Russian Church, inasmuch as they convinced Nikon, then Metropolitan of Novgorod, that many of the ceremonial observances of the Moscovite Church were contrary to the usage of the œcumenical churches of the East. Finally Nikon felt bound to submit in all things ecclesiastical to the authority of the Greeks, and it was largely due to his initiative that the eminent Kievlyans, Arseny Satanovsky, Damaskin Pitsky, and the still more famous Epifany Slavenitsky, were invited to Moscow, to instruct the Moscovite clergy, and translate Greek and Latin books, both religious and secular, into Slavonic for the use of the schools.

Thus the scholars of Constantinople and Kiev opened the eyes of Nikon to the fact that the Moscovite service-books were unorthodox, and subsequent, independent, investigations of his own, conducted with the assistance of the learned Slavenitsky, in the patriarchal archives, convinced him that the sooner these liturgies were rectified the better. With characteristic energy he at once (1654) summoned a properly qualified synod of experts to re-examine the service-books revised by order of the late patriarch Joasaf, and the majority of the synod decided that "the Greeks should be followed rather than our own ancients." But the minority included Paul, Bishop of Kolomna, and several of the old revisers, most of them members of the party of the protopops, who protested energetically against the decision of the council. Nikon thereupon addressed six-and-twenty interrogatories to Paisios, Patriarch of Constantinople, inquiring at the same time how he should deal with the dissentients. Paisios recommended excommunication, and authorised the holding of a second council to settle matters, to which Makarios, Patriarch of Antioch, and the metropolitans of Servia, Nicea and Moldavia, all of whom happened to be at Moscow, were invited. This second council, which assembled in the Uspensky Cathedral, in Orthodox Week, the first week of the great fast, 1656, sanctioned the revision of the service-books as suggested by the first council, and anathematised all who still persisted in crossing themselves with two fingers instead of three. The revision of the service-books was then entrusted to the learned Epifany Slavenitsky and the Greek monk Arsenios, and carried out in accordance with the wishes of Nikon and the suggestions of the council.

Heavily weighted with the fullest œcumenical authority, Nikon's patriarchal staff, never very gentle, now descended with crushing force upon those of his opponents who still refused to obey the precepts of the Church, as interpreted by himself. He was no rigorist indeed, and to those who repented and submitted, even at thc eleventh hour, he could be generous enough. Thus when Neronov, whom he had imprisoned in chains for outrageously abusing him at the council and appealing to the Tsar against him afterwards, when Neronov found it expedient to agree with his adversary quickly, remarking at the same time that, after all, the Greek authorities had not formally condemned the Moscovite service-books, Nikon assented. "Both are good," said he, "it is a matter of indifference, follow whichever you will." To those, however, who obstinately resisted his divine authority, the most holy patriarch could be as "a ravening bear of the forest." But among his opponents he was now to find men as rugged and as unbending as himself, men who, if they could not succeed in dominating the Church below, were quite prepared to join the army of martyrs in Heaven. Foremost among these irreconcilables, who were neither to be convinced by the testimony of Greek archbishops, nor silenced by the decrees of œcumenical councils, stood the protopop Avvakum. Not only pride and obstinacy, but conviction and conscience, moved the intrepid protopop to withstand, for the sake of what he believed to be the truth, the omnipotent and triumphant patriarch. He never realised that his position was absurd and untenable, and it is this which makes his heroic steadfastness so pathetic.

For, indeed, Nikon was so entirely in the right, that it requires a mental effort to imagine how anyone could ever have seriously believed him to be in the wrong. The patriarch stood firm for antiquity, a real antiquity, pruned of all the parasitical excrescences, the outcome of ignorance and misunderstanding, which had overgrown the Moscovite Church in the course of ages. His opponents, blinded by prejudice and suspicion, failed to see that his reforms were but a return to primitive antiquity, and denounced them as the inventions of Antichrist. Agreement was impossible. The question at issue had to be fought out till the bitter end. So long as there were men in Moscovy ready to be tortured to death rather than cross themselves with three fingers instead of two, or spell the name of our Lord with two iotas instead of with one iota, there could be no peace in the Church, especially as the martyrs of to-day might very easily have become the persecutors of to-morrow, toleration being accounted a mortal sin by both parties.

The patriarch certainly showed the schismatics no mercy. It was a rough age when gentle methods did not recommend themselves even to the mildest of men. Nikon was naturally hard if not cruel, and above all things he was thorough. His scheme of reform included not only the service-books and the Church ceremonies, but the ikons actually in use, which had widely departed from the ancient Byzantine models, being, for the most part, imitations of Polish and Frankish originals. The patriarch ordered a search from house to house to be made for these "new-fangled" ikons, and we are told by an eye-witness that his soldiers and servants were charged first to gouge out the eyes of these "heretical counterfeits," and then carry them through the town in derision. He also issued an *ukaz* threatening with the severest penalties all who dared to make or use such ikons in the future. Hundreds of pious Moscovites, who had grown up to venerate these holy images, naturally regarded such acts of violence as sacrilege and iconoclasticism. The plague which visited Moscow about this time was popularly supposed to be a divine judgment on the impiety of the patriarch. There was a loud murmuring, and for a time Nikon went in danger of his life.

Nevertheless he departed not a hair's-breadth from the narrow path. The utmost concession he would make to the timid remonstrances of the pious Tsar, whose sense of propriety had been shocked by the anathematising and trampling under foot of scores of offending ikons in the Uspensky Cathedral itself, in the presence of an immense and horror-stricken congregation, was that the degraded images should be privately and decently buried instead of being burnt publicly by the common hangman.

This ruthlessness goes far to explain the unappeasable hatred with which Avvakum and his followers ever afterwards regarded Nikon and all his works. The protopop was not the man to keep silence under the persecutions of Antichrist, and the virulence of his denunciations speedily led to his seizure. He was dragged, in full canonicals, from a loft which he used as a chapel after being expelled from his church, and was sent in chains to the dungeons of the Andronev Monastery. During his detention the party of the protopops was broken up, Vonafitev and the weaker members submitting to the patriarch, while the stronger spirits were flogged, tortured and exiled in all directions. On September 15, 1657, Avvakum's fate was also decided. He escaped the tonsure through the personal intercession of the Tsar, but was banished to Tobolsk with his wife and family. His adventures and sufferings are recorded in his autobiography.

MODERN CLOTHING

Another example of Russian conservatism is to be found in the following account of an attempt to change the Russian style of dress.

The clothing [of the Russians] was neither pretty nor practical, nor hygienic, but the people held to it and wanted nothing of changes.

And on this point the populace was not any more conservative than the former government, the upper hierarchy, the dignitaries. Once in the last years of the reign of the Tsar Alexis, a boyar rode to the hunt in Polish costume. It so happened that this clothing was subsequently burned at the order of the Patriarch. There were occasions when individual representatives of the higher circles were so bold as to wear German clothing, but the government looked askance at such a beginning. On August 6, 1675 an *ukaz* was issued to all court officials: under penalty of disgrace and degradation they were not to dare to assume foreign manners, to cut their hair in the way of foreigners, to wear foreign clothing, caps, or hats, or to allow their servants to wear such objects.

A few decades earlier the opposite had occurred. Foreigners living in Moscow had in part begun to wear Russian clothing. But this had also been forbidden, since it had happened that in a procession, the foreigners, who as heretics were unworthy of the blessing of the Russian church, nevertheless had participated in this blessing. The Patriarch, who gave the blessing,

---

Source: Alexander Brückner, *Beiträge zur Kulturgeschichte Russlands im XVII. Jahrhundert* (Leipzig, 1887), pp. 191ff.

had not been able to distinguish the Lutherans or the Catholics present from the Orthodox. The Church Prince noted the difference when the foreigns had not bowed toward the Patriarch as had the Russians, and he issued an order to all foreigners immediately to doff Russian clothing. According to a contemporary, this caused great difficulties because of a shortage of material and tailors.

It is known how the clergy opposed the shaving of beards. Patriarch Adrian, just before the introduction of shaving by Peter the Great, had issued a violent encyclical concerning beards, in which, among other things he noted that men who wore only mustaches without beards looked not like men but rather like cats and dogs. Adrian's predecessor, the Patriarch Joachim, in his testament, had issued the most categorical protest against the introduction of foreign manners and garbs. But still more: even such a man as the distinguished politician and diplomat Ordyn-Nashchokin, who understood the meaning of foreign manners, who had allowed his son to be educated by a Pole, and who was by no means a fanatic, had declared, "What are foreign ways to us? Our clothing is not to the taste of foreigners and their clothing is not to ours."

When Peter came forth with his reforms for beards and clothing, there was no opposition in the higher circles of Moscow's society. Patriarch Adrian, who had previously opposed shaving beards, was silent. The great ones accommodated themselves peacefully to all which the ruler demanded of them. Many could even see the use of such a reform and they sympathized with Peter. The marriage of a courtier in 1701 was celebrated in old Russian costume at Peter's order, according to a witness, in order to show the absurdity and foolishness of the former style. The boyars had exceedingly high caps, the women wore sleeves 12 ells long and heels five inches high. At court one accepted European clothing quickly, as the many pictures of Peter's contemporaries show. . . .

In the lower strata of the population one grumbled in a completely different fashion. Countless were arrested and punished because they permitted themselves to express opposition to the reforming Tsar. A resident of Dmitrov had declared, as he drew on the new clothing, "Whoever has introduced this clothing should be hanged." Already before Peter the sectarians had declared in their writings, "God has expressly forbidden the introduction of foreign clothes, these clothes are most unpleasing to him." Such a reform was therefore heresy, a defection from the true Church. Now the people grumbled against the Patriarch Adrian who was silent before such evil reforms, who allowed it all to happen without protest simply in order to keep his own position. Generally it was believed that shaving and the new clothes were only the beginning of still worse heresy, namely that the fast was not being observed at court or in the army. The rumor spread that Peter was not a true Tsar, but a foundling of German birth. As proof one pointed to the introduction of German clothing: a true Russian would not have done that. The wildest rumors were spread and believed, such as the legend that Tsar Peter had been killed while abroad and that the foreigners had sent another back in his place. The true Peter had been stuck in a barrel and thrown into the sea. Persons around Peter, such as Menshikov, were considered to be in league with the devil, since they wore wigs. The Tsar himself was repeatedly called the Anti-Christ. During the Astrakhan rising the people were told that the foreign military men and the high officials practiced idolatry and even carried their idols with them. The government learned of this and investigated the origin of such a story. It was learned that the wig stands, which the foreigners used for combing the wigs, were considered to be idols.

Russian clothing . . . needed a reform. It was rather effeminate. Men often had their wives' clothes remodelled for themselves. The old suits were also very costly and luxurious, using a great deal of material. . . . Peter himself liked to wear Dutch or French sailor's clothing. This permitted him the free movement necessary in shipbuilding or such activity. In the long Russian gowns with hanging sleeves one could not climb a mast or swing an axe or carry on any intensive activity. Soloviev has well noted that the manner of clothing corresponds to the manner of the people. The comfortable, indolent Asiatic always appears in a robe. If the Russian wanted to change into a European, to work, to produce, to advance in the western European way, he had to give up his oriental clothing which hindered activity. . . . The clothing reform was a historic necessity, not the result of a chance whim of an absolute ruler.

AN EXOTIC LAND

For many Europeans, however, Russia was still a strange, exotic land with odd customs. Travelers related fantastic stories, mixing fact with fiction. The following selection, originally written in Latin, illustrates this genre of travelogue.

Some dialogues and idiomatic expressions are added which contain phrases occurring in everyday life and particular constructions so as to

Source: Henricus Wilhelmus Ludolfus, *Grammatica Russica* (Oxford, 1696), Preface, pp. 91–97.

explain certain syntactical matters. To the dialogues I have added a German translation because the merchants of various nations make use of the German language in Russia. I have also found that not a few Russians know Latin and German. By the authority of the Patriarch a school has even been established in Moscow where Greek teachers teach Latin and Greek in such a way that the instructional program is not in conflict with the fundamental law of Russia, as is claimed by some. His present Royal Majesty indeed desires all the more that the talents of his subjects be cultivated.

Moreover, since many foreigners are forced to enter Russia not only for the sake of commerce and governmental negotiations, but also for the care of the foreign churches which by the clemency of the Tsar have received concessions in the trading center of Archangel and of Wolgoda, as well as in the capital city of Moscow itself, one or the other person might perhaps in some way profit from my work. If I should achieve this end, I shall regret neither the expended labor nor unfavorable opinions. Since I am not seized by a ridiculous ambition to seek fame through a work on grammar, my peace of mind will not be disturbed by the judgment of those who enjoy displaying their superior qualities by carping at others rather than by serving the public interest by their own effort in agreement with their capability.

Perhaps this example will convince the Russians that something can be printed also in their popular speech form as it would be both ornamental and useful for the Russian nation if they attempted to enhance their own language in the fashion of other nations and to publish good books in it. It is to be hoped that the Patriarch will lend a hand in this matter since he is seized by the laudable desire to promote good literature. To this end he has had Greek type made in Holland by the same craftsman who made these Slavic types for the use of the Oxford Academy.

*   *   *   *   *

Salt is obtained in three ways: (1) through evaporation in salt yards, the best known of which are in Perm, in Siberia; (2) by mining, it is dug out of the earth in large quantity in the province of Uffa; (3) produced by the sun, in the lake near Astracan and in Siberia. I was told that at Astracan the salt floats on the surface of the lake, while in Siberia it is extracted from the ground.

Nitrate and sulfur of excellent quality are found in Sinbiria, along the Volga, near the Kingdom of Kazan. Exportation into other countries, however, is prohibited by the Russians, since it is a source of gunpowder, in order to avoid supplying neighbors with a weapon of war.

Iron mines exist in the vicinity of the metropolis of Moscow and at the border of Sweden near Oloniza.

A talc called *sliuda* is found toward the trading center of Archangel, and from Russia the term "Muscovy glass" has been received by the English language. A large amount of crystal is obtained in the province of Uffa.

At the borders of Siberia, around the river Yenisei, ore is found which, because of its color and heaviness, was considered gold ore. But students of metallurgy who were sent there found out that it is not fire resistant, and in a talk with me, they called it gold sulfur, believing that if one could make it durable, it would be real gold. . . .

                    *   *   *   *   *

A matter of great curiosity is the *mammotovoi kost* which is dug out of the earth in Siberia. People tell miraculous stories about it; for they say that it is the skeleton of an animal which lives underground and exceeds in size all animals living on the earth. In medicine it is used in the same manner as the horn of the so-called unicorn. A piece of it was given me by a friend who said he had received it from a Russian Primate who had returned from Siberia. To me it looks like genuine ivory. More experienced people have told me that this *mammotovoi kost* are elephants' teeth. This would mean that they were carried there in the Deluge. . . .

                    *   *   *   *   *

Most curious among the plants is the *kosa trava*, "the scythe herb," which is said to grow in Siberia and to be able to break iron. If one hits it with a scythe, the scythe goes to pieces. Some trustworthy men who had been in Siberia have declared this to me so that I would appear to be of an obstinate nature if I refused to believe them.

On the other hand, I am quite aware of the fact that in Russia one has to use great caution concerning things reported by public opinion. For I have learned from better-informed men that the story about the plant *boranetz* is untrue. This plant is said to have the shape of a lamb, to be wrapped in wool, and to graze in a circle. The afore-mentioned men, who had been in those parts where said plant is supposed to grow, have never been able to find it, but they said that in some Tatar countries there are sheep whose lambs have such soft and nicely curled wool that their pelts are sold as pelts of the *boranetz* or lamb plant.

Widespread in Russia is the fame of a wound-healing root which grows in Siberia and is called *voltschnoi koren*, "wolf's root." It is said to have a the great quality of healing injuries. But that it really can, as I have been told, heal an injury in any part of the body merely by being chewed in the mouth—that I do not want to assert.

                    *   *   *   *   *

The People. The natives are mostly of a very robust constitution which with many of them manifests itself in a tall stature and a stoutness which is not at all vulgar. Attributable to this quality is also their fecundity which fills that country with a larger number of inhabitants than is usually believed. This conclusion may be reached from the gigantic armies which are levied, in times of war, in urban and rural areas on the basis of the number of inhabitants. I have been told by men worthy of belief and who had participated in a campaign in a commanding position, that when an army was raised a few years ago against the Prekopin Tatars, it consisted of more than 300,000 men. Since fasting with them takes up almost one half of the year, during which time the common people use food of very little nutritious value, such as cabbage and cucumbers, not cooked on fire, but merely conditioned with salt, this is also an indication of a strong stomach, the warmth of which they undoubtedly maintain with distilled spirits and garlic which is much used among them. Perhaps these two things are conducive to preserving their good health, especially the garlic which helps the stomach to dissolve viscuous matter to no less a degree than it is despised by many for its unpleasant impression on the nose. I have hardly noticed any epidemic disease among them, except for the disease common to the northern countries, namely scurvy. . . .

To the natural history of Russia belongs also the strange method of traveling used in the extreme parts of Siberia towards China; for they have sails on their vehicles. As long as the wind is favorable, they spread the sail out and proceed quite quickly over the frost-hardened snow, taking six dogs with them in the vehicle. When there is no wind, the sail is taken down, and those dogs are hitched to the vehicle. I have been told that those six dogs pull half a load of a team of horses.

The following commodities are exported from Russia: rhubarb (which, however, is inferior to the Chinese and the Turkish), castoreum, moss, honey, wax, tar for ships, cheaper linen goods, caviar, Russian leather (commonly called *jufften*), and hemp. The city of Yaroslav is primarily famous for the production of Russian leather, the largest part of which, as well as of caviar, is sent to Italy. The hemp is used by the English and the Dutch for equipping ships with hawsers. While I was staying in Moscow, some Dutch merchant obtained permission to export wheat and he then developed large business.

The English and the Dutch carry on commercial transactions with the Russians at the trading center of Archangel and in Narva, the former place being more visited by English boats and the latter by Dutch. In Narva great privileges had been granted by the King of Sweden to Armenian merchants living in Persia to enable them to ship their merchandise bought in Holland by that route. This can be done quite conveniently via the Baltic Sea, the Volga River, and the Caspian Sea. But not one of them has the right to return to Persia by way of Russia unless he has come from Persia by the same route. Thus they are forced to cross Russia both when coming from Persia and returning there. For it is more convenient for a person to go from Russia to Persia than from Persia to Russia, since he can use a second river which flows there.

Formerly, the Baneanes merchants, famous throughout India, used to come with their merchandise as far as the capital city of Moscow. Now, however, they are no longer allowed to go beyond Astrakhan, but are forced to carry out their business transactions at that place.

Trade between China and Russia is carried on by Russians who get silk clothes from China. They bring from there also the herb *the*, as well as a product which they call *temzui*, of golden-yellow color, aromatic odor, and chalky texture, and which they consider an excellent medicine for many diseases. The Mohammedan Buchartzi, as whose capital, if I am not mistaken, Samarkand was mentioned to me, often visit Tobolsk, the capital of Siberia, with their Indian merchandise. Perhaps it is for their sake that, as I have been told, Arabic is taught in the city of Tobolsk.

The Kalmuk Tatars bring to Moscow horses for sale mostly in the fall. A herd of this type of horses they call *tabun*, which consists of six, eight, twelve thousand horses, and sometimes even more.

These Tatars trade not only their horses but also children, and they often sell their sons to the Russians. When at one time I met a boy of this kind, who had learned Russian, I, prompted by curiosity, made some inquiries about their language. I asked him how he called God in his language. He said *Bog u nas niet*, i.e., we have no God. They do, however, have a religion of some kind and their highest priest is called *kutufta,* who, just as the *kutufta* of the Mugal Tatars, is appointed by the Dalailama, who lives at the border of China, in a place called Barantola, as I learned. The Lamas or priests of the Chinese are likewise said to stand under the command of that Dalailama and honor him as a divine being. His common reputation among them is that he is immortal, and thereby it is all the easier for him to keep the common people in that superstitious credulity, since he lets hardly anybody see him except the priests who are aware of the fraud. A certain man who had the function of envoy of the Tsar to the Chinese Emperor used to tell that he had been granted the honor of seeing the Dalailama, if he agreed to throw himself to the ground before him, but that he had not consented to that condition.

May God have mercy on the enormous masses of people who up to now have been shrouded in the utter darkness of idolatry and may He finally open to them the door to the recognition of their salvation. I believe that in this wish all those who seek the glory of their Redeemer and wish the salvation of the entire human race through the Spirit of Christ will join me.

RUSSIAN TRADE

A more detailed account of the development of Russian foreign trade in the 17th century is to be found in the following selection, written by Soviet historians.

Archangel occupied first place among the ports for foreign trade. In the middle of the 17th century the turnover in Archangel amounted to no less than 75% of all foreign trade.

The Archangel fair opened annually on August 1—after the middle of the 17th century, on July 1—and continued to October 1. Foreign ships arrived in June and July They usually came in convoys of four to six ships because of the danger of attack by pirates. Trading at the fair began relatively late. The great Russian exporters were in no hurry to conclude deals and they watched out that no Russian trader should lower his prices. They were interested only in large-scale trade, in which small purchases could not change the price set by wholesale purchases. Foreign merchants attempted to destroy the agreement of the Russian exporters by buying goods at low prices from small sellers, who in turn hurried to sell their goods before the opening of large scale trading. Large scale trade began only at the end of August or even in the middle of September. At the end of September the ships departed; the Russian merchants packed up and sailed up the Dvina. With the closing of the fair, the city of Archangel died until the following spring.

The number of foreign ships arriving in Archangel varied very greatly, depending on the general political situation in Europe and the state of the international market. At first, in the 16th century, eight to ten English ships came to Kholmogory. After the shores of the Bay of Finland had been seized by the Swedes and the Russians had finally lost Narva, the significance of the port of Archangel grew. At the end of the 16th century, already more than twenty ships came. The years of intervention were unfavorable for trade, but nevertheless the general turnover of trade at Archangel was even a little higher then than during the 16th century. At this time the Dutch took over first place in the number of ships and in the volume of export and import.

Source: K. V. Bazilevich and N. V. Ustiugov, "Torgovlia," in *Ocherki istorii SSSR, XVII v.* (Moscow, 1955), pp. 131–34.

SEVENTEENTH CENTURY 49

The Dutch merchant and diplomat Isaac Massa wrote in 1618 that 20 to 30 large Dutch ships travelled to Russia each year. In fact, in 1618 43 ships in all came to Archangel, of which 30 were Dutch and only 3 English. The Dutch ambassadors A. Burk and I. Feltdrill, in their report of a mission to Russia in 1630–1631, declared that they had counted 100 Dutch and several English ships in the port of Archangel. Such a gathering of merchant ships must be considered exceptional, since in the 1630s and 1640s the number of ships varied from forty to fifty. Before the second Polish war, the number of ships again rose to 80. In 1658 there were only four English ships among 80. After the issuance of the New Trade Statute of 1667, which introduced a protective tariff, the number of foreign ships arriving annually in Archangel remained almost constant. To be sure, in 1669, 47 ships were registered, but in 1670 there were again 80. With some variations the number apparently remained the same to the end of the century.

The collections of the Archangel customs grew steadily at the end of the 17th century, and the annual sum of duties in the 1670s rarely fell below 60,000 rubles. In 1675–1676 it reached 82,180 rubles, while in the first half of the 17th century it had varied between 26,000 and 40,000 rubles. The annual collection remained just as high in the 1680s. In 1687–1688, 82,600 rubles were collected.

The history of foreign trade through the port of Archangel shows the gradual decline of English trade with the Russian state and the growth of Dutch trade.

In the middle of the century, Sweden, strengthened as a result of the Thirty Years' War with Germany and the Peace of Westphalia of 1648, emerged as a third competitor in the struggle for the Russian market. After the Swedes had seized the southern shore of the Baltic Sea, that body became a Swedish lake. In connection with this a project arose in Sweden to transfer the basic route of Russian trade from Archangel to the Baltic Sea through Novgorod and the Baltic ports. At the end of the 1640s the Swedish resident in Moscow attempted to reach agreement in this question with the Dutch and English merchants, but the effort failed. In the mid-1650s another Swedish resident vainly sought to persuade the Russian government of the disadvantages of foreign trade through Archangel, and he pointed to the necessity of transferring Russian foreign trade to the Baltic Sea. Transferring foreign trade to the Baltic Sea without Russia's having its own port on its shore meant putting all foreign trade with Europe under the control of Sweden and also the loss of income at Archangel. Therefore the Russian government rejected the proposal.

Foreign trade through the western frontiers cannot compete in volume with the trade through Archangel, but for a number of cities (Novgorod, Pskov, Tikhvin, Smolensk) it has a great significance. Through these cities went the greatest quantity of hemp, flax, leather, linen, cloths, etc. Metals were imported—iron, copper, lead, and also industrial articles. Despite the extremely unfavorable conditions in which the Russian merchants were put, the constraint and arbitrary actions which they had to endure in Sweden, despite the difficulties of travel after the peace of Kardis in 1661, the number of Russian traders going to Stockholm increased. Some rather significant fortunes were made in this trade: in Novgorod the Stoianovs, in Pskov the Pogankins and Rusinovs, in Tikhvin the Samsonovs, Shpilkins, in Smolensk (in the 1670s) the Zhdankovs and Liubovetsky.

While Archangel was the chief port for trade with the countries of Western Europe, Astrakhan played this role for the eastern trade.

CONDITIONS IN MOSCOW

The rivalry between English and Dutch merchants in Russia also was mentioned in the memoirs of an Englishman, who had served as the personal physician of Tsar Alexei Mikhailovich. Apart from his personal respect for the Tsar, this writer had only scorn for the Russian way of life.

The Russian Government is perfectly Monarchical, it has offices call'd *Precauses;* the dispensation of their justice is commonly arbitrary, for they have very few written laws, they go much upon presidents (but money is their best president, which overthrows all the former). They waste abundance of paper in writing down things at large (as our common clerks do) all in rolls of a great length, and although they have a table before them, they cannot write but upon their knees, after the old fashion that St. Jerom is pictur'd. Their clerks they call *Podiacks*, and he that is Lord Deputy, *Diack*. They borrow most of their characters from the Greeks.

All things are transacted by way of petition, which is roll'd up like a wafer, and the petitioner holds it up before the *Boyar*, who if in a good humour puts forth his hand to receive it, and either reads it presently, or gives it to his *Diack*, who commonly must be brib'd for a remembrancer. His Imperial Majesty is a goodly person, two months older than King Charles the Second, of a sanguine complexion, light brown hair, his beard uncut, he is tall and fat, of a majestical deportment, severe in his anger, bountiful, charitable, chastely uxorious, very kind to his sisters and children,

Source: Samuel Collins, *The Present State of Russia* (London, 1671), pp. 43–45, 110–12, 116–17, 126–31.

of a strong memory, strict in his devotions, and a favourer of his religion; and had he not such a cloud of sycophants and jealous nobility about him, who blind his good intentions, no doubt he might be numbred among the best and wisest of princes: His father was a great lover of English men, and a man of peace; but this Emperour is of a warlike spirit, ingaged against the Crim, Polacks and Swedes, with what success let time declare. Thus much I know: This empire is impoverish'd, depopulated and spoil'd so much in ten years, as it will not recover its pristine prosperity in forty. Seven years ago the Plague carried away 7 or 8 hundred thousand people: And three years since the Crim carried away captive out of the borders 400,000 souls into perpetual captivity, besides 300,000 were consumed and kill'd by dint of sword in several armies; the best of the land is harass'd, the rest untill'd for want of men. For in five hundred *versts* travel up the river, you may see ten women and children for one man. All things are there become scarce; every thing six times the rate that it was formerly; and copper money is not valued.

* * * * *

I shall now give you a further description of the Czar. He is a goodly person, about six foot high, well set, inclin'd to fat, of a clear complexion, lightish hair, somewhat a low forehead, of a stern countenance, severe in his chastisements, but very careful of his subjects love. Being urged by a stranger to make it death for any man to desert his colours; he answer'd, it was a hard case to do that, for God has not given courage to all men alike. He never appears to the people but in magnificence, and on festivals with wonderful splendor of jewels and attendants. He never went to any subjects house but his governours when he was thought past all recovery. His centinels and guards placed round about his court, stand like silent and immoveable statues. No noise is heard in his pallace, no more than if uninhabited. None but his domesticks are suffer'd to approach the inward court, except the lords that are in office. He never dines publickly but on festivals, and then his nobility dine in his presence. At Easter all the nobility and gentry, and courtiers kiss the emperours hand and receive eggs. Every meal he sends dishes of meat to his favourites from his own table. His stores of corn, and dry'd flesh are very considerable, with these he pays his *Strelsies* or *Janzaries*, giving them some cloth, but very little money; for they have all trades, and great privileges.

The emperour with his pottash, wax and honey, he buys velvet, sattin, damask, cloth of gold and broad-cloth, with which he gratifies his officers for their service.

He hath now seven *versts* off Moscow, built workhouses for hemp and flax, in that good order, beauty and capacity, that they will employ all the poor in his kingdom with work. He hath allotted many miles of wast land for that design.

* * * * *

In the night season the Czar will go about and visit his chancellors desks, and see what decrees are pass'd, and what petitions are unanswer'd. He has his spyes in every corner, and nothing is done or said at any feast, publick meeting, burial or wedding but he knows it. He has spyes also attending his armies to watch their motions, and give a true account of their actions: these spyes are gentlemen of small fortunes, who depend on the emperours favour, and are sent into armies, and along with embassadors, and are present on all publick occasions.

'Tis death for any one to reveal what is spoken in the Czars pallace. I being curious to see the fine buildings for the flax and hemp, ask't to what end they were built, but not a workman durst tell me, though they knew it well enough; but they replied, God and the emperour know best, this was all I could get from them. The Czars children are attended with children of their own bred up with them, and there is none of them but know their distance, and their degrees of bowing to all sorts of persons. None dare speak a word what passes in their court.

* * * * *

The trade last summer was very low in Mosco, by reason of their late war, which had drein'd them of two fifths, besides the raising of their customs, and taking their goods by force for copper money, which fell from a hundred to one, till at last it was call'd in, to the undoing of many men. Divers hang'd themselves, others drunk away the residue of the states, and dyed with drinking.

English cloth is a drug, because dearer than the Dutch, which though slight, and shrinks a sixth part in wetting, yet the Russians like it, because they say none but new cloth will shrink, but we are to blame for not fitting them with the like. Again, we keep our old trade of cloth, but they bring silks, and all manner of pedlary ware, which vends better than cloth, the which grows now much out of fashion. *Sed si populus vult decipi, decipiatur.*

If the Persian and Indian silk trade prevail in Russia, the Czar, I fear will think it too great a boon to restore the English immunities, and 'twill be as hard for them to regain their priviledges, as it was for Pharoahs people to drive their charriots through the Red Sea, when their wheels fell off.

As I have nothing to say against the magnificence, splendor, clemency and vertue of the Czars own person, so I have no reason to recommend the Russes integrity, for the generality of them are false, truce-breakers, subtile foxes, and ravenous wolves, much altered, since their traffick with the Hollander, by whom they have much improv'd themselves in villany and deceit.

The Dutch, like locusts, swarm in Mosco, and eat bread out of the Englishmens mouths, they are more in number, and richer, and spare no gifts to attain their ends; whereas the English depending on their old priviledges, think 'tis enough to say with the Jews, We have Abraham to our Father, we are Englishmen, do us right, or we will complain: But the Russians are of Solomons opinion, that money answers all things.

If we would out-do the Dutch Trade, it must not be driven on by such as take up goods upon trust and time, as it has been these twenty years last past. At present they come like locusts out of the bottomless pit, and so they do all the world over, where there is a sun-shine of gain. In Russia they are better accepted than the English, because they gratifie the nobility with gifts, which they will have if they lend any assistance.

The Hollanders have another advantage, by rendring the English cheap and ridiculous by their lying pictures, and libelling pamphlets, this makes the Russian think us a ruined nation. They represent us by a lyon painted with three crowns revers'd and without a tail, and by many mastive dogs, whose ears are cropt and tails cut off. With many such scandalous prints, being more ingenious in the use of their pencils than pens. These stories take much with barbarous people, when no body is present to contradict them.

It would not be impertinent, in my opinion, if some intelligent person in Moscua should represent the state of his Majesty of Great Britains Kingdoms, forces and territories to the best advantage, and also his colonies in the West-Indies, with all their revenues, and drawing a map of the aforesaid places, present it to Afanasy Nashockin, to breed in him an opinion of his Brittish Majesties real greatness, which the Dutch have so much extenuated. Bogdan Matfoidg the chamber-favourite should not be neglected neither. He fancies rarities, and therefore should be presented with some. For as Nashockin maintains reason of state, so Bogdan must be the man to procure the Czars personal affection towards his Majesty of Great Britain.

The Russes are very proud of, and much pleased, with the honourable peace they have made with Poland, and now think no nation superiour; for they are never good natur'd but when they are either beaten or bribed. No master (to them) like Mars nor mistris like Luna, these indeed are the only planets which rule the world.

CHAPTER 3

Russia Becomes a European Power

RUSSIAN DIPLOMACY IN THE 18TH CENTURY

Russia's emergence as a major European power can be dated from Peter the First's victory over the Swedes at Poltava in 1709. Sweden was a small country, but it had played a major role in 17th century Europe. Now Russia, under the determined leadership of Peter I, began to realize its own potential as a European power. Peter reorganized Russia's administration, strengthened its army, and sought in general to reform his country's way of life. Some of his efforts ended in failure, but on the whole he made Russia a major factor in European affairs.

Diplomatic Institutions under Peter I

The breadth and complexity of foreign policy under Peter I necessitated the reorganization of the institutions conducting international relations and the creation of new diplomatic cadres. The Russian diplomats whom Peter I inherited from his predecessors were not up to the new tasks of foreign policy arising from the complicated international situation of the beginning of the 18th century. Under Peter the whole diplomatic service was reorganized with an eye to western European practices. Permanent diplomatic missions were established in foreign countries—the absence of these had already been strongly felt in the 17th century. In 1699 A. A. Matveev was sent to Holland with the title "extraordinary and plenipotentiary envoy"; in 1701 a "minister" was named to Vienna, etc. At the same time Russian consuls, protecting Russian commercial interests, appeared in the most important European cities and even in some cities outside Europe. On the other hand, permanent foreign missions were established at the Tsar's court at the end of the 17th century.

Source: S. V. Bakhrushin and S. D. Skazkin, "Diplomatiia evropeiskikh gosudarstv v XVIII v.," *Istoriia diplomatii,* I (Moscow, 1959), 344–69.

Peter asserted the principle of the personal inviolability of ambassadors with great persistence when the matter concerned the representatives of his country. In 1708 a great storm arose over the case of the Russian ambassador to England, A. A. Matveev, who was arrested for debts, insulted and even beaten. This incident aroused great alarm among the whole diplomatic corps in London which saw in the outrage to the Russian ambassador a violation of international diplomatic law. Matveev was freed. All the ministers, "to a man," visited him, "shuddering at the affront, unheard of and unrivaled in history." The English government hoped to smooth the incident over by offering Matveev a large gift of money, but the Russian refused the gift, declaring that in his person the Tsar himself had been outraged. In order to emphasize the significance of the incident, as well as his own dissatisfaction, Matveev, despite the requests of the English ministers, demanded his passport and departed for Holland without taking leave of the Queen, refusing to accept the customary present from the Queen and not wanting to use the yacht offered him for his departure.

Fearing retaliation by the Russian government against English citizens in Russia, the English government directed its envoy Whitworth to spare neither effort nor expense in order to regulate the matter. Queen Anne expressed her regrets. Peter demanded the death sentence for those persons who had outraged his ambassador. The guilty ones were in fact prosecuted. In regular session the parliament called the action against Matveev a crime "against both English law and that international law on which the privilege of envoys is based." A special act was introduced "for the protection of the privileges of ambassadors and public ministers," defining a number of questions connected with ambassadorial inviolability. The diplomatic corps took part in the preparation of the text of the law. Although the death penalty was not applied to the guilty persons, the English government sent an extraordinary embassy to Peter I with apologies. In the document from Queen Anne, Peter I was called "Caesar," i.e. emperor, and therefore it was decided henceforth to use this title in reference to the Tsar when dealing with the English government. The embassy was received with great ceremony, and Peter, "taking into account the attitude of the nation as expressed in the parliamentary act and also the honor shown him by the Queen in the present embassy," did not persist in his demands. Thus, thanks to Peter's energetic action, this incident served as an occasion for the development of ambassadorial law.

Peter himself, however, sometimes took extreme measures toward foreign representatives who interfered in Russia's internal affairs. In 1718 he arrested the Dutch resident in St. Petersburg who was charged with having sent false, unfavorable reports on Russia to his government and also with having carried on suspicious relations with subjects of the Tsar. The ambassador was put under guard. All his papers were seized, and the Tsar himself conducted the investigation. Peter demanded his recall by the Dutch states.

The old Ambassadorial Department could not meet the new demands of government for an efficient organ of foreign relations. Already at the end of the 17th century, alongside it, an "Ambassadorial Chancery" arose, which gradually took over all functions of the department. In 1716 the collegial principle was introduced into the Ambassadorial Chancery, and it was re-named the "Ambassadorial College." Finally, in 1720, a special College of Foreign Affairs was formed which replaced the old Ambassadorial Depart-ment. . . .

In the course of the reorganization of the organ of foreign relations, there took place a unique mixture of European ways with the old ways and customs of Russian diplomacy. In particular, great attention was given as before to questions of the sovereign's honor. Proper forms of etiquette were the first thing taken from foreign practice. "The Russians," wrote the Danish envoy in 1717, "will give up none of their old Russian ways which can serve for their exaltation, and at the present time they are studying foreign ways suit-able for maintaining and increasing their dignity and honor." Foreign am-bassadors were offended because Russian officials would never make the first visit. As regards ceremonies, the diplomats of Peter I were often as capricious as those of his father. In the signing of the Russo-Danish treaty of 1710 a dispute arose over the order of the signatures of the plenipoten-tiaries. The Danish plenipotentiary agreed that the signatures of the Russian plenipotentiaries be first on the Russian copy, but he demanded that the Danes' signatures be first on the Danish copy. The Russian ministers yielded, but they resorted to the following trick: The Chancellor signed and put his seal on the last line, the Vice-Chancellor above him, and the Danish envoy on the first line. "The Russians thus wanted to imply that they considered the last place first and vice versa." . . . Even Peter himself did not renounce old conceptions of honor. In receiving foreign ambassadors he wore "neither a hat nor anything else on his head," obviously so as not to have to take off his hat at the mention of a foreign title. The Tsar would stand under the very edge of a canopy, leaving no room for an ambassador beside him. All these contrivances, still practiced in the first decade of the 18th century, were but remnants of the past, alien to Peter's active nature, and, feeling encumbered by them, he soon abandoned them altogether.

As for foreign ambassadors, they were sometimes not treated with the respect which Peter demanded for his own ambassadors. Before their ar-rival in the capital they were kept as before under careful and capricious surveillance. Their servants could not leave the dwelling, and the ambas-sadors themselves could go out only with the permission of the local com-mandant.

The diplomatic skills necessary for the conduct of policy were not developed suddenly. In 1708 the ministers of Louis XIV reacted very unfavorably to the Russian envoys in France, who, in their words, "sought nothing from the king for the benefit of their sovereign and they made only arrogant inquiries." Characteristic, however, was the great caution of Russian diplomats. They rarely agreed to give answers in writing, not wanting thereby to tie themselves down. In some ways diplomatic receptions resembled the receptions of the 17th century. In 1710 Tsarist ministers demanded that the Danish envoy give them his credentials in cipher with a translation on the back. When he refused on the grounds that this would reveal the cipher, they disingenuously replied "that there would be nothing wrong with that since there should be no secrets between the Tsar and the Danish King."

Such were the cadres with which Peter began his diplomatic work on a new, broader and bolder scale. The quick successes of the young Petrine diplomacy are thereby all the more striking. In the second half of Peter's reign a new generation of able and fine diplomats arose who oriented themselves well in international relations and who worked with great dexterity and with outstanding tact.

B. I. Kurakin was an outstanding diplomat of this period, ably defending Russia's interests with dignity. He long held the post of ambassador to Holland, often carrying out very important missions for Peter in England, Hannover, France, at the Congress of Utrecht. Kurakin was in effect a Vice-Chancellor abroad. Russian representatives in the other countries of Europe wrote to him and acted according to his "counsel."

Another talented coworker of Peter in the diplomatic sphere was the clever and steadfast P. A. Tolstoi, who for many years represented Russia's interests at the difficult and even dangerous post of ambassador to Turkey. It was he who brought about Tsarevich Alexei's return to Russia from Austrian territory, and in 1719 he travelled to Berlin with the special mission of restraining the Prussian king from concluding a separate peace with Sweden and an alliance with England.

The instruction given by Peter in 1718 to the delegates to the Aland Congress is undoubtedly a model of diplomatic tact and art. Peter proposed "to draw the Swedish delegates deeply into negotiations . . . and deal with them delicately." The basis of the talks should be not only "to conclude peace with Sweden but also to establish friendship." In a special instruction to Osterman, Peter wrote, "When the previous enmity and hatred between the two powers is eradicated and an eternal friendship is established, then we can not only protect ourselves from others but we can also keep the balance in Europe." Therefore the Tsar considered it necessary to propose acceptable terms to Sweden. "We know," he wrote to Osterman, "that even though by force of arms we might bring the Swedish king to concede all which we have won, Sweden would then always seek means of regaining what it has lost. War will not be ended this way. Therefore we will propose the following means for eradicating all controversies: if the king will yield to us the provinces which we now hold, besides Finland, then we will undertake to help him make up his losses in another place, where he needs it." In conclusion, Peter developed the thought of the unity of interests of all the allies warring against Sweden. Therefore he rejected a separate peace: "If there are no terms for the Prussian and Polish kings, then peace will be weakly founded. We cannot leave them at war."

*   *   *   *   *

The functions of Russian diplomats under Peter became extraordinarily complex. Among other things, they had to conduct a literary struggle with political currents abroad harmful for Russia. When the news of the battle of Narva reached The Hague, Matveev, the Russian ambassador, presented a memorial to the states, seeking to dispel the bad impression made by the news. The Swedish ambassador had to issue a refutation. Later Prince Kurakin, while in The Hague, had to watch the newspapers for items objectionable to Russia and to refute anything printed of that sort. He even complained to the Dutch government about newspapermen. . . . Peter used various means of informing foreign governments about his foreign policy. This was the purpose of P. P. Shafirov's "Discourse" on the "legal reasons" for the war with Sweden, published in 1717 and which was the first Russian treatise on international law. . . . In The Hague Matveev "every week had a gathering of all the leading local figures in his home for conversation and cardplaying and other pleasures" . . . In 1707, an order better to orient Russian representatives abroad, a system of mutual information on the most important military and political events, negotiations, etc., was instituted.

Petrine diplomacy masterfully exploited internal contradictions of enemy countries for purposes of influencing their policies.

Russian diplomats made use of information and friendly relations with leading representatives of the ruling circles of various governments in the interest of their own country. Thus, in 1703, P. A. Tolstoi, the ambassador to Turkey, informed the sultan, through his mother, of the treacherous activities of the vizier in inciting a rising of the Crimean tatars against the Sultan. As a result, the vizier, who was hostile to Russia, was not only removed from his post but also punished. Under Peter, as under his predecessor, valuable information about the situation in Turkey, about the plans and intentions of the Turkish government in regard to Russia, was obtained from the Christians languishing under the Turkish yoke, who had long looked to Russia with hopes for their liberation. In particular, the Russian government received important information from the nephew of the Patriarch of Constantinople. In addition, the Russian representatives in Constantinople received secret information also through secret agents in the Turkish court and in the embassies of other countries. In 1719–1720 the Russian envoy Dashkov received detailed reports about the very secret talks between the vizier and the ambassadors of England and Austria, which permitted him to block the efforts of these ambassadors to bring about a renewal of the war between Russia and Turkey. In the last years of the Northern War the Russian government was well informed, through the reports of its secret agents, about the internal situation of Sweden, the condition of its economy, the number, arms and equipment of its army and fleet, and about the differences of opinion in Swedish ruling circles. After the end of the war, Russian diplomacy supported the party of "patriots" in Sweden. Russian diplomacy conducted an especially complicated and difficult struggle in the last stage of the Northern War with the power most dangerous to Russia, England. The Russian resident in London, F. P. Veselovskii, pointed out to the English that their government, in carrying out a policy sharply hostile to Russia, was not considering England's interests but rather the personal interests of King George I and of the ruling family of Hannover. In order to restrain George I and the English government from an attack on Russia, St. Petersburg for a while carried on relations with the pretender to the British throne, James Stuart, and with his partisans, the Jacobites. But in this the Russian government avoided any concrete promises and obligations in regard to the Jacobites.

One of the basic "channels" through which the policies of foreign governments were to be influenced was bribery, a means which often obtained valuable political information. In concluding peace with Turkey in 1711 it was necessary to give large bribes not only to the vizier but also to the mufti, and later, at the time of the treaty's ratification, also to the English and the Dutch ambassadors. In 1720, in order to obtain a "permanent peace" with Turkey, it was necessary to give presents not only to the Turkish dignitaries but also to the French ambassador and his wife.

Bribes were necessary not only in Constantinople. In 1701 the envoy to the Viennese court, Prince P. A. Golitsyn, complained about having insufficient funds for bribery, since "not only the men but even more the wives of the ministers shamelessly take it." . . . In 1706 Matveev, the ambassador in England, was directed to win the favor of the all powerful Duke of Marlborough, although Peter had doubts about success: "he is rich beyond measure, but offer him about 200,000 more." Marlborough requested a principality in Russia. Peter at that time was so interested in an alliance with England or else in England's benevolent mediation between Russia and Sweden that he was ready to agree to give the Duke a choice of Kiev, Vladimir or Sibir, with an annual income of 50,000 *efimki*, the largest ruby in the world, and the order of Andrei the First Called. Nothing came of this transaction.

Foreign governments also came to use the same methods in Russia. Especially guilty of taking bribes was Peter's Vice-Chancellor, the clever but greedy Shafirov.

Peter I as a Diplomat

Peter held all the threads of Russian diplomacy firmly in his own hands. He participated personally in all talks, often fulfilling the functions of both ambassador and foreign minister. Twice he travelled abroad on diplomatic missions and he personally concluded such important treaties as the agreement in Rava (1698) and the treaty of Amsterdam (1717). At home the Tsar dealt directly with foreign ambassadors and he spoke with them informally. . . .

Peter had his own principles of international politics. His usual rule was a political scrupulousness and a fidelity to obligations. "It is better to see us deserted," he wrote, "than that we should desert our allies, for the honor of our word is more dear than anything else."

The strength of Peter's foreign policy consisted in the fact that Peter concentrated on one problem. To this one problem he directed all his diplomatic efforts, refusing to take up other problems not on the first order of business. Thus, the Polish question existed for Peter only in the framework of the Northern War. The only time Peter, against his will, had to deviate from this basic principle was in 1711 at the time of the war with Turkey. Peter's foreign policy is distinctive in this regard from the vacillating and contradictory policies of his predecessors. Nor was such firmness in carrying out a determined line to be found in the policies of his immediate successors.

Russian Diplomacy under Peter I's Successors

The lack of firmness in Russia's foreign policy opened for foreign powers the possibility of conducting unceremonious intrigues in St. Petersburg and of openly interfering in the internal affairs of the Russian empire. As is known, Elizabeth Petrovna was enthroned in 1741 by the guard with the active participation of the French ambassador Chetardie, who hoped to bring about a rapprochement between France and Russia. Chetardie financed the coup and at first enjoyed a great influence at the court. But he met a serious and clever opponent in the person of the Chancellor A. P. Bestuzhev. While Chetardie was gone from St. Petersburg, the Austrian ambassador, the Marquis Botta-Adorni, inspired by the success of his French colleague, conducted talks among opposition elements among the Russian nobility about the possibility of reestablishing the overthrown Ivan Antonovich on the throne. In order to discredit Bestuzhev, his enemies attempted to involve him in this plot. This effort failed. In 1744 Chetardie returned to St. Petersburg with the mission of drawing Russia into the war of the Austrian succession on the side of France and Prussia. He openly declared that he intended to oust the Chancellor. Chetardie's ally was the Princess of Anhalt-Zerbst, a devotee of Frederick II, and the mother of the bride of the Grand Duke Peter Fedorovich, the future Catherine II. Bestuzhev acted with his characteristic decisiveness. At his order, all Chetardie's coded correspondence was deciphered by a Professor of Mathematics of the Academy of Sciences, Goldbach, and immediately delivered to the Chancellor. Thanks to this Bestuzhev succeeded in compromising the French ambassador and in achieving his expulsion from Russia. Later, in 1756, the English ambassador Charles Williams worked out with Grand Duchess Catherine Alekseevna a plan whereby she would seize power after the death of Elizabeth Petrovna. The foreign diplomats apparently reckoned on the ease with which bands of guards carried out coups in 18th century Russia.

The Russian government was in this regard less enterprising. It carried on large scale intrigue only in Sweden where the continued struggle of the Swedish nobility with royal power offered such an opportunity. Significant sums were expended in order to create a Russian party among the Swedish nobility in counterweight to another grouping which received support from the French government. In this field, in contrast to earlier times, the English diplomacy in the 1740s worked hand in hand with Russian diplomacy, undertaking a significant part of the expenses on its own account. In 1740, for example, the Russian and the English envoys agreed on giving 50,000 *efimki* each to the common cause. . . .

[In 1747] the new Russian envoy N. I. Panin, in a letter to the Russian chancery, proposed a program of action in the event of the death of the sick Swedish king. In his words, Russia faced three tasks: not to allow the establishment of an autocracy in Sweden, to overthrow the present ministry, and to put in its place ministers of the good "patriots." Panin proposed to "win over" some influential member of the French party, but at the same time he insisted on the use of armed intervention: "the distribution of money will be of no use."

The same system of bribery in conjunction with military intervention was also practiced in Poland and in Kurland. In the unending struggle for influence in foreign governments throughout Europe in the middle of the 17th century, not only private persons but also ministers were bribed. Thus, in 1737, expensive presents were sent from St. Petersburg to the Hofmeister of the Swedish King, Horn. He long demurred, but he nevertheless accepted the gifts with great circumspection. The draft was received at the bank, as if in payment for goods, and he gave a receipt. The next day the Russian envoy gave him back the receipt.

Foreign governments spent a great deal of money bribing Russian ministers and dignitaries. In 1725 the French ambassador was empowered by his government to spend up to 6000 *chervontsy* for the "public and secret gratification" of persons who could be useful to France, beginning with the all-powerful Menshikov, the chancellor Golovkin, Osterman and others, and ending with women close to Catherine I. Regular annual pensions would be paid to leaders of Russia's foreign policy, and the most outstanding political figures of that time did not disdain taking such remuneration from several courts at the same time. The English ambassador Williams described such a situation not without humor. "Already for some time," he wrote in 1756, "the Chancellor (Bestuzhev) had asked me for a large pension from the King, saying that they pay him here only 7000 rubles annually, and on such compensation he cannot live up to his station; that he understands the interests of his country are linked with those of England, and that therefore whoever served Russia well also serves England. Thus he can serve the king without doing anything contrary to his own conscience and without bringing harm to his country . . . But he was surprised when on Monday I told him, 'The King has granted you a lifetime pension of 12000 rubles a year.' He was perplexed and he did not believe me. He did not thank me, and at my departure he paid no attention to his pension." Only later, when the Banker Wolff assured him of the truth of this statement, did the Chancellor hasten to express his gratitude to Williams. "Tell him," he asked, "that we will get along in the best way and that I will do everything possible for him."

All governments attempted to have their own agents in foreign governments, through whom they could receive necessary information. The Russian intelligence service did this too. Under Anna Ioannovna the Russian envoy in Turkey, Nepliuev, had an agent close to the French ambassador and through him he received news about his rival's actions. In Sweden in 1747 it was even necessary to change the system of correspondence in the Chancery since the Russian envoy, Baron Korf, was able to learn all the government secrets. In 1726 it was learned that the Prussian councillor Ferber reported to St. Petersburg about all his sovereign's intimate talks. Ferber was executed.

Russia's enemies, England and Prussia, made still bolder use of secret agents. In this respect they were able even to use the future Empress, the Grand Duchess Catherine Alekseevna, born a German princess. Her mother was an agent of Frederick II until she was exiled from Russia by order of the Empress Elizabeth. The English ambassador Williams was able to win access to Catherine both through his secretary Stanislaw Poniatowski (the future Polish King) and also through large loans, made to her from the largess of the English King.

A final characteristic of this period was the strengthening of secret diplomacy, carried on outside official representatives and organs set up to conduct foreign policy. The Empress Elizabeth Petrovna and the French King Louis XV carried on a secret correspondence without the knowledge of their ministers.

The artful web of diplomatic intrigues and means of influencing the policies of neighboring countries clearly shows the complexity of international politics in Europe on the eve of the French bourgeois revolution of 1789. Russian diplomacy of this epoch was able not only to consolidate the gains of Peter I but it also played an important role in the affairs of western Europe. Retarded in comparison with western Europe, Russia of the 18th century suffered less than its neighbors from the contradictions between feudalism and newly developing capitalism which hampered countries standing on a higher level of economic development. Therefore, despite changes of faces on the throne, its government could conduct a more decisive policy.

The presence of outstanding diplomats in the government also facilitated Russia's international successes. Such was the renowned Andrei Ivanovich Osterman, who began his career under Peter I as a negotiator with Sweden. He took an active role in the conclusion of the brilliant Treaty of Nystadt. His experience and natural gifts developed in him exceptional diplomatic qualities. "Often," Manstein wrote of him, "foreign ministers would talk with him for two hours and upon leaving, they would know no more than they did when they came. Whatever he wrote, whatever he said, could be understood in two ways. Subtle, skilled in dissimulation, he could control his own feelings and when necessary he could break out in tears. He never looked anyone in the eye. Out of fear that his eyes would betray him, he would hold them immobile." They said of Osterman that he had an attack of gout in his hand whenever he had to sign a dangerous document.

A. P. Bestuzhev-Riumin was a man of a different type, ambitious, sly, in command of all the secrets for diplomatic success, but far from able to control his feelings like Osterman. Bestuzhev conceived a definite political system, which he systematically brought to life. As the foundation he posited an alliance of Russia with Austria in opposition to the growing power of Prussia and for purposes of attacking Turkey.

Diplomatic Methods of Catherine II

Under Catherine II some new methods of diplomatic work came into use. Catherine paid great attention to the problem of diplomatic propaganda abroad. In particular, her own correspondence with Voltaire, Grimm, Diderot and other representatives of the "enlightened epoch" served this purpose.

In addition, Catherine actively followed foreign publications which could bring harm to Russia or to her personally as Empress. She succeeded in preventing the publication of a book by Rulhiere on the coup of 1762. At her direction "Antidote" was published in Amsterdam as a refutation of a book about Russia which had appeared in Paris. Also to be included in the list of new diplomatic methods is her invitation of foreign diplomats to participate in the travels of the Empress through Russia—for example in 1785 to see the water route from the Baltic Sea to the Volga and in 1787 to the Crimea. Here, in unconstrained conversation with the Empress herself or with Potemkin, they discussed matters and often even resolved complex diplomatic questions. The French ambassador Segur, in his notes, loquaciously describes how he exploited these trips for propagandizing the idea of Franco-Russian friendship. During the trip of 1785 the basis was laid for the conclusion of a Franco-Russian trade pact.

Direct conversations with foreign sovereigns also had great significance. Catherine conducted a lively correspondence with Frederick II. Not satisfied just by correspondence, Catherine set up personal meetings too. Thus she proposed that Frederick II's brother, Prince Henry, in Sweden on a visit in 1770, travel from there on to St. Petersburg. In 1780 Joseph II and Catherine met in Mogilev. She gained his participation in 1787 in her trip to Taurida despite the emperor's obvious desire to avoid a meeting. During these meetings of "crowned heads," problems of international politics were resolved between the entertainments and the meals.

Of the former methods of diplomatic activity, especially great use was made under Catherine II of agitation among the Orthodox populations of foreign countries. It is known how Tsarist diplomacy exploited the dissident question in order to intervene in the affairs of the Polish Commonwealth. During the first Turkish war a rising of the Christian population on the islands of the Archipelago broke out against Turkish rule, greatly easing the tasks of the Russian armed forces. At the end of the war, the treaty of Kuchuk-Kainarji contained the first articles concerning religious rights of the Christian population of Turkey. Catherine employed the same policy in regard to the Crimea, where she assumed the role of protectress of the local Christians, Greek and Armenian, from oppression by the Tatars.

In diplomatic etiquette, Russia differed in no way from western Europe in the second half of the 18th century. In fact, Russian practice introduced a few refinements in details. Thus, in 1750, Elizabeth Petrovna decided to receive in audience only ambassadors, envoys and "plenipotentiary ministers." All other representatives were to deliver their credentials to the College of Foreign Affairs. Under Catherine II there was an innovation aimed at emphasizing Russia's great position among the European states. At an official presentation to the Empress, foreign ambassadors were to use French, the international language of that time, and the Empress would reply in

French. But if the ambassador gave his greeting in his own language, then she replied in Russian, even though, as is known, she did not speak Russian entirely correctly. Thus when Lord Buckingham greeted Catherine in English, she answered in Russian. His successor, Macartney, in order to curry favor with the Empress, spoke in French. The demand that the ambassadors kiss the Empress's hand during the presentation had the same purpose, that of emphasizing the stature of the head of the Russian government. Thereby, in 1762, arose a conflict with the Austrian Ambassador, Count Mersy, who at first refused to carry out this ceremony on the grounds that it was not done at the Viennese court, and then he demanded that the Russian ambassador in Vienna kiss the hand of the Austrian Empress. He had to yield.

Catherine's government also showed great care in the question of her title. In 1766 the French court refused to add "Imperiale" to the title "Majeste," asserting that such an addition was contrary to the rules of the French language. The resolution written by Catherine on this subject declared, "It is against the rules of language and Russian protocol to accept a document without the proper titles."

RUSSIAN STRENGTH

In 1735, in connection with the war of the Polish succession, Russian troops first appeared in western Europe. By 1756 Russia had become an integral part of the European balance of power. Details of Russia's economic and military strength, as presented in the following selection, therefore became all the more important for western observers.

Number of Inhabitants

According to the last numbering in the years 1744 and 1745, of the people of those provinces which properly constitute Russia, there were seven millions of males, from the age of four years to that of sixty, who pay the capitation or poll-tax. Seven millions might be allowed for women, children, and old men. The Russian nobility, with their families, might be computed at five hundred thousand. The officers of the revenue and clerks of the chancery, who form a class apart, are, with their wives and children, reckoned about two hundred thousand. For Livonia, Ingwa, and Finland provinces, which are not comprehended in the capitation, there are allowed six hundred thousand souls. As for the Cossacks of the Ukrain, of the Don, and of the Jaick,

---

Source: C. H. von Manstein, *Memoirs of Russia* (London, 1770), pp. 380–407.

as well as for the different nations of heathens that inhabit Siberia and the frontiers of Auria and Japan, they are computed at a million eight hundred thousand. The total making about eighteen millions four hundred thousand individuals.

Revenue

Neither is the revenue which the sovereign draws from these vast dominions proportioned to their extent. They amount at most to twelve or thirteen millions of rubles, which makes pretty near sixty-five millions of French livres, reckoning five livres to the ruble (not three millions sterling). I have been at a great deal of pains to come at the knowledge of the specific sums of all the different branches of receipt, in order to give a more satisfactory account on this head, without being able to get at any thing authentic, as the several colleges which administer the revenue keep a profound secret upon it.

The capitation is levied on none but the males, from the age of four to sixty. The inhabitants of town and country are comprehended in it. Every citizen pays a hundred and twenty copecs a year, and every peasant twenty-four. Some years ago, the Empress Elizabeth augmented the capitation by ten copecs a head, in aid of the extraordinary expences she was obliged to be at in raising fifty new battalions.

Though these revenues appear so little in proportion to the greatness of the empire, they are, nevertheless, sufficient, not only for the common expences of the state, but for extraordinary exigences.

Peter I. found them enough for those great enterprises and new establishments which he executed in his reign. This was the easier, for that the greatest part of his ministers, and even the chancellor himself, served without any salary; and both the Russian officers and soldiers received a very small pay.

But under the Empress Anne, there was some appearance of the state's being threatened with a want of money soon. The luxury which had been introduced from the very beginning of her reign, consumed immense sums. At the same time too, the pay of all the officers was augmented, and put upon an equal footing, as I have set forth in the Memoirs. And yet for all this, there was money enough found to carry on the war with Poland and with the Turks, without the need of raising new taxes.

Count Munich, who was at the head of the military, made such good arrangements, that the army, which in time of peace was not used to be paid but every four months, and even that not till after the term, was paid every month beforehand. And the court had, moreover, wherewithal to bestow gratifications as often as the troops had suffered extraordinary fatigues, or done some great action. . . .

It must, however, be owned, that this could not have held on, if there had been a necessity of making two more campaigns against the Turks, the expences of that war being very considerable, as I have shewn in my relation of those campaigns.

It must also be granted, that the Russian army cannot make, for any series of years together, campaigns at a distance from their frontiers, especially in countries where the provisions and necessaries for the maintenance of the troops are dearer than in Russia, for their pay, which is sufficient for the army when it remains within the Russian territories, where every thing is comparatively very cheap, is too little on its coming into parts where every thing is at a higher price. And, accordingly, the court has been obliged to raise the pay one-half as often as it has detached a body of auxiliary troops; as when the Empress Anne, in 1735, sent eight regiments of foot to the Rhine; or Elizabeth, eleven thousand men under Keith to Sweden; and, in 1748, succours to the house of Austria against France.

It may, in general, be demonstrably averred, that there is a scarcity of money in Russia; nothing being more common than to pay twelve, fifteen, and even twenty per cent. interest for it.

Under the ancient Czars, the revenues were yet smaller than they are at present. It is only since Peter I. that they have augmented. The continual wars in which that Prince was engaged during his reign, and the great enterprises executed by him, obliged him to encrease the taxes to the double of what they were before.

One of the principal reasons that render money so scarce in Russia, is that distrustfulness of theirs, which being the predominant weakness of that nation, extending even to their nearest relations, a great many merchants, after having gained anything of a sum in trade, bury it in places, of which they reserve to themselves alone the knowledge, and, not unfrequently, die without discovering to any one the secret; so that it is reckoned there is in Russia much more money under ground than above, otherwise that empire ought to be very rich; for, within these two hundred years, there have immense sums entered it, and little went out; except indeed, that lately, the two circumstances of luxury and of the sending troops out of the country, occasion some outlets, which, however, are comparatively trifling. There is no nation in Europe that has any trade with Russia, of which the balance does not turn in favor of this empire.

Trade

As to trade, Russia is so admirably well situated, and has so many conveniencies for it, that few other states in Europe have the like. The immense extent of the empire furnishes it with an incredible quantity of merchandise, and with almost every thing desirable for human life; so that if in one province there should be a want of any thing, it can be supplied by another. There are a number of navigable rivers, the course of which is in so advantageous a direction, that from Petersburgh to the frontiers of China, there is a water carriage for everything to within the space of about five hundred wersts, or about two hundred eighty English miles. This convenience much facilitates the transport of provisions and merchandise.

But even land-carriage itself is very cheap; for from Moscow to Petersburgh, a distance of above four hundred English miles, the common charge, in winter, when every thing is carried on sledges by the *poud*, or weight of forty pounds, is not above eight, nine, or at most twelve copecs, which are four German gross, or a little more than half a French livre, or scarce an English sixpence.

It is on the account of this advantage, that the *inland* trade of the empire, both wholesale and retail, has been always exclusively appropriated to the Russian subjects, and that foreigners have never obtained the permission of carrying their merchandise into the interior parts of the country, nor of purchasing in the provinces Russian commodities, to be brought at their expence to the sea ports.

According to the laws, no foreign merchant has even leave to buy, in the sea ports, goods of another foreign merchant; he must buy them of a Russian. A foreign merchant is, however, at liberty to make contracts in any provincial or countrytown; but the goods cannot be delivered to him but at a port.

The sovereigns of Russia have always carefully preserved to their subjects this commercial privilege; and when, in 1716, the English solicited a free trade at Kasan and Astracan, Peter I. chose to refuse an advantageous alliance, which he might then have concluded with that nation, rather than grant this request.

Of old none but the Armenians had the liberty of transporting foreign goods from Astracan to Petersburgh, there to export them to foreign countries, as also to make use of the same means of carriage back of the returns from Europe. But there are great precautions taken against their selling anything in Russia. Their bales are carefully sealed up with many seals at their entry into the Russian ports, which they are obliged to produce unbroken at the places of exportation.

As this trade brings in a considerable revenue, and is prejudicial in nothing to the Russian subjects, there has hitherto been no obstruction to it.

Some years ago the English, it is true, obtained a grant of liberty of trade with Persia, by the Caspian Sea; but neither do they presume to sell their goods, by the way, in Russia.

The commerce of the Russians with foreigners may be considered in a twofold light; the trade by land, and the trade by sea.

By land, the Russian trade with China, the Calmucks, the Buckhars, Persia, Crimea, Turkey, Poland, Silesia, and Prussia.

For the trade by sea, there are, at present ten ports principally used, Riga, Perno, Revel, Narva, Petersburgh, Wybourg, Fredericsham, Kola and Astracan. It is reckoned that there come into these ports, every year, from fifteen hundred to seventeen hundred sail of foreign ships.

The first treaty of commerce that ever Russia concluded was with England, in the reign of queen Elizabeth. At that time, and even until the present century, the only known port that Russia had, was Archangel. But Peter I. having conquered Livonia, Ingria, and Finland, he acquired with these provinces other ports, and having established his residence at Petersburgh, he appointed it the staple of all the merchandise that his immense dominions may produce.

This Prince, at the first, endeavoured to induce his subjects to transport their merchandise to his new residence, by granting several privileges, and by lowering the customs on the goods they should bring to Petersburgh; but never could the Russian dealers be persuaded to come into this innovation. The Emperor was at length obliged to use his absolute authority to determine them to it. In 1722, he expressly prohibited the carrying of any goods to Archangel, but such as belonged to the district of that government. This ordinance raised, at first, a great outcry among the traders, both Russians and foreigners, and caused several bankruptcies; but the merchants, accustomed themselves little by little to come to Petersburgh, found their account in it better than at Archangel, where the ships cannot make but one voyage a year, whereas they can make two to Petersburgh; not to mention other advantages which the merchants derive from the proximity of several trading towns, and which they were formerly forced to do without, on account of the distance at which they were, in Archangel, from all the rest of Europe.

The most considerable articles of trade that Russia furnishes are corn, leather, iron, linens, hemp, wood, potash, pitch and tar, wax, honey, great quantities of furs or peltry, rhubarb, hides, caviar, ising-glass, matts, etc.

In balance against these, the Russians must have from foreign countries, cloth, the finest sort of linen, spices, wine, and, in general, the articles of luxury, which constitute now a very great object, as may have been remarked in the preceding Memoirs.

During the two years 1740 and 1741, that the baron de Mengden was at the head of trade, the annual profit to Russia amounted to three hundred thousand rubles, about sixty thousand pounds, exclusive of the customs. The profit might be much greater, if the Russian nation did not prefer its love of ease to the risques of navigation.

Peter I. during his reign, took all the pains imaginable to make his subjects good merchants, and to engage them not to sell any longer the merchandises produced in his dominions at second hand by foreigners, but to carry on their trade directly in goods laden on Russian bottoms to foreign countries, in the manner practised by other commercial nations.

In the beginning of this century, the Emperor made a trial of this kind. He sent a Russian merchant, called Soloview, to Amsterdam, there to establish a Russian factory, or house of trade; and that he might succeed the better, he not only gave him several commissions of the court, but there were also granted to him great advantages on the rest of his trade to Russia. As Soloview was really a man of parts, and had all the necessary capacity, he knew so well how to avail himself of all these circumstances, that he had, in a few years, gained a considerable capital, at the same time that his civil behavior had won him the friendship and confidence of all the Dutch merchants. But Peter I. being in 1717 in Amsterdam, some of the great men of the court, who had taken a pique against him, because he would not satisfy the extortions of their avarice, found means to blacken him in the opinion of the Emperor, who, having caused this merchant to be carried off, had him embarked on board of a ship for Russia. This occasioned the Russian trade's falling into a great decline in Holland, the dealers of Amsterdam being thereby grown afraid of trusting any Russian merchant, so that it has not since been possible to form there any solid establishment.

Peter I. would try another scheme. He resolved to procure the sale of the merchandise of his empire in those states which had no direct trade with Russia, and, for that purpose, obliged some of the most substantial merchants of his country to load considerable parcels of hemp, of flax, of cables, of wax, on vessels furnished them by the admiralty: to these he added a great quantity of iron-guns, of mortars, bomb-shells, cannon-balls, and anchors, and sent all this to Bourdeaux and Cadiz, where there had been previously placed Russian consuls. But this trade succeeded so ill, that the charges of merchandise absorbed a good part of the capital, and the adventurers never saw but very little returns.

At length, this Prince flattered himself that he should inspire his subjects with a taste for trade to foreign countries, and for navigation, by publishing an edict, in which it was ordained, That if any freeman of a town would trade upon his own account, on a Russian bottom, he should have a quarter of the customs abated to him, both on exports and imports. But this produced no effect, for, during his life, there was not a merchant found to risque an undertaking upon that foot.

Fabric of Arms

Among the manufactures established by Peter I. that of arms is one of the most worthy of remark. Formerly, this empire had none made at home, but was obliged to have from other countries all the arms it wanted. But Peter I. having levied an army, and built a fleet, judged it indispensably necessary to have arms fabricated in his dominions; and as the iron in them is of an excellent kind, there is nothing wanting but good armorers and gunsmiths. He caused to be engaged the best masters that could be found in other nations; gave them great salaries, and established two manufactures, one at Toula, a small town, situated at 180 wersts on the other side of Moscow, the other at Susterbeck, a little town, or rather village, about 27 wersts from Petersburgh.

In these two places, every thing is so well ordered, that the *connoisseurs*, who have seen them, agree that they are masterpieces in their kind. The whole is conducted there by water-works.

At Toula they make every thing requisite for the land-armies. The cannon and small arms are excellent, but they do not as yet excel in the cock-plates. The manufacture at Susterbeck, which was particularly designed for the supply of the marine, fell into decline during the reigns of Catherine and Peter II. The best masters, whom Peter I. had procured at a vast expence from foreign countries, were dead or turned off, or dispersed. . . . .

Military

I come now to speak of the changes in the military. When Peter I. came to the throne, he had hardly any other troops in his empire than the *Strelitzes*. This militia had been formed by the patriarch Philaret, father of the Czar Michael Feodorowitz, to curb the nobility and the great of that country. There is no comparing them to any thing so fitly as to the Janizaries; they fought in the same manner, and had much the same privileges as these have. They might amount to forty thousand men, divided into different regiments; part of them served in the guards about the Czar's person, the rest were distributed in garrison on the frontiers. Their arms consisted of musquets and sabres; their pay was not above four rubles a year (sixteen shillings), but as they had great privileges in trade, they might very well subsist on it. Even several rich citizens inrolled themselves in this body, who did no duty in time of peace, and in time of war they could easily exempt themselves from marching, by giving a competent present to the commander, and by sending a man in their room.

The militia having been raised to counterbalance the nobility, care was taken, from the very first of its institution, to place none at the head of it but soldiers of fortune, or some foreigners that had distinguished themselves in the wars of Poland. This had caused, and kept up the hatred between this body and the nobility. No gentleman would ever list in it, holding it shameful to serve persons of an inferior condition.

For a long time, Russia maintained no other troops in time of peace than this infantry. However, there were always kept collaterally in reserve, a number of colonels and other officers, of whom the greatest part were foreigners, and to whom there was allotted in time of peace a slender pay. As soon as a war was coming on, each colonel had a particular district assigned him, in which to levy men; and every village was obliged to furnish him the number specified for its contingent. Easy it is to judge that these people were ill disciplined, ill clothed, and ill armed. Indeed, they took whatever weapons came next to hand, and few had any fire-arms; the most of these had a sort of battle-ax, called in the Russian language *berdish;* the rest had wooden clubs. Such troops, one may readily imagine, were not capable of great services; and, accordingly, they were hardly trusted with any thing but guarding the baggage. As soon as the campaign was over, every soldier returned to his village; and if the war continued, there was a necessity of entirely new-raising the regiment for the next campaign. In short, these troops could not be compared to any but to those which the Turkish Bashaws bring into the field with them, excepting that these last are better armed, and have more courage.

All that is here said concerns only the infantry.

As to the cavalry, it was composed of the lesser nobility, and was called in Russia *Dieti Boiarsky*, or *Boyars Children;* they were dispersed over all the provinces where they possessed hereditary fees. At the opening of the campaign, each repaired to the general rendezvous, with a certain number of servants in proportion to his estate. These gentry had no pay, and were obliged to maintain themselves and their servants at their own expence during the whole war. Their common arms consisted in bows and arrows, sabres and half-pikes: some had also firearms; that is to say, such as could pay for them.

Such a cavalry opposed to disciplined enemies, would hardly have stood a very good chance; but the Tartars and Poles, against whom they had the oftenest to combat, were not much better in that respect than themselves, so that they might serve tolerably well.

Besides this cavalry composed of the nobility, Russia maintained some thousands of Tartars, who had submitted to this empire, on the terms of preserving their liberty of conscience, after the conquest of the kingdom of Kasan.

In the case too of the Czars, their wanting a more numerous cavalry, they could take a great number of Calmucks into their pay, to whom they paid no more than a ruble (four shillings) a year, and a mantle made of a sheep's skin.

But when the Cossacks had, at length, put themselves under the protection of Russia, its troops were augmented by a hundred thousand horse.

Among the ancient Czars, there were some that had a foreign guard; as for example, Iwan Basiliwitz, to whom the historians have given, though wrongfully, the appellation of tyrant, for he was one of the greatest men that ever Russia produced.

The Czar, Michael Feodorowitz, in the last years of his reign, and his son, Alexis Michaelowitz, had already had the design of putting the army upon another foot. During the war they had with Poland, they had formed some regiments of infantry upon the foot of other European troops, and had given the command of them to foreign officers. The regiment of Boutinsky had subsisted ever since the year 1642; one Dalziel commanded it: this regiment was composed of fifty-two companies, each of a hundred men. There are also to be seen ancient lists of the regiment of the first Moskowsky, of the year 1648; a general, Drummond, was the commander.

The Czar, Alexis Michaelowitz, caused to be translated into the Russian language, a book on the military art (which had been published in German) to serve for the instruction of his officers. He also sent for from Brescia eight thousand carabines, which are actually now at Moscow.

But as there was, at that time, a necessity for keeping measures with the Strelitzes, who beheld with a jealous eye these new troops; as the Boyars also, who had great influence at court, would not consent to lose entirely the peasants belonging to their lands, and who, according to ancient custom, were not obliged to serve but only in time of war, and then, no longer than the campaign lasted; especially too, as the clergy, who had great power, were afraid that foreign heretics might gain too great an ascendant over the sovereign; this project of reformation came to little or nothing.

It was under the reign of Alexis Michaelowitz, that about three thousand Scotch arrived in Russia, who had quitted Great Britain after the defeat and imprisonment of King Charles I. These were very well received; they had a place assigned them contiguous to the town of Moscow, where they built houses, and formed that part of this great town, which is distinguished to this day by the name of *Inostranaya Sloboda*, or habitation of strangers.

Peter I. having ascended the throne, the various troubles with which the beginning of his reign was agitated, obliged him to put himself into the hands of foreigners, and to shake off those prejudices which had hindered his father and grandfather from executing the project of alteration they had begun. After this Prince had rid himself of the Strelitzes, his first care was to root out of the higher nobility that prejudice as to their quality, from which they held it an indignity for a man of a great birth to serve under a man of an inferior one. To succeed in this design he fell upon the following expedient. He formed out of the youths, who were brought up with him, according to the custom of that time, a company of fifty, under the name of *Poteschnie* (or for amusement), and made them be clothed in one uniform, and exercised in the foreign manner; declaring at the same time, that he would have no prerogative over his comrades. He began with serving in the lowest degree, not even so high as a private soldier, but in quality of drummer. He renounced all his authority as to the military rank, depositing it in trust in the hands of the Prince Romandonowsky, who was to advance him accord-

ing to his merit, and without any favor: and so long as Prince Romandonowsky lived, which was till 1714, it was always he that advanced Peter I.
to the ranks of general and admiral, when he would take them upon him.

By this means the Emperor arrived at his end, for the nobility seeing
that their master did not make any distinction of quality in the service,
submitted also to the like; and though they could not forget the prerogative
of their birth, they were, however, ashamed of pretending upon it to a right
of which the Emperor had divested himself.

Little by little the Emperor augmented this company, and at length
formed two regiments of infantry, whom he declared his guards in 1706.
Blomberg was colonel of the first, and the marshal Prince Gallitzin of the
second: they were clothed, armed, and exercised after the manner of the
other troops of Europe. Some time afterwards he established some more
regiments of infantry on the same footing, and gave orders to all his ministers at the foreign courts to engage as many officers in his service as
they could find. In a few years he had a considerable number of very good
ones.

The Emperor wanted also to form his cavalry upon the same foot as that
of the rest of Europe. For this purpose, he took some hundreds of Saxon
reysters or horsemen into his service, that were to serve for a model; but
having discovered that there were not to be found in all Russia horses proper
for remounting the heavy cavalry, and that, if he had recourse to foreign
ones, the expences would be too great; he was obliged to abandon this
project, and content himself with raising regiments of dragoons.

Among the foreigners who came to Russia, the principal was the marshal
Ogilvy: it is to this general that the Russians are indebted for the first establishment of order and discipline in their army, and especially in the infantry.

As to the dragoons, it was the general Ronne, a Courlander, that was in
charge of them; but as almost all the officers, and particularly the generals
who entered into the service of Peter I., had never served but in the infantry;
the exercises and evolutions of the cavalry were much neglected, and the
dragoons learn'd no other part of the exercise than what belonged to them
when dismounted to act on foot: they had scarce any knowledge of evolutions a horseback.

The Empress Anne having raised three regiments of cuirassiers, the dragoons learned of them their evolutions, and are now better exercised than
they were formerly.

Some years before the death of Peter I. this Emperor established for his
army perpetual quarters, in the different provinces of his empire, where the
regiments were to remain in time of peace. Houses were built there for the
officers, and the scheme was to found some great villages, where the soldiers
were to be lodged. These villages have never been entirely finished, and the

regiments which had been distributed among the provinces since the year 1723 to 1732, have had their quarters in towns, and in the neighbouring villages.

Peter I. planned this establishment in imitation of the Swedes. I have, I think, before mentioned in Memoirs, that this Emperor had once entertained a design of imitating in every thing the Swedish arrangements, but the great difficulties he met with in it made him relinquish the project.

In the time of the Empress Anne, these perpetual quarters were totally abandoned, and have never been thought of since.

When Peter I. died, his army consisted of two regiments of guards, of which the first had four battalions, and the second three; of fifty regiments of infantry, of thirty regiments of dragoons, of some squadrons of hussars, sixty-seven regiments in garrisons, and six of militia; the whole might amount to about two hundred thousand men.

There was no considerable change made in the army during the reigns of Catherine and of Peter II. but the Empress Anne having ascended the throne, she began, as I have observed in that part of my Memoirs relative to her life, by augmenting the army. There were added to the guards five squadrons of cavalry, and three battalions of infantry; she formed some time afterwards three regiments of cuirassiers, and increased the militia, by fourteen regiments, for the guard of the lines of the Ukrain. At her death, the Russian army amounted to two hundred and forty thousand men.

It was during the reign of this Princess, that, through the good arrangements made by marshal Munich and the general officers who commanded under him, the finishing hand was put to the introduction of good order and discipline into the army, insomuch that all who have seen it have been obliged to confess, that the infantry might rank among the best in Europe.

It was at that time that Russia had in her service such good generals, that few powers in Europe could boast the like. Munich, Lacy, Keith, Lowendal, have illustrated their names enough for it to be presumable, that they will descend to the latest posterity. Be this observed, without particularly naming here all the other generals who commanded under them, among whom there were some who might have done honor to any service in the world.

After the accession of Elizabeth to the throne, she was obliged to yield to the importunity of some old Russian generals, and especially to those of the marshal Knez Dolgoroucky, who prevailed on her for the abandoning the new exercises, and, in general, all that had been introduced of new into the army under the preceding reign. By this means, indiscipline and disorder, little by little, crept in among the troops. The best generals, and a number of good officers, extremely disgusted at the bad procedure towards them, quitted the service; so that none remained in it but those to whom the permission of retiring was absolutely refused, or who did not know where else to go.

The good officers, who are still there, are too timid, too much out of heart, to undertake the correction of the insolence of their subalterns; and the rest have not a capacity for it if they would.

Among the great number of foreigners who came to this empire since the beginning of this century, there were certainly some excellent officers; but there were also some of the most abject wretches that Europe could produce. Some adventurers, at their last shifts, and who did not know how to dispose of themselves otherwise, got to Russia, and even made their way in the services as well as the best.

During the war with Sweden, the Empress Elizabeth broke four regiments of infantry, to put the men into the marine; but to make amends for this, she, in 1747, augmented the army with fifty new battalions; so that at present it amounts to two hundred and seventy thousand seven hundred and ninety-one men, without reckoning the light troops of the Cossacks and Calmucks, of whom there might be, without any difficulty, raised as far as sixty thousand horse.

Yet all these troops are hardly sufficient to cover such an immense extent of country, and Russia cannot employ in its campaigns above 120,000, or 130,000 regulars at the most; the rest must be reserved for the garrisons and frontiers.

In the wars against the Turks and against Sweden, there were all the troops assembled that it was possible to muster for the campaign, and yet the different armies of it could never amount at a time to 100,000 combatants.

The irregular or light troops, of which Russia has so prodigious a quantity, are capable of very good services against the Turks and Tartars, but would rather embarrass an army than be useful to it in an inhabited country. Their consumption of the forages is so great, that they would soon bring a scarcity upon a camp; to say nothing of the ravages they commit for some miles round in a country, and by which they would intercept and destroy the provisions necessary for the main army.

ENLIGHTENED DESPOTISM

From 1725, the time of Peter's death, until 1762, when Catherine II overthrew the government of her husband, Russia changed rulers frequently in a series of palace coups, executed by the palace guard. Catherine estab-

lished herself by gaining the favor of the guard and of the nobility in general. She also sought to make her name as a woman of the Enlightenment. She corresponded with the French philosophes, and she herself wrote prodigiously. One of her most famous works was her Nakaz, an instruction to an assembly convened to reform Russia's laws.

All the provinces of Russia, not excepting the barbarous nations who dwell in the remotest parts of that vast empire, had orders to send deputies to Mosco, to present their ideas on the laws that were the fittest for their peculiar exigencies. Catharine herself repaired to that ancient capital. The opening of the states was held with extraordinary pomp. It was surely an interesting and novel transaction, to see deputies of numerous people, different in their manners, their dress, their languages; and they themselves must have been astonished at being here thus assembled for the purpose of discussing their laws, people who had never thought about law any farther than to obey the arbitrary will of a master, whom it often happened that they did not know.

The empress, desirous to leave to this assembly the appearances of the completest liberty, had a sort of gallery constructed in the hall in such manner, that, without being perceived, she could see and hear all that passed. The business was begun by reading the instructions translated into the Russian language, the original whereof in French, almost entirely in the handwriting of Catharine, has since been deposited, enclosed in a magnificent case of silver gilt, in an apartment of the imperial academy of sciences at St. Petersburg.

"The sovereigns of Russia possessed the most extensive dominions in the world, and every thing was yet to be done: at last," says M. de Voltaire, "Peter was born and Russia was formed;" that is, doubtless, to say, that at this period it arose out of chaos. The bare idea of forming it was grand, and its execution might justly excite astonishment. Tzar Alexey Michailovitch, his father, had already sketched out the work, and it must be confessed that Peter advanced it to a surprising degree. To leave his country, that he might return to govern it with greater glory; to go and seek light in all parts where it enlightened mankind; to submit for several years to be the disciple of other nations, in order to become the master and the reformer of his own; to work as a simple carpenter at Saardam, to prepare himself for creating a navy that should be formidable to his enemies; to lower himself to a common soldier, in order to become a great commander; to form on all hands establishments of great utility, till then unknown to his subjects; to attack at once all the abuses both in church and state, in the manners and customs that had been

Source: William Tooke, *Life of Catherine II*, 3d ed. (London, 1799), I, 479–97.

most sanctioned by inveterate habit; to extend reformation, and care to every particular that was deserving of them; to temper the severity of his discipline by the total abolition of the word slave: to mix pomp with toil, and annex prosperity to triumphs; all together characterised him as the great genius, the great man, and the great monarch.

But if that prince, so justly renowned to all posterity, polished his country in so many respects; if he made regulations worthy of admiration and praise, with all this he framed no permanent laws, and much less a system of legislation that should embrace all objects. That great work* was left for Catharine II. She alone conceived the grand idea of undertaking it, and she alone had the courage to put it in execution. A code of laws, and especially laws founded on wisdom, is the noblest present that can be made to a people: no woman had yet been a legislatrix; and that part the empress of Russia resolved to act.

The reading of the instructions was frequently interrupted by bursts of applause. All present extolled the sagacity, the wisdom, the humanity of the sovereign. But fear and flattery had a greater share in these exclamations than an admiration proceeding from a just knowledge of the matter. It was hoped, perhaps, by that means to attract the favour of the empress, or at least to escape Siberia. The deputies of the Samoyedes alone had the courage to speak freely. One of them stood up in the name of his brethren, and said:— "We are a simple and honest people. We quietly tend our rein-deer. We are in no want of a new code: but make laws for the Russians, our neighbours, that may put a stop to their depredations."

The following sittings did not pass so quietly. Much had been said about giving liberty to the boors. Some thousands of this oppressed class of beings were preparing to support by force what they expected from equity. The nobility dreaded an insurrection; they dreaded, above all, a defalcation of their revenues; and some nobles were rash enough to assert, that they would poignard the first man who should move for the affranchisement of the vassals. Notwithstanding this, however, count Scheremetoff, the richest individual of all Russia, got up, and declared that he would willingly agree to this affranchisement. The debate was carried on with great warmth, which grew to such a height, that fatal consequences were to be apprehended; and the deputies were dismissed to their respective provinces.

However, previous to the dissolution of this assembly, the members were required to signalize the meeting by some conspicuous act of gratitude. It was thought right that, though the benefit that was intended for the subjects should be lost to them, it ought not to be so to the sovereign who had con-

---

* This work may be chiefly taken from the writings of Montesquieu, and several others of the French philosophers; but it must always resound to the glory of Catharine that she had the liberality of mind to draw from such sources.

ceived the noble idea of it. Accordingly, by a general acclamation, the titles Great, Wife, Prudent, and Mother of the Country, were decreed to that princess; but when she was petitioned to accept of those titles, she answered, with an assumed modesty, "That if she had rendered herself worthy of the first, it belonged to posterity to confer it upon her; that wisdom and prudence were the gifts of heaven, for which she daily gave thanks, without presuming to derive any merit from them herself; that lastly, the title of mother of the country was the most dear of all in her eyes, the only one that she could accept, and which she regarded as the most benign and glorious recompence for her labours and solicitudes in behalf of a people whom she loved."

Proud of the work which had obtained her such flattering marks of homage, Catharine eagerly dispatched copies of her instructions to the sovereigns whose approbation she most coveted. They complimented her on her laborious enterprise, and made no hesitation to pronounce that it would be an eternal monument to her glory. The king of Prussia, who knew how sensible she was to praise, and who was always lavish of it with less delicacy than ease, wrote to her a long letter, which, among other things, contained this flattering observation: "No woman has hitherto been a legislatrix. That glory was reserved for the empress of Russia, who well deserves it."

The empress received this letter at Kazan, having had a desire to visit her provinces in Asia, and the famous shores of the Volga.

Count Solms, minister of the king of Prussia, on sending this letter to count Panin, wrote him a note to the following purport:

I hasten to transmit to your excellency the letter which the king my master has had the honour to compose, in answer to that with which her imperial majesty was graciously pleased to accompany the present of her instruction for the formation of the new code in Russia, ordering me to cause it to be presented to her imperial majesty. He subjoins, with his own hand, in the dispatch which he has addressed to me, "I have read with admiration the work of the empress. I was not willing to tell her all that I think of it, because she might have suspected me of flattery; but I may say to you, with due deference to modesty, that it is a masculine performance, nervous, and worthy of a great man. We are told by history, that Semiramis commanded armies. Queen Elizabeth has been accounted a good politician. The empress-queen has shewn great intrepidity on her accession to the throne; but no woman has ever been a legislatrix. That glory was reserved for the empress of Russia, who deserves it."

It certainly redounds much to the praise of Catharine, that these instructions are founded on the principles of an enlightened humanity; and that, though autocratrix and of unlimited power, she recognizes no legitimate authority but that which is founded on justice; every particular in her laws has a tendency to enervate despotism, and to render a just authority respectable. Her purpose is to form a solid, and not an arbitrary legislation. Her whole plan is directed to prevent all those who govern under her from exercising a capricious and cruel authority, by subjecting them to invariable laws, which no authority should be able to infringe.

The accomplishment of this grand design, however, did not proceed so smoothly as the first steps gave room to expect. Either it was found that the plan of a convocation of the nation by its deputies was beginning at too high a pitch, and that in an assembly composed of such a diversity of tribes, manners, and tongues, it would be impossible to come to any common conclusions; or the whole apparatus was used only as a machine, and suffered to fall when it had answered the end for which it was contrived.

A few articles in these instructions will suffice to show the principles on which they are drawn up:

The spirit of the nation, the nation itself, ought to be consulted in the framing of laws.

These laws should be considered no otherwise than as a means of conducting mankind to the greatest happiness.

It is our duty to mitigate the lot of those who live in a state of dependence.

The liberty and the security of the citizens ought to be the grand and precious objects of all laws; they should all tend to render life, honour, and property, as stable and secure as the constitution of the government itself.

The liberty of the subjects ought only to be restricted concerning what it would be disadvantageous to them to do.

In causes purely civil, the laws should be so clear and precise, that the judgments resulting from them be always in perfect unison in the same cases, in order to remove that jurisprudence of decisions which is so often a source of uncertainties, of errors, or acts of injustice, according as a cause has been well or ill defended at one time or at another, gained or lost according to influence or circumstances.

We read with equal pleasure the instructions she prescribes to be followed in the criminal constitution:

It is incomparably better to prevent crimes than to punish them.

The life of the meanest citizen is of consequence; and no one should be deprived of it, except when it is attacked or required by the country.

In like manner his liberty should be respected, by being difficult about imprisonment, by carefully distinguishing the cases where the laws will dispense with it, as also those in which the public safety requires arrestation, detention, or formal imprisonment, and in this case even concerning different prisons.

In the methods of trial, the use of torture is contrary to sound reason. Humanity cries out against this practice, and insists on its being abolished.

A prisoner is not to be sacrificed to the torrent of opinions. Judgment must be nothing but the precise text of the law; and the office of the judge is only to pronounce whether the action is conformable or contrary to it.

Concerning punishments:

The aim of punishment is not to torment sensible beings.

All punishment is unjust when it is not necessary to the maintenance of the public safety.

The atrocity of punishments is reprobated by the compassion that is due to human nature; whenever it is useless, it is a sufficient reason to regard it as unjust, and, as such, to reject it.

In the ordinary state of society, the death of a citizen is neither useful nor necessary.

All that follows under this head, touching the proportion that should be observed between crimes and punishments; on the rarity of the cases where the crime deserves death; on the rule to be observed in confiscations, which the empress would not extend beyond acquired property, and a number of other ideas are such as could only proceed from goodness of heart and profound meditation. The whole amount of the articles of her instructions is in number 525; and the very publication and dispersion of the book throughout the empire has been attended with salutary effects. It was doubtless a great and arduous undertaking and worthy of an exalted mind.

The instruction of the empress is not a lawbook itself. She only says, "Such regulations should be made.—In the first place it should be examined, whether," etc. But it must be confessed, that excellent suggestions are thus delivered, which certainly have produced, and must continue to produce, great effects. Thus we find it said, chap. xi., "Peter I. promulgated a law in 1722, that persons who were not of sound mind, and who oppress their serfs, should be put under guardians. The former point of this law has been kept up; why the latter is not enforced is not known."—Again, chap. xii.:

It seems too, that the new manner in which noblemen exact their dues from the peasantry is hurtful to population. There is scarcely a village which does not pay certain tributes to its lord in money. The lord, who never, or but very rarely, sees his village, imposes on every head a tax of one, two, and even to five rubles, without concerning himself how the peasant is to pay that sum. It will be absolutely indispensable to prescribe laws to the nobility, obliging them to act more circumspectly in the manner of levying their dues, and to require of the peasant tributes of such a nature as shall remove him as little as possible from his house and family. By this means agriculture will be better followed, and the population of the empire be increased. At present, a labourer leaves his home at the age of fifteen to go and seek his subsistence in distant towns; roams about the empire, and pays his dues annually from what he earns.

If, for some political reason, it be not practicable to free the boors throughout the empire from their vassalage, yet means should be thought of to enable them to acquire property. In pursuance of this idea, should not a method be devised for gradually bettering the condition of this lower class of people?

Is not such language, which evinces so much sagacity and benevolence, the fittest for the mouth of a monarch who is desirous of making improvements, without undertaking the boisterous and intemperate part of an austere reformer? It is a great matter, if a prince shews that he understands the vices of the country, and knows how they may be remedied. Suppose even that nothing farther is done, must not every considerate spectator feel himself inclined to believe that this sagacity and this benevolence have met with difficulties which were absolutely not to be overcome? But such words are never lost: under Catharine much was effected by what she planned with prudent moderation. In some places, however, she expresses herself decisively, and with command; and wherever this is the case, the instruction retains the virtual force of a law.

The whole performance is an excellent compendium of choice observations, of just maxims, and of generous sentiments; and at the same time a beautiful collection of striking passages from the celebrated philosophers of Greece and Rome, of apt examples from ancient and modern history, from the manners of cultivated and savage nations, and even from such nations as are not very much known to the rest of Europe, the Chinese and other Asiatics. Whoever would make himself acquainted with the philosophy of legislation, might reap considerable advantage by taking it as his manual.

In addition to the passages above cited from this work, as a specimen of the sentiments of Catharine, it will not be amiss to extract a few others, if it be only to shew, that upwards of thirty years ago a monarch delivered the best of those which, in the opinion of some, were first discovered by the republicans of the present day. A lofty philosophical station is taken in the 6th chapter:

Several things influence mankind, religion, climate, laws, maxims of government, examples of things past, manners, customs, from which, as the result, a public mind is formed.

Elucidations of this maxim from the various nations succeed to this. Then,

It is the business of the legislator to follow the temper of the nation; for we do nothing better than what we do voluntarily, and in pursuance of our natural disposition. For establishing a more perfect legislation, it is necessary that the minds of men should be previously prepared for it. But in order to defeat the pretext usually alleged, that it is not possible to do good, because the minds are not yet disposed to admit it, take the pains to prepare them for it: this will be already a great step advanced.

When it is intended to make great changes in a nation, that may turn to its benefit, that which has been established by laws should be reformed by law; and what custom has brought into practice should be changed by custom; and it is very bad policy to change by laws what ought to be changed by custom.

[Chap. viii. of punishments:] Examine with attention into the cause of all relaxations, and it will be seen that they arise from the impunity of crimes, and not from the moderation of punishments. . . . It often happens that a legislator, who intends to correct an evil, confines his thought to that correction: his eyes are open to that object, and shut to the inconveniences attending it.

[Chap. ix.:] If you consider the forms of law in regard to the trouble a citizen has to obtain his right, or to get satisfaction for some injury, you will doubtless find them too many; if you regard them in the relation they bear to the liberty and security of the citizens, you will often find them too few, and you will see that the punishments, the expences, the delays, even the danger of the decision are the price that every citizen pays for his liberty.

Not to be farther tedious, we will conclude with the following:

Would you prevent crimes; contrive that the laws favour less the different orders of citizens, than each citizen in particular. Let men fear the laws and nothing but the laws. Would you prevent crimes; provide that reason and knowledge be more and more diffused among mankind. To conclude; the most sure, but the most difficult method of making men better is by rendering education more complete.

Nothing that relates to government is left untouched in this little book. The maxims of politics, of toleration, and of justice, are thus loudly and powerfully delivered from the throne, and have thereby received, as it were, one sanction more.

Still proceeding on the same enlarged and enlightened plan which we have before had occasion to commend, the empress continued to cultivate and encourage the arts and sciences; to make her empire an asylum to the learned and ingenious; and to reform the manners and instruct the minds of the people, through the extent of its most distant provinces.

The transit of the planet Venus over the sun, which was to happen in the summer of 1769, added a new opportunity of shewing as well the munificence of Catharine as the attention she paid to astronomy. This great princess wrote a letter from Mosco with her own hand, to Count Vladimir Orloff, director of the academy of sciences at Petersburg; wherein she desires the academy to inform her of the most proper places in her dominions for the making of those observations; with an offer to send workmen and artists, and to construct buildings in all those places which the academy might think proper for the purpose, and to grant every other assistance requisite to the undertaking. She also desired, that if there were not sufficient astronomers in the academy to make observations in all the places required, to give her notice, that she might send a proper number of the officers of her marine, to qualify themselves under the eye of the professors in the academy, for that undertaking. Such is the extent of that vast empire, that the observations which were made, both on the transit and exit of this planet, the one in the frozen regions towards the pole, and the other on the borders of the Caspian, were made within its own limits; to some part of which astronomers from every corner of Europe went to behold that remarkable occurrence.

The academy at Petersburg applied to a member of the royal society of London, to procure the necessary instruments for the purpose of proceeding successfully in that important observation. Mr. Ramofsky, who was the writer upon this occasion, candidly acknowledged the great joy of the academy, and their obligations to Mr. Short, for procuring them those instruments; and confessed their doubts of being able to answer the views of the empress, till they had received his letter.

What appears somewhat surprising is, that while Catharine was striving to build her fame upon a solid basis, she made it a matter of much importance to obtain from all the powers of Europe, the title of Imperial majesty, which some of them had refused her. The king of Sweden had long since given it to Catharine; but the Swedish diet could not be brought to grant it till the commencement of this year.

CATHERINE II

Catherine won great renown in her day, and her Memoirs *did a great deal toward winning the sympathies of later historians. Not all commentators, however, have been kind. What follows is Alexander Herzen's biting account of 18th century Russia, written as an introduction to one of the first translations of Catherine's memoirs.*

Elizabeth, absorbed in pleasures and petty intrigues, little thought of overturning the government. She was led to believe that the Regent intended to shut her up in a convent. She, Elizabeth, who spent her time in the barracks of the guards, and in licentious excesses . . . better make herself Empress! So also thought La Chétardie; and he did more than think; he gave French gold to hire a handful of soldiers.

On the 25th of November, 1741, the Grand Duchess, dressed in a magnificent robe, and with a brilliant cuirass on her breast, presented herself at the guardhouse of the Preobrajensky regiment. She exposed to the soldiers her unhappy condition. They, reeking with wine, cried out, "Command, mother, command, and we will slaughter them all!" The charitable Grand Duchess recoils with horror, and *only* orders the arrest of the Regent, her husband, and their son—the *baby*-Emperor.

Source: A. Herzen, ed., *Memoirs of the Empress Catherine II* (New York, 1859), pp. 11–16.

Once again is the old scene repeated.

Anthony Ulrich, of Braunschweig, is awakened from the most profound slumber; but this time he cannot relapse into it again, for two soldiers wrap him up in a sheet and carry him to a dungeon, which he will leave only to go and die in exile.

Again is the *coup d'état* accomplished.

The new reign seems to go on wheels. And once more nothing is wanting to this strange crown . . . . but an heir. The Empress who will have nothing to do with the little Ivan, seeks one in the Episcopal palace of the Prince-Bishop of Lubeck. It is the nephew of the Bishop whom she selects, a grandson of Peter I, an orphan without father or mother, and the intended husband of the little Sophia Augusta Frederica, Princess of Anhalt-Zerbst-Bernburg, who resigned all these sonorous and illustrious titles to be called simply . . . . *Catherine II*.

And now, after all that has been said, let the reader picture to himself what must have been the nature of the medium into which destiny had cast this young girl, gifted, as she was, not only with great talent, but also with a character pliant, though full of pride and passion.

Her position at St. Petersburg was horrible. On one side was her mother, a peevish, scolding, greedy, niggardly, pedantic German, boxing her ears, and taking away her new dresses to appropriate them to her own use; on the other, the Empress Elizabeth, a coarse and grumbling virago, never quite sober, jealous, envious, causing every step of the young Princess to be watched, every word reported, taking offence at everything, and all this after having given her for a husband the most ridiculous Benedict of the age.

A prisoner in the palace, she could do nothing without permission. If she wept for the death of her father, the Empress sent her word that she had grieved enough. "That her father was not a king, that she should mourn him longer than a week." If she evinced a friendship for any of her maids of honour, she might be sure the lady would be dismissed. If she became attached to a faithful servant, still more certain was it that that servant would be turned away.

Her relations with the Grand Duke were monstrous, degrading. He made her the confidante of his amorous intrigues. Drunk from the age of ten, he came one night in liquor to entertain his wife with a description of the graces and charms of the daughter of Biren; and as Catherine pretended to be asleep, he gave her a punch with his fist to awaken her. This booby kept a kennel of dogs, which infested the air, at the side of his wife's bed-chamber, and hung rats in his own, to punish them according to the rules of martial law.

Nor is this all. After having wounded and out-raged nearly every feeling of this young creature's nature, they began to deprave her systematically.

The Empress regards as a breach of order her having no children. Madame Tchoglokoff speaks to her on the subject, insinuating that, *for the good of the state*, she ought to sacrifice her scruples, and concludes by proposing to her a choice between Soltikoff and Narichkine. The young lady affects simplicity and takes both—nay, Poniatowsky into the bargain, and thus was commenced a career of licentiousness in which she never halted during the space of forty years.

What renders the present publication of serious consequence to the imperial house of Russia is, that it proves not only that this house does not belong to the family of Romanoff, but that it does not even belong to that of Holstein Gottorp. The avowal of Catherine on this point is very explicit—*the father of the Emperor Paul is Sergius Soltikoff.*

The Imperial Dictatorship of Russia endeavours in vain to represent itself as traditional and secular.

One word before I close.

In perusing these Memoirs, the reader is astonished to find one thing constantly lost sight of, even to the extent of not appearing anywhere—it is *Russia and the People.* And here is the characteristic trait of the epoch.

The Winter Palace, with its military and administrative machinery, was a world of its own. Like a ship floating on the surface of the ocean, it had no real connection with the inhabitants of the deep, beyond that of eating them. It was the *State for the State.* Organized on the German model, it imposed itself on the nation as a conqueror. In that monstrous barrack, in that enormous chancery, there reigned the cold rigidity of a camp. One set gave or transmitted orders, the rest obeyed in silence. There was but one single spot within that dreary pile in which human passions reappeared, agitated and stormy, and that spot was the domestic hearth; not that of the nation—but of the state. Behind that triple line of sentinels, in those heavily ornamented saloons, there fermented a feverish life, with its intrigues and its conflicts, its dramas and its tragedies. It was there that the destinies of Russia were woven, in the gloom of the alcove, in the midst of orgies, *beyond* the reach of informers and of the police.

What interest, then, could the young German Princess take in that *magnum ignotum*, that people *unexpressed*, poor, semi-barbarous, which concealed itself in its villages, behind the snow, behind bad roads, and only appeared in the streets of St. Petersburg like a foreign outcast, with its persecuted beard, and prohibited dress—tolerated only through contempt.

It was only long afterwards that Catherine heard the Russian people seriously spoken of, when the Cossack Pougatcheff, at the head of an army of insurgent peasants menaced Moscow.

When Pougatcheff was vanquished, the Winter Palace again forgot the people. And there is no telling when it would have been again remembered had it not itself put its masters in mind of its existence, by rising in mass in 1812, rejecting, on the one hand, the release from serfdom offered to it at the point of foreign bayonets, and, on the other, marching to death to save a country which gave it nothing but slavery, degradation, misery—and the oblivion of the Winter Palace.

This was the second *memento* of the Russian people. Let us hope that at the third it will be remembered a little longer.

CHAPTER 4

Tsar Alexander I

THE EARLY YEARS

The character of Alexander I, Catherine's grandson, has been subjected to considerable scrutiny by historians. Torn in his youth between Catherine and his father Paul, an accomplice to the assassination of his father, Alexander was indeed a paradoxical figure. In his youth, he enjoyed the loyalty of a number of liberals, including Prince Adam Czartoryski of Poland.

As soon as I came in, the Grand-Duke took me by the hand, and proposed that we should go into the garden, in order, he said, that he might enable me to judge of the skill of his English gardener. We walked about in every direction for three hours, keeping up an animated conversation all the time. The Grand-Duke told me that my conduct and that of my brother, the resignation we showed in a position which must be painful to us, and the calm indifference with which we had received both the smiles and the frowns of fortune, had gained us his esteem and confidence; that he divined and approved our sentiments; that he had felt it necessary to let us know what he really thought, and that he could not bear the idea that we should judge him otherwise than as he really was. He added that he did not in any way share the ideas and doctrines of the Cabinet and the Court; and that he was far from approving the policy and conduct of his grandmother, whose principles he condemned. He had wished for the success of Poland in her glorious struggle and had deplored her fall. Kosciuszko, he said, was in his eyes a man who was great by his virtues and the cause of humanity and of justice. He added that he detested despotism everywhere, no matter in what way it was exercised; that he loved liberty, to which all men had a right; that he had taken the strongest interest in the French Revolution, and that while condemning its terrible excesses, he wished the French Republic success and

Source: Adam Gielgud, ed., *Memoirs of Prince Adam Czartoryski* (London, 1888), I, 110–13, 115–21, 256–63.

88

rejoiced at its establishment. He spoke to me with veneration of his tutor, M. de la Harpe, as a man of great virtue, of true wisdom, of strict principles, and of energetic character. He owed to him all he knew and any good qualities he might possess—especially those principles of truth and justice which he was happy to bear in his heart and with which M. de la Harpe had inculcated him.

While we were walking about in the garden we several times met the Grand-Duchess, who also was taking a walk. The Grand-Duke told me that he confided his thoughts to his wife, that she alone knew and shared his sentiments, and that I was the only person besides herself to whom he had dared to speak of them since his tutor had gone; that he could not mention them to any Russian, as none were as yet capable even of understanding them; and that I must therefore feel how great a pleasure it would be for him to have in future some one with whom he could talk openly and in entire confidence.

This conversation was, as may be imagined, occasionally interrupted by demonstrations of friendship on his part, and of astonishment, gratitude, and devotion on mine. He bade me farewell, saying that he would try to see me as often as possible, and urging on me the greatest circumspection and secrecy, though at the same time he authorised me to communicate to my brother the subject of our conversation.

I was deeply moved, and could hardly believe my ears. That a Russian Prince, Catherine's successor, her grandson and her favourite child, whom she would have wished to see reigning after her instead of her son, and of whom it was said that he would continue her reign, should disavow and detest his grandmother's principles—should repel the odious policy of Russia—should be a passionate lover of justice and liberty—should pity Poland and wish to see her happy—seemed incredible. And that such noble ideas and great virtues should be able to grow and flourish in such an atmosphere and with such surroundings, was surely little less than a miracle.

I was young, full of exalted sentiments and ideas; extraordinary things did not long astonish me, for I readily believed in anything that seemed to me great and virtuous. I was subjugated by a charm which it is easy to understand: there was so much candour, innocence, resolution which seemed unshakeable, and elevation of soul in the words and countenance of this young prince, that he seemed to me a privileged being whom Providence had sent to this world for the happiness of humanity and of my country. My attachment to him was boundless, and the feeling with which he inspired me at that moment lasted even after the illusions which had given birth to it successively disappeared; it resisted the attacks which Alexander himself made upon it, and it never died in spite of the many events and sad misunderstandings which might have destroyed it. I told my brother of our conversation, and after giving a free rein to our surprise and admiration, we plunged into reveries of a radiant future which seemed to be opening before us. It should be remembered that at that time so-called liberal opinions were much less prevalent than they are now, and had not yet penetrated into all the classes of society and even into the Cabinets of sovereigns. On the contrary, everything that had the appearance of liberalism was anathematised in the Courts and salons of most of the European capitals, and especially in Russia and at St. Petersburg, where all the convictions of the old French régime were grafted in an exaggerated form on Russian despotism and servility.

It was assuredly a most fortunate and important incident that in the midst of these elements there should be a prince, the future ruler of Russia, who would necessarily exercise immense influence in Europe, holding such decided and generous opinions entirely opposed to the existing state of things. Now that I look back, forty years afterwards, upon the events which have taken place since that conversation, I see only too well how little they have realised the picture that our youthful imaginations had drawn.

*   *   *   *   *

We often returned to Tsarskoe-Selo, and soon after we settled there for the season. Our relations with Alexander naturally aroused much interest: it was a kind of freemasonry, but the Grand-Duchess was let into the secret. An intimacy whose object was at that time so recent and so ardently discussed furnished material for conversations which were suspended only to be resumed on the next opportunity. Political opinions which now seem trite and hackneyed were at that time startling on account of their novelty, and the mystery we had to preserve, the idea that we were expressing these opinions under the eyes of a Court encrusted with the prejudices of absolutism and of Ministers puffed up with their supposed infallibility, added interest and piquancy to these relations, which grew more frequent and intimate every day.

The Empress Catherine looked favourably upon the connection which was establishing itself between her grandson and ourselves; she approved it, of course without guessing at its true motive or at its probable consequences. Probably, with her old ideas as to the splendour of the Polish aristocracy, she thought it would be useful to attach an influential family to her grandson. She in no way suspected that this friendship would confirm him in the opinions which she detested and feared—that it would be one of the thousand causes of the progress of liberty in Europe, and of the re-appearance—only for a time alas!—of Poland, which she had thought she had buried for ever, on the political scene. Her approval of the marked preference shown us by Alexander closed the mouths of all objectors, and encouraged us in continuing our relations, which were so attractive to us in all respects.

The Grand-Duke Constantine, from a spirit of imitation, and seeing that his doing so pleased the Empress, now made great professions of friendship to my brother, invited him to his rooms, and admitted him to the intimacy of his family; but there was no question of politics in this connection. My brother was not in this respect as fortunate as I was; none of the motives which had bound us to Alexander existed in the case of Constantine, and his capricious and violent character, not admitting any impression but that of fear, rendered all intimacy with him undesirable. Alexander, however, requested my brother to take Constantine's overtures in good part, at the same time charging him not to reveal the secret of our political conversations.

At first Alexander was quartered in the palace, and did not yet live in the separate building in the park which the Empress had ordered to be built for him, and which had just been completed. We used to go there for our afternoon walks until Alexander established himself in the new building, when he was much more free to see us. He often had either my brother or myself to dinner, and a day seldom passed but one of us supped with him also, when the rooms at the palace were quite finished. In the morning we used to take long walks together; the Grand-Duke was very fond of walking and of visiting the villages in the neighbourhood, and it was especially on these occasions that he used to talk of his favourite subjects. He was under the charm of early youth, which creates images and dwells upon them without being checked by impossibilities, and which makes endless projects for a future which seems to it eternal.

His opinions were those of one brought up in the ideas of 1789, who wishes to see republics everywhere, and looks upon that form of government as the only one in conformity with the wishes and the rights of humanity. Although I was myself at that time very enthusiastic—although born and brought up in a Republic where the principles of the French Revolution had been accepted with ardour—yet I had constantly to moderate the extreme opinions expressed by Alexander. He held, among other things, that hereditary monarchy was an unjust and absurd institution, and that the supreme authority should be granted not through the accident of birth but by the votes of the nation, which would best know who is most capable of governing it. I represented to him the arguments against this view, the difficulty and the risks of an election, what Poland had suffered from such an institution, and how little Russia was adapted to or prepared for it. I added that now at any rate Russia would not gain anything by the change, as she would lose the man who by his benevolent and pure intentions was most worthy of acceding to the throne. We had incessant discussions on this point. Sometimes during our long walks we talked of other matters. We turned from politics to nature, of whose beauties the young Grand-Duke was an enthusiastic admirer. One had to be a great lover of nature to discover its beauties in the country we walked in; but everything is relative in this world, and the Grand-Duke flew into ecstasies about a flower, the greenness of a tree, or the view over an undulating plain. There is nothing uglier or less picturesque than the neighborhood of St. Petersburg. Alexander loved gardens and fields, and was fond of agriculture and the rustic beauty of village girls; the occupations and labours of the country, a simple, quiet, and retired life in some pretty farm, in a wide and smiling landscape—such was the dream he would have liked to realise, and to which he was always returning with a sigh.

I knew well that this was not the thing best suited to him; that for so high a destiny more elevation, force, ardour, and self-confidence were necessary than Alexander seemed to possess; that it was not right for a man in his position to wish to rid himself of the enormous burthen which was reserved for him, and to yearn for the pleasures of a quiet life. It was not enough to perceive and feel the difficulties of his position; he should have been filled with a passionate desire to surmount them. These reflections occasionally presented themselves to my mind, and even when I felt their truth, they did not diminish my feelings of admiration and devotion for Alexander. His sincerity, his frankness, his self-abandonment to the beautiful illusions that fascinated him, had a charm which it was impossible to resist. Moreover, he was still so young that his character might yet gain the qualities in which it was defective; circumstances and necessities might develop faculties which had not the time or the means of showing themselves; and although he was afterwards much changed, he retained to the last a portion of the tastes and opinions of his youth.

Many people—my countrymen especially—in later years reproached me for having placed too much confidence in Alexander's assurances. I have often maintained against his detractors that his opinions were sincere. The impression produced by the first years of our relations could not be effaced. Assuredly, when Alexander, at the age of eighteen, spoke to me with an effusiveness which relieved his mind, about opinions and sentiments which he concealed from everybody else, it was because he really felt them, and wished to confide them to someone. What other motive could he have had? Whom could he have wished to deceive? He certainly followed the inclination of his heart and expressed his real thoughts.

Besides our political discussions, and the ever-welcome topic of the beauties of nature, and the dream of a quiet country life after the destinies of free Russia should have been secured, Alexander had also a third object to which he ardently devoted himself, and which was not at all in accordance with the others, namely, the army, which was his hobby, as it was that of his father, the Grand-Duke Paul. This prince lived during the summer in his country-house of Pavlovsk, half-a-league from Tsarskoe-Selo. The Empress Catherine had allowed him to keep there for his amusement some battalions of marines. He was Grand-Admiral, and this honorary title gave him certain privileges. The Empress pretended not to perceive that Paul made too large a use of them, and that following the example of Peter III, his unfortunate father, he had created for himself a sort of little army, which he clothed and endeavoured to drill according to the system he had observed in Prussia when he visited Frederick the Great at Berlin. This army was, I believe, composed in all of twelve very small battalions, some cuirassiers, dragoons, and hussars, and some guns; and all promotions in this force were in the Grand-Duke's hands. The uniforms were very eccentric in cut, and were in striking contrast to the uniforms of the Russian army in this respect; they were a caricature of the uniforms of the troops of Great Frederick. Many people of society and of the Court had obtained permission to wear these uniforms, and they were the only courtiers whom Paul allowed to attend at his country-houses. Among them was M. Rostopchin, who played an important part after Paul became Emperor, and was afterwards much talked about at the time of the fire of Moscow. These courtiers took their uniforms with them whenever they went to Pavlovsk or to Gatchina, another country-house belonging to the Grand-Duke, or even to his soirées in the Winter Palace, for Paul never went to his mother's in the evening. People only appeared in this costume, however, in Paul's apartments; everywhere else it was tabooed so long as Catherine lived, and people laughed at it with impunity.

* * * * *

The opinions and sentiments which had seemed to me so admirable in Alexander when he was Grand-Duke did not change when he became Emperor; they were somewhat modified by the possession of absolute power, but they remained the foundation of all his principles and thoughts. They were for many years like a secret passion which one dares not acknowledge before a world incapable of comprehending it, but which constantly dominates us and colours our actions whenever its influence can make itself felt. I shall often have occasion to return to this important subject in explanation of Alexander's character, for at other times the Emperor, being thoroughly aware of his power and the obligations it imposed upon him, might have been compared to a man who still likes to amuse himself with the toys of his childhood, and leaves his favourite recreation with regret in order to return to the occupations and duties of real life.

There was no longer any question of the old reveries of extreme liberalism;

the Emperor ceased to speak to me of his plan of giving up the throne, or of the document he had made me write. But he was constantly thinking of more practical matters, such as the administration of justice, the emancipation of the masses, equitable reforms, and liberal institutions; this was his diversion when he was alone with me. He understood the often insurmountable obstacles which the most elementary reforms would meet with in Russia; but he wished to prove to those with whom he was intimate that the sentiments he had expressed to them were still the same, notwithstanding the change in his position. It was necessary, however, not to disclose them, and still less to take a pride in them, in the presence of a public which was at that time so little prepared to appreciate them, and would have regarded them with surprise and horror. Meanwhile the government machine continued to work according to the old routine, and the Emperor was obliged to take part in its management. In order to remedy the discrepancy between Alexander's opinions and his acts, he established a Secret Council composed of persons whom he regarded as his friends and believed to be animated by sentiments and opinions in conformity with his own. The first nucleus of this Council was formed by the young Count Paul Strogonoff, M. de Novosiltzoff, and myself. We had long been in near relations with each other, and these now became more serious. The necessity of rallying round the Emperor and not leaving him alone in his desire of reform drew us more closely together. We were regarded for some years as models of intimate and unshakeable friendship. To be superior to every personal interest, and not to accept either presents or distinctions, was the principle of our alliance. Such a principle could not take root in Russia, but it was in accordance with the ideas of Alexander's youth and inspired him with special esteem for his friends. I was the sole author of the principle, which indeed was specially suited to my peculiar position. It was not always liked by my companions, and the Emperor himself afterwards grew tired of servants who wished to distinguish themselves by refusing to accept rewards which were so eagerly sought by everyone else.

The understanding between us had, as I have shown, begun at the coronation of the Emperor Paul at Moscow, and we had for a long time been on intimate terms, as we met daily at Court Strogonoff's. The fourth member admitted by the Emperor to the Secret Council was Count Kotchoubey. Being the nephew of Count Bezborodko, a Minister who had been held in high esteem by the Empress Catherine, he was sent when still very young to the embassy at Constantinople, and was recalled under the Emperor Paul to give place to M. Tamara. While at Constantinople he conducted himself to the satisfaction of his Government, and was perhaps the only Russian who was well treated in the capital. This was at the time of our grand Diet, and during the reign of Leopold, when Russians used to be received by ladies in drawing-rooms in a manner anything but flattering. I remember the Countess Caroline, afterwards Lady Guildford, being asked by Count Tchernitcheff to insult him in order to enable him to gain a wager, upon which she said: 'You are a Russian.' But to return to Count Kotchoubey. He had acquired a certain European varnish and grand manners which made him a favourite in society. Vanity, a general defect among men, and especially among Russians and Slavs of all kinds, exposed Kotchoubey to sarcasms from other vain people, but he was too good-natured to resent them. He was also accustomed to business, but he had not much knowledge; his intelligence was clear, but not deep, and he had more good-nature and sincerity than are usually found in Russians. This did not save him from certain weaknesses characteristic of his nation—a great wish for place, for distinction, and especially for a fortune to cover his expenses and those of his family, which had become very numerous. He showed an extreme readiness to adopt any opinion that might be in fashion and to follow any lead imposed upon him by a superior will or by the conventions of society. When he was with us he professed liberalism, though with a certain reserve, as it was not to be reconciled with his real opinions. His vanity was such that it betrayed itself when he strove most to conceal it, which exposed him to the satire of my two colleagues. I did not join in their jokes, as he had estimable qualities and showed me much friendly feeling, of which I had strong evidence some years later.

We were privileged to dine with the Emperor without a previous invitation, and we used to meet two or three times a week. After coffee and a little conversation, the Emperor used to retire, and while the other guests left the palace, the four members of the Secret Council entered through a corridor into a little dressing-room, which was in direct communication with the private rooms of their Majesties, and there met the Emperor. Various plans of reform were debated; each member brought his ideas, and sometimes his work, and information which he had obtained as to what was passing in the existing administration and the abuses which he had observed. The Emperor freely expressed his thoughts and sentiments, and although the discussions at these meetings for a long time had no practical result, no useful reform was tried or carried out during Alexander's reign which did not originate in them. Meanwhile the Official Council, namely, the Senate and the Ministers, governed the country in the old way. Directly the Emperor left his dressing-room he came under the influence of the old Ministers, and could do nothing of what had been decided upon in the Secret Council; it was like a masonic lodge from which one entered the practical world.

This mysterious Council, which was not long concealed from the suspicions, or ultimately from the knowledge, of the Court, and was designated 'the young men's party,' grew impatient at not obtaining any result whatever from its deliberations; it pressed the Emperor to carry out the views he had expressed to us and the proposals he considered desirable and necessary. Once or twice an attempt was made to induce him to adopt energetic resolutions, to give orders and make himself obeyed, to dismiss certain superannuated officials who were a constant obstacle to every reform and to put young men in their place. But the Emperor's character inclined him to attain his end by compromises and concessions, and moreover he did not yet feel sufficiently master of the position to risk measures which he thought too violent. In our Council Strogonoff was the most ardent, Novosiltzoff the most prudent, Kotchoubey the most time-serving, and I the most disinterested, always striving to curb undue impatience. Those who urged the Emperor to take immediate and severe measures did not know him. Such a proposal always made him draw back, and was of a nature to diminish his confidence. But as he complained of his Ministers and did not like any of them, an attempt was made in the Council, before inducing him to change them, to discuss the matter in a practical spirit, apart from the abstract considerations of reform which had previously occupied us. Strogonoff accepted the post of Procurator of the First Department of the Senate; and Novosiltzoff was appointed one of the Emperor's secretaries, a place which gave him many advantages, as every letter addressed to the Emperor passed through his hands, and he had a right to publish the Emperor's ukases. His special department, however, was at first to deal with promoters of public undertakings, who are sometimes men of talent, but more often adventurers of very doubtful honesty who flock to Russia from abroad at the beginning of each new reign. This was a duty for which he was qualified by his varied knowledge in matters of finance and industry, and it was at the same time a school which did much to form his character. I must not here forget the fifth member of the Secret Council, M. de la Harpe, Alexander's tutor, who had come on a visit to his former pupil. He did not take part in the after dinner meetings, but he used to have private conversations with the Emperor, and frequently handed to him memoranda reviewing all the branches of the administration. These memoranda were first read at the secret sittings, and afterwards passed on from one member of the Council to the other to be considered at leisure, as they were interminably long. M. de la Harpe was at that time about forty-four years of age; he had been a member of the Swiss Directory, and always wore the uniform of that appointment, with a large sword fastened to an embroidered belt outside his coat. We were all of the opinion that he did not merit his high reputation and the esteem in which Alexander held him. He belonged to the generation of men nourished with the illusions of the last part of the eighteenth century, who thought their doctrine a sort of philosopher's stone, or universal remedy which removed all difficulties to the regeneration of society. M. de la Harpe had his own particular panacea for Russia, and he explained it in such diffuse papers that Alexander himself had not the courage to read them. One of his favourite phrases was *organisation réglementaire;* an important idea no doubt, but he used to repeat it so often and with such emphasis that it was at last attached to him as a sort of nickname.

The Emperor, perhaps without admitting it to himself, began to think less of the capacity of his former tutor, though he was always seeking reasons for raising him in our esteem; his character he always continued to value highly. He did not like us to cast ridicule on the inanity of M. de la Harpe's papers, and he was always much pleased when we praised any of his former tutor's suggestions. But in truth M. de la Harpe had little or no influence on the reforms which Alexander afterwards introduced. He had the good sense to hold aloof from our meetings, and the Emperor himself preferred this, in order, I suppose, to avoid the scandal which might have been produced by an ex-director of the Swiss Republic and a recognised revolutionist preparing reforms for the Russian Empire. He was, however, recognised as one of our colleagues; there was always a chair ready for him at our meetings, and when he left St. Petersburg he assured us that he would still in spirit take part in our deliberations.

NAPOLEON'S INVASION

Alexander's great test came in 1812, when Napoleon's Grand Army invaded Russia. Alexander had acceded to a peace and a treaty with Napoleon in 1807, but a further test of arms had been virtually inevitable. Russia could not voluntarily remain under Napoleon's influence, and the French Emperor in turn could no longer tolerate Russia's independent policies.

The war eventually meant Napoleon's downfall and Russia's ascendancy in Europe. Alexander's own contradictory tendencies came out clearly at this time. To some Europeans he represented national freedom, to others national oppression. He came to regard himself as almost a prophet.

The first part of the following selection was written before Napoleon's attack of 1812, the second part, after.

The last campaign in Poland, distressing as it was to the French, is nothing to what they must experience, if they dare again to invade it. At that time the sudden overthrow of Prussia enabled them to seize on many fine and

---

Source: Alexis Eustaphieff, *The Resources of Russia in the Event of a War with France*, 2d ed. (Boston, 1813), pp. 84–108.

fertile provinces, which furnished them with necessary supplies; but which are now exhausted, or will be prevented from furnishing any. The more men Buonaparte brings with him, and the farther he penetrates into Russia, the nearer he will draw to the fate of Charles XII. Again the Russian peasants will be removed, again their habitations will be destroyed, and again whole fertile regions will be, for safety, converted by the Russians into a barren wilderness. The French, if they advance, will see nothing but the Russian bayonets bristling in front, and receding only to strike with surer aim; nothing but fugitive Cozaks hanging on their wings, who, used to this distressing mode of warfare, will harass them by day and night; and nothing behind or around them but sterility, famine, and desolation.

The French soldiers feel this; Buonaparte knows it too, and hence is his delay; for Russia has taken a decisive stand against him, ever since she refused to adopt his continental system, the darling child of his ambition, and the constant object of his dreams and visions. His character is too well known to suppose he would not have long ago marched his myrmidons against Russia, if he were not somewhat deterred by the hazard of the undertaking. The policy of Russia, on this occasion, seems replete with wisdom. While she is conscious of her own strength, she leaves to him the choice of war, and preserves for herself the incalculable advantage of not appearing the aggressor, but of appealing, with a resistless voice, to her people in self-defence, and in revenge of that violation of sacred engagements which France in attacking her must necessarily commit. Whether Russia repents of her alliance or not, her strict observance of the treaty, and her steady adherence to her promises, while they shew the value and constancy of her friendship, and cover with confusion those who doubted it, teach Europe to rely in future on her fidelity and perseverance, and may possibly raise against France powerful and determined enemies, even where they are least expected.

Let, therefore, France buckle on her armour; and in hostile array march against Russia. Let clouds, portending disaster, gather on; and the threatening tempest again spread wide its rapid wings, and pour its deluge upon the north: Russia undismayed, awaits, nay, invites the blow. Next to Providence, she relies on the tried heroism of her people; and on the prayers of the suffering millions, whose champion she now stands forth. Her struggles will be against universal tyranny; and her success will be the deliverance of all. Her safety will be the protection, and her independence the relief and security of the oppressed. Her cause is the cause of freedom; and every soil, trod by the foot of a freeman, shall yield to it a tribute of sympathy. Her cause is the cause of humanity; and wherever man draws the breath of life, blessings shall be its enviable portion.

It is with Russia that the fallen nations can even hope to rise. The frowning idol, under whose iron foot numberless victims daily expire may yet be

hurled from its ensanguined throne, and awe the world only by its tremendous ruins! The overgrown colossus, from whose fatal grasp Europe in vain
strives to free herself, can only on its own element be crushed. The thunder
of Albion has only struck at its shadow on the ocean; but the huge substance,
in which all the ingredients of mischief are consolidated, still remains the
same. Some of the distant sparks have only been intercepted; while the main
furnace, wherein such horrid conflagrations are engendered, still remains un-
extinguished. Even in the regions of the now respiring Lusitania, only some
of the monster's limbs have been shattered; the enormous body is still animated with life and vigour, is still fed by daily torrents of human blood, and
endowed with the unnatural power of renovating and increasing its strength
at pleasure. To assault its extremities is only to provoke its rage and fury;
but to encounter it at once, in all its dimensions, heart to heart, is the only
chance of destroying it. This may yet be hoped from the invasion of Russia.

*   *   *   *   *

How far the statements and opinions, contained in the preceding pages,
have been justified by subsequent events, it is now in the power of every
man to decide—of every man, whose judgment is not warped by prejudices,
or who has not sworn, under the illusion of Gallic enchantment, to believe
Napoleon infallible, and exempt from all the vicissitudes of human nature.
The immense armies, raised by Russia to match a world in arms, show the
extent of her resources, and the sufficiency of her population; the noble
perseverance of Alexander proves how unjustly he was distrusted and
blamed; and the voluntary sacrifices, and indissoluble union of the Russian
people of all classes, while they furnish a severe satire on the officious mor-
alist, who pretended to pity their fancied misery and prescribe rules for
their imaginary happiness, cover wtih shame and confusion the eager slanderer, who, judging perhaps from his own disposition, doubted their loyalty,
and conceived treachery to be their inmate. How little was Russia understood! and how little was it anticipated, that she should give posterity the
unprecedented example of a nation of more than 40,000,000 souls without
a single traitor! Such, however, is the fact. She alone was proof against
that contagion of French influence, which has penetrated into every other
part of the civilized world; and which, if it really was exerted in Russia to
the extent stated, failed where it was most expected to succeed. Not a solitary
instance of treason has occurred, and even the famous plot of Speransky, so
much spoken of, on inquiry proved groundless, and the supposed culprit,
whose innocence was afterwards clearly established, was endowed with a
pension of 20,000 rubles a year. But the Russian talent and national character have in no instance been more strikingly illustrated than in the conduct
of Count N. Romantzow, the Russian chancellor and prime minister.

This distinguished nobleman, son of a hero whose name will ever shed a lustre on the Russian history, though of acknowledged probity and honour, was suspected, even by some of the Russians, of being a French partisan, as far at least as he was influenced by his own political sentiments and predilections. His apparent cultivation of the French interest, his seeming preference of those who were supposed employed in misleading him, his affected hostility to Great Britain, and above all, his journey to Paris, which looked like a slavish homage to Buonaparte, had exposed him to such undisguised obloquy and such galling and disgraceful aspersions, as none, but patriots like himself, could have had the courage and magnanimity to endure with patience. In proportion to this public denunciation were public gratitude, astonishment, and joy, when it was found, from the diplomatic correspondence between him and the French minister, that his deportment was only modified by circumstances, but wholly rested on the firm principle of pure patriotism; that, by exposing and humbling himself, he was securing and raising his country; that, while the crafty Frenchmen considered him their tool, they were caught in their own toils; and that the fruits of his profound policy, were, finally, the conquest of Finland, the most precious gem in the Russian crown; a formidable army, prepared, increased, and organized under the auspices of the treaty of Tilsitz, which was so much censured because so little understood; and a glorious peace with Turkey, at a most critical juncture, when Russia wanted every soldier at home—a peace, which annexed to her empire the Moldavian provinces as far as the Pruth; which secured her triumph over all the counteracting influence of the French; and shewed, that the Turkiesh divan had a better knowledge of the means of Russia, than all the cabinets of Europe, and that it acted with better policy and foresight as to the issue of the impending contest.

Alexander himself is entitled to equal credit for having, by a temporary humiliation, consented to an interview on the Niemen, the object of which was the ultimate salvation of his country. He was suddenly involved in a war, in which, through the nefarious conduct of the British "talent" administration, he beheld himself abandoned by those very men by whose solicitation, and for whose interest, he had recourse to arms; and while he alone had to withstand the gigantic force of France, bringing in her train all the subjugated nations of Europe, his prospect of relief was yet distant, as his armies, scattered over the face of his vast empire, could not be collected in time enough to arrest the progress of the enemy. Thus circumstanced, he accepted of the peace of Tilsitz, which added to his territories considerable possessions; and, strange as it may seem, secured to him all its essential advantages, inasmuch as Buonaparte, though the eclat of the negotiation rested with him, lost thereby the favourable opportunity of invading Russia, and allowed Alexander all the necessary time to strengthen himself against such an attempt in future. At the very moment that the submission of the Russian emperor was a theme of universal reprobation, and with many an object of senseless and unceasing clamour, he was contemplating the approaching crisis of his empire, and was preparing for a contest, in which there would be no compromise, and in which Russia was to conquer and be the first power on the European continent, or to fall, and be erased from the list of nations. No sooner had he finished his preparations, no sooner had he surveyed with an eye of intelligence his own resources, and the unanimous exertions of his people, determined to support him to their utmost, than he took an elevated ground from which France could not drive him, but by force. He sought no war, but was determined rather to encounter it, than to recede an inch; and far from fearing it, he left the choice of it to his adversaries. Nay, he sent forth a noble defiance in the person of the duke of Oldenburgh, who, being deprived of his dukedom by Buonaparte, was invited to Russia, and received the hand of Alexander's sister, the very princess who was refused to the French emperor. Finding such unequivocal tokens of the resentment of Russia, Napoleon was willing to appease her by indemnifying the duke of Oldenburgh; but she would not even listen to his proposals, unless they should be preceded by his withdrawing all his troops from the Prussian territories. This fixed demand, an unequivocal proof of confidence and readiness to meet the foe—of deliberate resolution, not of despair and necessity, to confront the danger, that, by a trifling compromise, might early have been averted, was too galling to Buonaparte's pride; and his refusing to comply, produced the extraordinary campaign which has completely verified the fourth section of the preceding tract, relating to the military prowess of Russia, and of which a sketch is attempted here, as far as the scantiness of information from official sources, and the author's moderate abilities, could favour such an undertaking.

THE WAR OF 1812

The French had first advanced into Russia easily, but as time went by, their situation became more difficult. The Russians avoided a pitched battle, a showdown, until they stood at Borodino, which in itself was an indecisive battle. Contrary to Napoleon's hopes, Alexander refused to negotiate peace, vowing that Russia would resist to the end. The French could only plod ahead in frustration, at least until they reached Moscow.

Source: Eugene Labaume, *The Campaign in Russia* (London, 1815), pp. 160–73, 192–94, 203–7, 327–34.

After the battle of the Moskwa, our triumphant army marched in three columns towards the capital of the Russian empire. Napoleon, impatient to get possession of it, pursued the enemy with his accustomed vigour, on the high road of Smolensko; while Prince Poniatowski, at the head of the fifth corps, marched on the right, by way of Kaluga. The Viceroy, commanding the fourth corps, continued on the left flank, and taking the road of Zwenighorod, proceeded towards Moscow, where the whole army was to assemble.

We could judge of the consternation that reigned in this capital, by the terror with which we inspired the country people. Our arrival in Rouza (9th of September), and the cruel manner in which we had treated the inhabitants were no sooner known, than all the villages on the road to Moscow were instantly abandoned. The country presented one uniform scene of horrible desolation: for most of those who fled, burnt, in despair, their houses, their *chateaux*, and the grain and forage, which were scarcely gathered. All these unhappy beings, terrified by the fatal and useless resistance of the inhabitants of Rouza, threw away the pikes with which they had been armed, and swiftly fled to conceal their wives and their little ones in the thick forests at a distance from our route.

On approaching Moscow, we had hoped that civilization, which enervates the soul, and especially an attachment to property, so natural to the inhabitants of large towns, would have induced the people not to quit their habitations. We were convinced that the rapacity of our soldiers was principally excited by the deserted state in which we found the villages. But the country around Moscow does not belong to the inhabitants of that beautiful city; it was the property of the lords who had declared against us, and their peasants, equally enslaved and oppressed with those of the Nieper and of the Volga, obeyed the orders of their masters. They had been enjoined, on pain of death, to fly at our approach, and to hide in the woods whatever could be useful to us.

We perceived the execution of this fatal measure on entering the village of Apalchtchouina. The houses deserted, the castle abandoned, the furniture dashed to pieces, and the provisions destroyed, presented a spectacle of the most frightful desolation. All these ravages shewed us what sacrifices a people sufficiently magnanimous to prefer independence to riches, will cheerfully make.

Near Karinskoé, a village half way towards Zwenighorod, whither we were marching, the cossacks appeared. According to their custom, they made no stand against our advanced-guard, but contented themselves with observing us, by marching on an eminence at our left, parallel to the high road. On the summit of this height, in the midst of a thick wood of birch, rose the grey walls and the steeples of an ancient abbey. At the foot of the hill stood the little town of Zwenighorod, built on the banks of the Moskwa. On this point the cossacks formed themselves into several bodies, and skirmished for some time with our light troops, but they were gradually dislodged from their ambuscades, and we took post around Zwenighorod.

The abbey situated above this little town, commands the course of the Moskwa. Its embattled walls, more than twenty feet in height, and between five and six feet thick, are flanked by four great towers, with embrasures. This edifice, constructed in the thirteenth or fourteenth century, reminds us of the times when the Moscovites, filled with veneration for their priests, suffered the sacerdotal authority to take precedence of that of the nobles; and when the Czar marched, on days of ceremony, before the patriarch of Moscow, holding the bridle of his horse. But these monks, so powerful and so formidable before the time of Peter I., were brought back again to the simplicity of the apostles, when this great monarch, on founding his empire, confiscated their property and diminished their number.

To conceive a proper idea of the changes produced by this reform, it was sufficient to enter the abbey of Zwenighorod. At the sight of these lofty towers and enormous walls, we supposed that the interior contained an agreeable and commodious residence, and that we should find among these monks the wonted abundance of all richly-endowed abbeys. A large iron gate, strongly barricaded, confirmed us in the persuasion that this convent was well supplied with every thing that our soldiers needed. We were about to force the entry, when an old man, whose flowing beard was whiter than his robe, came to admit us. He was desired to conduct us to the abbot. On entering the court, we were much surprised at finding that this vast edifice did not correspond with the high opinion we had conceived of it; and that our guide, instead of introducing us into the apartments of the superior, conducted us to a small chapel, where we saw four monks prostrate at the foot of an altar, constructed in the Grecian style. These venerable old men, when they perceived us, threw themselves at our feet, and, embracing our knees, entreated, in the name of the God whom they adored, that we would respect their church, and the graves of some bishops of which they were the faithful guardians. "You may judge by our miserable appearance," they addressed us by means of an interpreter, "that we can have no hidden treasures; and our food is so coarse that many of your soldiers would scorn to eat it. We have no other possessions than our relics and our altars. Deign to respect them from a reverence for a religion so similar to your own." This we promised, and our assurance was confirmed on the arrival of the Viceroy, who established his head-quarters in this abbey, and thereby preserved the church and the convent, from the pillage with which they were threatened.

While this asylum, formerly so peaceful, was a prey to the tumult unavoidable on such occasions, I perceived one of these pious monks, who, to conceal himself, took refuge in a cell almost under ground, the simplicity of which presented nothing to excite our avarice. This friar, sensible of my attentions to him, rewarded them by acknowledging that he spoke French, and that he wished to have the pleasure of conversing with me. Charmed with his candour, I profited by it, to inform myself of every thing relating to the sentiments and character of a nation, from whom we had conquered more than two hundred and fifty leagues of territory, without becoming acquainted with them. When I mentioned Moscow, he told me that it was the place of his nativity, and I perceived that deep sighs interrupted his speech. I judged by his silent grief that he mourned over the misfortunes to which this great capital would soon be exposed. I sympathized with him; but, anxious to know the state of affairs in that city which we were on the point of entering, I ventured at length to ask him concerning it.

"The French have entered the territory of Russia with immense force," said this venerable monk; "they come to ravage our beloved country, and they advance even to the sacred city—the centre of our empire and the source of our prosperity. Unacquainted with our manners and our character, they think that we shall bend under their yoke, and that, compelled to choose between our homes and our independence, we shall, like too many others, submit to their dominion, and renounce that national pride in which consists the true power of a people. No, Napoleon is mistaken. We are too wise not to abhor his tyranny; and we are not sufficiently corrupted to prefer slavery to liberty. In vain he hopes to force us, by his numberless armies, to sue for peace. He does not remember that the population of Russia is at the absolute control of the nobility. Our seigneurs, able at their pleasure to cause whole districts to emigrate, will order their peasants to fly into the deserts at the approach of the invader, or, if necessary, will destroy every town and village, rather than give them up to a true barbarian, whose tyranny is more dreadful to us than death itself.

"We are aware too," added he, "that Napoleon relies much on the dissensions which used formerly to exist between the monarch and the nobles; but the love of our country has stifled every ancient feud. He flatters himself likewise, that he will be able to arm the people against the great. Vain efforts! the people are, from religion, obedient to their masters; nor will they confide in the deceitful promises of him, who burns their cottages, murders their children, devastates their country, and subverts their temples. Besides, has not the whole of Europe witnessed the most striking instances of his perfidy? Is he not the scourge of Germany, of whom he professed to be the protector? Spain too, having trusted to the sincerity of his alliance, is become one vast burying-place! The Pontiff who crowned him, and raised him from a private station to the first throne in the world, what reward has he received for that diadem? An ignominious captivity! And even your own country, which, for the sake of a foreigner, seems to have forgotten the race of St. Louis, what advantages does she derive from her submission? Incessant new taxes to maintain a crowd of worthless courtiers, or to gratify the luxury of a family insatiable in their pleasures. In addition to this, you have proscriptions and secret executions without number. Your very thoughts are fettered, and whole generations are destroyed. In truth, your mothers have often been reduced to the sad necessity of deploring their fecundity. This," said the venerable old man to me, "this is the situation in which your tyrant has placed you: a tyrant, who is the more vain and odious, because he sprung from an obscure family; and who, formerly having scarcely one domestic to serve him, is now desirous that the whole universe should crouch at his feet, and that even kings should be compelled to wait in his ante-room. If I did not fear to disgrace the majesty of that monarch who loves us as we love him, I would draw a comparison between your monarch and ours,—but such a comparison would only produce a shocking contrast, as it would place vice in constant opposition to virtue."

Struck by the energy of this priest, whose strength of mind had suffered nothing from age, I remained silent; and was at the same time charmed with his candour. Affected by the confidence with which he had honoured me, I thought I might cast off all reserve, and derive much useful information from his conversation. "As you have just mentioned the Emperor Alexander," said I to him, "pray tell me what is become of him? Since we passed the Wilia we have never heard any thing of him; and at Witepsk, in a public audience, Napoleon announced with much satisfaction, that this monarch had shared the fate of his father, having fallen a victim, at Wiliki-luki, to the treachery of his courtiers."

"He cannot have much greatness of soul," answered the old man, smiling, "who triumphs at the death of an enemy. But to prove to you the falsity of that report, and to shew you how much harmony exists among all classes at this critical moment, and how beloved our sovereign is, I will read you a letter, which was sent to me from Moscow, a few days after Alexander had arrived there from the army." At these words he took out the letter, translating it to me as he went on.

Moscow, July 27

This day will add new lustre to our annals, and the remembrance of it will descend to the remotest posterity, as an eternal testimony of Russian patriotism and loyalty. It will record the ardent attachment, which our illustrious nobility, and every class of citizens, feel for our beloved sovereign. After a notification published in the evening, the nobility and the merchants assembled at eight o'clock on the following morning, at the palace Slobode, to wait the arrival of our most gracious Emperor. Notwithstanding the object of this meeting had not been communicated, every one attended, full of those loyal feelings which the appeal of the father of his country to his children, in the capital of his empire, would naturally inspire. The silence which reigned in this vast assembly clearly proved their union, and their disposition to submit to any sacrifice. When the manifesto of His Imperial Majesty was read in the presence of the governor of Moscow, appealing to the nation at large, and calling on every one to defend his country against an enemy 'who, with craft in his heart, and seduction on his lips, was bringing fetters and indissoluble chains for Russia,' the illustrious posterity of the Pojarskies, animated by the most ardent zeal, immediately testified their readiness to sacrifice the whole of their property, and even their lives. They immediately resolved that levies should be made in the government of Moscow, to form an army of the interior, consisting of ten men out of every hundred, who should be armed to the utmost of their ability, and provided with clothing and pay. The manifesto being afterwards read in the assembly of the merchants, this body, animated by the general zeal, resolved that a sum of money should be levied on each of them, proportionate to their respective capitals, to defray the expense of the army of the interior. Not satisfied with this, the greater part of them were desirous of making further sacrifices. They demanded permission to open a voluntary subscription for that purpose, and in less than an hour, the sum subscribed amounted to more than one million and a half of roubles.

Such was the disposition of these two bodies, when His Majesty, who had attended divine service at the church of the palace, appeared among the nobles. After assuring them, in a short speech, that he considered the zeal of the nobility as the firmest support of his throne; and, acknowledging that they had at all times, and under all circumstances, shewn themselves the guardians and faithful defenders of the integrity and glory of their beloved country, he condescended to give them a brief sketch of the state of military affairs, which then required extraordinary measures of defence. When he was informed of the unanimous decision of the two bodies, who had resolved to furnish, to clothe, and to arm, at their own expense, eighty thousand men for the defence of Moscow, he received this new proof of attachment to his person, and of love to the country, with the feelings of a father who loves his children, and who is proud of their courage. Yielding to the emotions which overpowered him, he exclaimed 'I did not expect less, you have fully confirmed my opinion of you.'

Afterwards his Imperial Majesty condescended to proceed to the saloon where the merchants were assembled, and being informed of the zeal they had shewn both in the resolution of levying a sum on the whole body, and making an extraordinary voluntary subscription of a million and a half of roubles, he expressed his gracious satisfaction in terms dictated by wisdom itself. His speech was followed by the general exclamation of 'We are ready to sacrifice for our father, not only our fortunes, but our lives.' These were the words of the descendants of the immortal Minin. The scene of that morning requires the pen of a new Tacitus; while the pencil of a second Apelles alone would do justice to the picture, which represented the monarch and the father beaming kindness and benevolence, receiving from his children who thronged around him, the sacrifices which they were offering on the altar of their country.

*   *   *   *   *

Approaching, however, towards the centre of the town, and especially in the neighbourhood of the Bazar, we began to see some inhabitants assembled around the Kremlin. These deluded beings, deceived by a national tradition, had believed that this citadel was impregnable, and had attempted the preceding day to defend it for an instant against our valiant legions. Dismayed by their defeat, they contemplated, with tears, those lofty towers which they had hitherto regarded as the *palladium* of their city. Proceeding further on, we saw a crowd of soldiers, who exposed to public sale a vast quantity of articles which they had pillaged; for it was only at the grand magazines of provisions that the imperial guards had placed sentinels. Continuing our progress, the number of soldiers multiplied; they were seen in troops, carrying on their backs pieces of cloth, loaves of sugar, and whole bales of merchandize. We knew not how to account for this shocking disorder, when at length some fusileers of the guards informed us that the smoke which we had seen on entering the town, proceeded from a vast building, full of goods, called the Exchange, and which the Russians had set on fire on their retreat. "Yesterday," said these soldiers, "we entered the city about twelve o'clock, and towards five, the fire began to appear. We endeavoured at first to extinguish it, but we soon learned that the governor had sent away all the engines. It is also believed," added they, "that this fire, which cannot be subdued, has been kindled by the nobility, with an intention of exciting us to plunder, and destroying our discipline; and likewise with the determination to ruin those merchants who opposed the abandonment of Moscow."

A natural curiosity made me proceed. As I advanced towards the fire, the avenues were still more obstructed by soldiers and beggars carrying off goods of every kind. The less precious articles were despised, and soon thrown away, and the streets were covered with merchandize of every description. I penetrated at length into the interior of the Exchange; but, alas! it was no more the building so renowned for its magnificence; it was rather a vast furnace, from every side of which the burning rafters were continually falling, and threatening us with instant destruction. I could still, however, proceed with some degree of safety under the piazzas. These were filled with numerous warehouses which the soldiers had broken open, every chest was rifled, and the spoil exceeded all their expectations. No cry, no tumult was heard in this scene of horror. Every one found abundantly sufficient to satisfy his thirst for plunder. Nothing was heard but the crackling of the flames, and the noise of the doors that were broken open; and occasionally a dreadful crash caused by the falling in of some vault. Cottons, muslins, and in short all the most costly productions of Europe and of Asia, were a prey to the flames. The cellars were filled with sugar, oil, and vitriol; these burning all at once in the subterraneous warehouses, sent forth torrents of flame through thick iron grates, and presented a striking image of the mouth of hell. It was a spectacle both terrible and affecting. Even the most hardened minds were struck with a conviction that so great a calamity would on some future day, call forth the vengeance of the Almighty upon the authors of such crimes.

*   *   *   *   *

The most heart-rending scene which my imagination had ever conceived, far surpassing the most afflicting accounts in ancient or modern history, now presented itself before our eyes. A great part of the population of Moscow, frightened at our arrival, had concealed themselves in cellars or secret recesses of their houses. As the fire spread around, we saw them rushing in despair from their various asylums. They uttered no imprecation, they breathed no complaint, but carrying with them their most precious effects, fled before the flames. Others, of greater sensibility, and actuated by the genuine feelings of nature, saved only their children, who were closely clasped in their arms. Many old people, borne down by grief rather than by age, had not sufficient strength to follow their families, and expired near the houses in which they were born. The streets, the public places, and particularly the churches, were filled with these unhappy people, who, lying on the remains of their property, suffered even without a murmur. No contention or noise was heard. Both the conqueror and the conquered were equally hardened: the one from excess of fortune, the other from excess of misery.

The fire, whose ravages could not be restrained, soon reached the finest parts of the city. Those palaces which we had admired for the beauty of their architecture, and the elegance of their furniture, were enveloped in the flames. Their magnificent fronts, ornamented with bas-reliefs and statues, fell with a dreadful crash on the fragments of the pillars which had supported them. The churches, though covered with iron and lead, were likewise destroyed, and with them those beautiful steeples, which we had seen the night before, resplendent with gold and silver. The hospitals too, which contained more than twenty thousand wounded, soon began to burn. This offered a harrowing and dreadful spectacle; almost all these poor wretches perished. A few who still lingered, were seen crawling, half burnt, amongst the smoking ruins; and others, groaning under heaps of dead bodies, endeavoured in vain to extricate themselves from the horrible destruction which surrounded them.

How shall I describe the confusion and tumult, when permission was granted to pillage this immense city! Soldiers, suttlers, galley-slaves, and prostitutes, eagerly ran through the streets, penetrating into the deserted palaces, and carrying away every thing which could gratify their avarice. Some covered themselves with stuffs, richly worked with gold; some were enveloped in beautiful and costly furs; while others dressed themselves in women's and children's pelisses, and even the galley-slaves concealed their rags under the most splendid court-dresses; the rest crowded into the cellars, and forcing open the doors, drank the most luscious wines, and carried off an immense booty.

This horrible pillage was not confined to the deserted houses alone, but extended to those which were inhabited, and soon the eagerness and wantonness of the plunderers, caused devastations which almost equalled those occasioned by the conflagration. Every asylum was soon violated by the licentious troops. The inhabitants who had officers in their houses, for a little while flattered themselves that they should escape the general calamity. Vain illusion! the fire, progressively increasing, soon destroyed all their hopes.

Towards evening, when Napoleon no longer thought himself safe in a city, the ruin of which seemed inevitable, he left the Kremlin, and established himself, with his suite, in the castle at Peterskoë. When I saw him pass by, I could not, without abhorrence, behold the chief of a barbarous expedition, who evidently endeavoured to escape the decided testimony of public indignation, by seeking the darkest road. He sought it, however, in vain. On every side the flames seemed to pursue him, and their horrible and mournful glare, flashing on his guilty head, reminded me of the torches of the Eumenides, pursuing the destined victims of the Furies!

The generals likewise received orders to quit Moscow. Licentiousness then became unbounded. The soldiers, no longer restrained by the presence of their chiefs, committed every kind of excess. No retreat was now safe, no place sufficiently sacred to afford any protection against their rapacity. Nothing more forcibly excited their avarice than the church of St. Michael, the sepulchre of the Russian Emperors. An erroneous tradition had propagated the belief that it contained immense riches. Some grenadiers presently entered it, and descended, with torches, into the vast subterranean vaults, to disturb the peace and silence of the tomb. But instead of treasures they found only stone coffins, covered with pink velvet, with thin silver plates, on which were engraved the names of the Czars, and the date of their birth and decease. Mortified at this disappointment, they again searched every part of the building, and at length perceived, at the end of a dark gallery, a lamp, the half-extinguished light of which fell on a small altar. They immediately proceeded towards it, and the first object which presented itself to their notice, was a young female elegantly dressed, and in the attitude of devotion. At the noise of the soldiers, the unhappy girl screamed violently, and fell into a swoon. In that situation she was carried before one of our generals.

*   *   *   *   *

Marching from Smolensko, a spectacle the most horrible was presented to our view. From that point till we arrived at a wretched ruined hamlet, at the distance of about three leagues, the road was entirely covered with cannon and ammunition-waggons, which they had scarce time to spike, or to blow up. Horses in the agonies of death were seen at every step, and sometimes whole teams, sinking under their labours, fell together. All the defiles which the carriages could not pass, were filled with muskets, helmets, and breast-plates. Trunks broken open, portmanteaus torn to pieces, and garments of every kind were scattered over the valley. At every little distance, we met with trees, at the foot of which the soldiers had attempted to light a fire, but the poor wretches had perished ere they could accomplish their object. We saw them stretched by dozens around the green branches which they had vainly endeavoured to kindle; and so numerous were the bodies, that they would have obstructed the road, had not the soldiers been often employed in throwing them into the ditches and the ruts.

These horrors, far from exciting our sensibility, only hardened our hearts. Our cruelty, which could no more be exercised on the enemy, was extended to our companions. The best friends no longer recognised each other. Whoever discovered the least sickness, if he had not good horses and faithful servants, was sure never to see his country again. Every one preferred to save the *plunder of Moscow*, rather than the life of his comrade. On all sides we heard the groans of the dying, and the lamentable cries of those whom we had abandoned. But every one was deaf to their supplications, or, if he approached those who were on the point of expiring, it was to plunder, not to assist them; it was to search whether they had any remains of food, and not to afford them relief.

Arrived at Loubna, we were able to save only two miserable barns from destruction, one for the Viceroy, and the other for his staff. We had scarcely established ourselves there, when we heard a loud cannonade in our front. As this noise appeared to come from our right, some thought that it was an engagement with the ninth corps, which, not having been able to relieve Witepsk, was obliged to retreat before a superior force; but they who were best acquainted with the country, believed that it was the Emperor and his guard, who had been attacked by Prince Kutusoff, before his arrival at Krasnoë. That prince had marched from Elnïa, and passed our army while we halted at Smolensko.

We can scarcely imagine a picture more deplorable than the bivouac of the staff. Twenty-one officers, confounded with as many servants, had crept together around a little fire, under an execrable cart-house scarcely covered. Behind them were the horses ranged in a circle, that they might be some defence against the violence of the wind, which blew with fury. The smoke was so thick that we could scarcely see the figures of those who were close to the fire, and who were employed in blowing the coals on which they cooked their food. The rest, wrapped in their pelisses or their cloaks, lay one upon another, as some protection from the cold; nor did they stir, except to abuse those who trod upon them as they passed, or to rail at the horses which kicked whenever a spark fell on their coats.

(November 16th) We recommenced our march before the dawn of day, and the road was again covered with the wrecks of our baggage and artillery. The horses could no longer draw, and we were obliged to abandon our cannon at the foot of the slightest hill. The only duty which then remained to the artillery-men, was to scatter the powder of the cartridges, and to spike the pieces, lest the enemy should turn them against us. We were reduced to this extremity when, at the distance of two hours' march from Krasnoë, the Generals Poitevin and Guyon, who were in the van-guard, saw a Russian officer coming towards them, followed by a trumpeter, who announced that a herald was advancing. Surprised at an appearance so unexpected, General Guyon halted, and, permitting the officer to approach, demanded whence he came, and what was the object of his mission. "I come," said he, "from General Miloradowitch, to tell you, that yesterday we beat Napoleon, with the imperial guard; and that to-day the Viceroy is surrounded by an army of twenty thousand men. He cannot escape us, and if he will surrender, we offer him honourable terms." To this General Guyon replied with indignation, "Return quickly whence you came, and announce to those who sent you, that if you have twenty thousand men, we have here four times twenty thousand." These words, uttered with a confident air, so confounded the herald, that he immediately returned to the camp of the enemy.

While this was going on, the Viceroy arrived, and listened to the intelligence with mingled surprise and indignation. Although his corps was so dreadfully weakened, and he probably had some knowledge of the serious affair which had taken place on the day before, between the advanced-guard of Kutusoff, and the imperial guard, yet, reflecting on the boasting manner in which this had been related, he conceived the hope, that by forcing a passage, he might in a short time rejoin the Emperor. He was likewise fully determined to fall honourably in the field, rather than accept of conditions incompatible with his fame. He immediately ordered the fourteenth division to front the enemy, carrying with them the only two pieces of cannon which remained; then calling General Guilleminot, he conferred with him for a long time, and the result of their conference was, that it was absolutely necessary to force our way through the enemy. In the meantime our troops had marched on, and the Russians, permitting them to advance to the very foot of the hill on which they were encamped, suddenly unmasked their batteries, and directed them on their squares. Their cavalry soon after descending from their position, completed the destruction of our troops, and captured their cannon, of which they had made but few discharges through want of ammunition.

General Ornano advanced across the fire of the enemy, with the remains of the thirteenth division, to succour the troops of the fourteenth, which were so cruelly beaten, when a cannon-ball passed so near him that he fell from his horse. The soldiers thought that he was dead, and ran forward to plunder him, when they perceived that he was only stunned by the violence of the fall. The Prince then sent his aide-de-camp, Colonel Delfanti, to endeavour to reanimate the troops. That brave officer, rushing forward amidst a shower of balls and grape-shot, encouraged his soldiers by his exhortations, and by his example; when, receiving two dangerous wounds, he was compelled to retire from the ranks. A surgeon having applied a slight dressing, he returned with difficulty from the field of battle. On his way he met Monsieur de Villeblanche, who, in the capacity of auditor of the council of state, had quitted the town of Smolensko, of which he was the intendant, with General Charpentier, who was the governor. Unfortunately he had obtained leave of the Viceroy to accompany him. This generous young man, perceiving Colonel Delfanti wounded, and leaning on an officer, listened to the dictates of his sensibility and offered him his arm also. As all three were slowly retiring from the field, a cannon-ball struck the colonel between the shoulders, and carried off the head of the brave Villeblanche. Thus perished two young men, who, in different professions, had proved their talents and their courage. The first fell a victim to his bravery, the other to his humanity. The Prince, deeply affected by this unhappy catastrophe, shewed the regard which he felt for the memory of Colonel Delfanti, by an act of benevolence towards the author of his being; and he would have afforded the same consolation to the father of Villeblanche, if the death of his only son had not shortly brought him to his grave.

Many officers of distinguished merit perished on that bloody day. We particularly regretted Major D'Oreille, whose intrepidity was so well known, and the captain of engineers, Morlincourt, whose modesty was equal to his talents. The cannonade yet continued, and carried destruction through all our ranks. The field of battle was covered with the dead and the dying. Great numbers of the wounded, abandoning their regiments, took refuge in the rear, and increased the crowd of stragglers. The firing, which had proved fatal to our first ranks, extended its ravages to the rear of our army, where the dismounted officers were stationed. The Captains Bordoni and

Mastini perished there. They constituted a part of the small number of the Italian guards who yet survived.

BORODINO

In Soviet historiography, the war of 1812 is called the "First Great Patriotic War," the second being the struggle against Hitler, 1941–45. The following article illustrates the role which the war effort of 1812 plays in Soviet historical thought.

Borodino. 1812. The name and date have been inscribed for ever in the annals of Russian national glory. The years, the decades, the centuries go by; the cavalcade of historical events opens up broader and broader horizons, but the date of a decisive event in the destiny of a people, once imprinted in their mind, never fades. Borodino is such a great event; it remains a memorial to the courage, heroism and boundless loyalty of the Russian people to their motherland, and a monument to the glory of Russian arms. Since then the best minds of Russia have been fixed on the event: it was the source of the spiritual and political upsurge which produced the Decembrist movement. The heroic theme of Borodino was an inspiration to the poet Lermontov; it gave the world Leo Tolstoi's majestic epic; it is embodied in Russian music and painting.

Famous historical battles have come down to us in the annals of mankind: Thermopylae, Cannae, Poitiers, Kulikovo. The battle of Borodino ranks among them.

What happened at Borodino on September 7, 1812? Thanks to Tolstoi's remarkable epic tale and the painstaking research of scholars, who in these 150 years have made a profound and all-round study of the history of that war, we know all the details. But it is not of them I will speak here. I want to emphasise that Borodino was the culminating point of the heroic year of 1812, a year which determined the future not only of Russia, but of Europe and the whole world for many years to come.

On the night of June 23, 1812, Napoleon's "Grande Armée" crossed the Russian frontier along the Niemen. It was an army the like of which the world had never seen: 420,000 soldiers were marching along the roads of Russia; 160,000 Austrians and soldiers of other Powers dependent on Napoleon were in the reserve. This gigantic army of 600,000 men was hurled

Source: A. Manfred, "Borodino: 150 Years Later," *International Affairs* (Moscow), 1962, No. 9, 79–83.

against the Russian armies, which numbered slightly more than 200,000.

It was not only the "Grande Armée" that invaded Russia: in June 1812, the artillery captain, who became Emperor of France, King of Italy, Mediator of Switzerland and Protector of the Rhine Union threw the whole of Europe against Russia. "Sixteen foreign nations, languishing under the iron sceptre of his ambition, were led by him to do battle against Russia," wrote Barclay de Tolly.

By 1812, Bonaparte had become the ruler of almost the entire European continent; his possessions stretched from the coast of the Netherlands and Northern Germany to the Adriatic. Before Napoleon set out against Russia, the Emperor of Austria, the King of Prussia, the King and Queen of Saxony, all the big and small monarchs, obedient to his will, came to pay homage to him at Dresden; he left them on their thrones, submissive, to do the will of their suzerain.

The fame of the invincible commander sped before his terrible army, which was marching along the roads of Russia. In effect, until 1812 the history of his Empire, as of his Consulate, was a succession of military triumphs, lightning victories, dazzling campaigns. Toulon, Arcole, Marengo, Austerlitz, Jena, Wagram, each could be the making of a commander.

Napoleon was rightly reputed to be the most outstanding general of his day, but this alone cannot, of course, explain his numerous victories. The éclat of the successes of the young Corsican officer who became Europe's ruler in a matter of 15 years is due to the fact that up to a certain stage there had unquestionably been elements of the progressive in his political activity, especially his foreign policy.

At that time, Napoleonic France, although ruled by her First Consul and then Emperor with an iron hand, had a more progressive social system than the rest of the world. It was a bourgeois empire fighting feudal empires and monarchies. Success followed upon success because Napoleon resolutely swept away the survivals of feudalism in the countries he conquered, clearing the path for bourgeois relations that at the time were new and progressive.

By the time the man who had once been a friend of Augustin de Robespierre became a powerful dictator and lord of millions of enslaved people in various countries, the progressive element in his policy had petered out. Acting, in the final analysis, in the interests of the French bourgeoisie, Emperor Napoleon, at the zenith of his fame and power, ceased to reckon with such factors as national awareness and great patriotic ideas. This was something that could not be roughly credited against items like the number of divisions or cannon; it could not be expressed in terms of cash. For Emperor Napoleon the sentiments that agitated the nations were an "unreal" category, something beyond his comprehension. He began to ignore these "unreal" factors in policy, and life was quick to take revenge for such carelessness.

Napoleon first came up against the fierce resistance of an enslaved people in Spain. He intensified his punitive measures against the Spaniards; he gave his brother, whom he had installed on the throne of Spain, the most rigid instructions, he sent his best marshals to Spain and reinforced his troops. He massacred the people fighting for their independence with incredible brutality, but neither the fusillades nor the repressions could break down the resistance of the Spanish peasants who refused to accept alien rule.

However, when he undertook the campaign against Russia, he had not assessed or even realised the profound meaning of the lessons of the Spanish people's war, which should have been a strict warning.

By the time Napoleon set out against Russia, the progressive element in his policy had disappeared altogether. The war against Russia was a war of conquest. In his dream of ruling the world, he was intent on conquering its biggest country and even laboured under the illusion that, once done with Russia, he would extend his rule to the borders of India. This was adventurism pure and simple, based on a conceited overestimation of his possibilities.

From the standpoint of elementary arithmetic, his campaign in the summer of 1812 might have been a winning move; on paper, his 600,000 men were three times as strong as the force at Russia's disposal, but elementary arithmetic is a poor counsellor in grand strategic schemes.

When Napoleon's troops entered Russia they saw that things were not going the way their leader had anticipated. Napoleon could have realised how strong and brave the Russian army was by following Suvorov's campaigns, which had taken place within his recollection, and by analysing the battles at Austerlitz and especially at Preussisch-Eylau and Friedland. But he refused to ponder this. "Russia is being impelled to her doom," he wrote in a proclamation addressed to his army as it stepped on Russian soil after crossing the Niemen in three places. But that was a grave error: it was he who was being inexorably led to his own doom.

The Russian army did not allow itself to be destroyed in the very first encounters, as Napoleon had hoped. It retreated, evading any decisive engagement, wearing down the enemy by long marches, making him extend his communications and weaken his striking force as he went deeper and deeper into the heart of Russia. This retreat continued for 10 weeks.

The impression was that Napoleon was once again winning out and that the summer campaign of 1812 would be a brilliant page in the roll of his military victories. But soon he and his more perspicacious aides realised that this war was different.

Napoleon was marching across a hostile country. Although he styled himself the bearer of the ideas of a new social system, yet when he entered a country where the peasants were groaning under the yoke of serfdom he did nothing to destroy it. The Russian people saw him only as a conqueror, an oppressor, a plunderer, and they rose against the alien invader. The war became a people's war, a patriotic war in the full sense of the word, because not only the troops but the broadest masses of people stood up in defence of the country.

This is not the place to discuss the limits to which the Russian army ought to have gone in its retreat, the extent to which Barclay de Tolly's initial military plan, the only correct one, was a reflection of the mood of the army and the people, or the motives which prompted the tsar to heed the unanimous demand of public opinion and appoint Kutuzov commander-in-chief of the Russian army, in spite of his personal dislike for the general.

In those anxious days Kutuzov, that remarkable general and wise politician, felt, as did all Russian soldiers, that it was no longer possible to continue retreating, that at some point the enemy had to be fought. Kutuzov realised the advantages of the tactics of retreat which had been followed. These were the only correct tactics, considering the relation of forces between the Russian army and the army of the invader at the outset. But the time had come to make a stand. The battle which has gone down in history was fought on September 7, within sight of the walls of Moscow.

By that day, the relation of forces between the two armies had changed from what it was at the start of the campaign in June-July 1812. The French army, worn down by the fighting against the regular army and the partisans, now numbered about 135,000 men and 587 cannon, including the reserves pulled up at the time of the battle. The Russian troops under Kutuzov's command numbered 120,000 men and had 640 cannon. The enormous numerical superiority enjoyed by Napoleon at the beginning of the campaign had been lost by the time he reached the approaches of Moscow. The strength of the sides had been almost equalised.

The great battle of Borodino was fought with extreme bitterness and much effort on both sides. It did not bring decisive success to either, at first glance, at any rate. It was the bloodiest battle on record, and its field was covered with the dead. The French army lost 50,000 or 60,000 men and 47 generals; the Russian army—40,000 or 50,000 men and 23 generals. And yet, although the high command ordered the Russian army to withdraw from Borodino, and the French troops entered Moscow, it was the battle of Borodino that marked the beginning of the end of Napoleon's fame, Napoleon's army and Napoleon's Empire.

He had hurled almost his entire force into the fierce battle, and had failed to win. Having failed to win, Napoleon's army had, by the same token, lost the battle, because its faith in the invincibility of French arms was undermined, and its hope of winning the war and securing peace with honour, dashed.

The story that the French army had been defeated in Russia by "General Frost" was subsequently circulated by the beaten French generals and picked up by many scholars. For a long time it roamed the pages of foreign treatises and magazine and newspaper articles.

No version of the event could be more false. It was not "General Frost" but the Russian army and the Russian people who defeated the French. Irrefutable proof that this story is false has been left by an authoritative eyewitness, the famous writer, Stendhal. As a French officer, Marie Henri Beyle, he was with the French army in its 1812 campaign and had been in Moscow.

"It would be a mistake to think," he wrote, "that the winter of 1812 was an early one; on the contrary, the weather in Moscow was excellent. When we were leaving it on October 19, it was only 3 degrees below zero, and the sun was shining brightly."

And so, the sun was shining brightly when the remnants of Napoleon's "Grande Armée", which had but recently made all Europe tremble, retreated from Moscow. That was the end. The French army had suffered a defeat, and the order to retreat was issued in the light of a bright autumn sun. It was not the mythical "General Frost" but the Russian people, the Russian army and the Russian commander Kutuzov who had won.

What happened after that is widely known. The rout of the "Grande Armée" as it retreated along the old Smolensk road was becoming a disaster. These starved, exhausted, bedraggled men who had thrown away their arms and packs and were helplessly dragging their feet were a far cry from the troops that had only a short while ago marched in triumph through the capitals of the vanquished European states.

They were no longer an army when, in early December 1812, according to the testimony of General Rochegodart, 20,000 freezing, starving fugitives burst into Vilno and began plundering the city. They were a herd, crazed with suffering and fear, incapable of doing their soldier's duty. Napoleon's "Grande Armée" had ceased to exist.

When the Russian people beat back the onset of the French army and inflicted irreparable losses on it at Borodino, they predetermined the early liberation of the enslaved peoples of Germany and Central, Western and Southern Europe from Napoleon's rule.

News of the Russian victory was met with jubilation not only in many European capitals but all over the world. This is attested by the reports, published recently for the first time, from Russian diplomatists in Britain, Austria, Spain and other European countries, and even from far-off United States and Brazil.

It is true that the overthrow of Napoleon's dictatorship did not lead to the establishment of freedom in Europe: the existing social system was not replaced by a more progressive one; that, however, is something that could not have happened because feudal monarchies were in the coalition of Powers which overcame Napoleonic France. Nevertheless, the liberation of enslaved peoples from alien rule and the restoration of the state and national independence of the countries conquered by Napoleon was of tremendous historical significance.

I shall not here analyse the impact of the Patriotic War of 1812 on the social movement in Russia. The movement of Decembrists, who first rose in struggle for the just cause of freedom sprang from the post-1812 spiritual upsurge in Russian social life.

The year of 1812 and Borodino for ever remain a historical lesson in international relations. The year of 1812 was a source of experience, it played a great part in the development of the art of warfare and introduced many new elements into military science. And when a century later, in the early 20th century, the German imperialists began to work out a new variant of world domination, they took into account the military lessons of 1812.

Schlieffen's famous plan, designed to avoid a simultaneous war on two fronts, envisaged that a blow would be dealt in turn against France and against Russia, first in the West and then in the East, with strategic success guaranteed by operations in the West. According to Schlieffen's plan for a blitzkrieg before the onset of autumn, the main solution lay in victory on the Western and not on the Eastern front.

However, when the German high command headed by Moltke, Jr., tried to put through Schlieffen's plan in the autumn of 1914 it failed, one of the essential reasons being its underestimation of the mobility and military might of the Russian armies. The Russian offensive in East Prussia forced the German high command to withdraw considerable forces (more than two corps) from the Western front and to transfer them to the Eastern front, against the Russian troops, thereby weakening the German strike force against the French troops. The German army was defeated in the battle of the Marne in September 1914. Hopes for a blitzkrieg were upset.

The war of manoeuvre slowed down into trench warfare, a war of attrition. When in the following year of 1915, the German high command decided to send its main forces to the Russian front to score a decisive victory in the war against Russia, warnings were sounded by some of its generals. "Napoleon's experience does not warrant imitation," said General von Falkenhayn, who was at the time the real commander of the German armed forces. "A campaign against Moscow leads us into the realm of the boundless," he added, and with good reason. But Hindenburg and Ludendorff, in their conceit, continued to dream of a decisive victory over Russia.

However, the German high command did not have the strength to repeat Napoleon's experiment. The German offensive of 1915 was stopped by the resistance of the Russian troops; the front was once again hardened in trench warfare.

The lessons of 1812 were so vivid that even the Hitler adventurers found it necessary to give them thought. In the 1930s, when Nazi Germany was only preparing to start the Second World War, Goebbels and his propaganda machine repeatedly said that they would avoid Napoleon's mistakes. Very soon, however, they forgot even their own warnings.

German imperialism unleashed the Second World War in September 1939, and Hitler's Third Reich crushed and enslaved many European countries in a matter of two years. Hitler conquered Austria, Czechoslovakia, Poland, Norway, Denmark, Yugoslavia, Greece, Belgium, the Netherlands and France. It seemed that history was repeating itself, that Hitler's empire was another Napoleonic Empire, outwardly, at any rate.

After literally the whole of Europe had been turned into an armoury supplying Nazi Germany with weapons, after Italian, Rumanian and Hungarian military units had been mobilised on the orders of Hitler's obedient vassals, he started his campaign against Soviet Russia, on June 22, 1941, almost on the same day on which Napoleon had started his.

At once, the tremendous difference between the old, tsarist Russia, and the mighty Soviet state became evident.

The whole Soviet people rose in defence of their Socialist country. Napoleon's army crossed the border on June 23 and reached Moscow on foot in September. The Nazi army, consisting mainly of tank, motorised, mechanised and air force units, managed to reach Moscow only in mid-October. But it never entered the capital.

The myth of the Wehrmacht's invincibility was dispelled in December 1941, within sight of the walls of Moscow. The battles of Moscow and the Volga, Kursk and Orel marked the rout of Hitler's war machine. The Soviet people liberated from Nazi tyranny not only their own country but also the peoples of Europe.

On April 30, 1945, the Soviet soldiers who destroyed the Nazi lair, Hitler's headquarters in Berlin, hoisted the Red Flag over the Reichstag. The idea of marching on Moscow and vanquishing our people was proved to be disastrous.

There is a historical continuity between 1812 and 1941–1945, even if the circumstances are different. The lessons of these two patriotic wars, these two trials of arms remain fully valid for our own day.

Any historical parallels between "this age" and a "bygone age" are, of course, irrelevant and quite pointless, because in the 150 years since Borodino the world has changed beyond recognition. Our own country has been affected most by these changes. But mention must be made of one aspect of these changes—the most essential and important in principle.

In the early 19th century, at the time of the Patriotic War of 1812, tsarist serf-owning Russia was one of the most reactionary and backward countries in economic and socio-political development. It knew nothing of the bourgeois revolutions through which Britain and France had by then passed; it was still to experience the savage regime of Arakcheyev, the deadening oppression of Nicholas I, and the long years of reaction. Fettered by tsarism and serfage, the Russian people still found the strength not only to beat back the onslaught but to overcome Napoleon's mighty empire.

The Soviet people, the descendants of the heroes of Borodino, have established the world's most progressive social system. The Soviet Union is a great country, whose people are building Communist society and, in community with the fraternal Socialist countries, are leading humanity. But the Soviet people have not merely established the most advanced socio-political system; they have transformed the backward, peasant Russia of 150 years ago into a mighty industrial state of high-quality engineering, intercontinental rockets and space conquest.

The Soviet people, animated by great creative endeavour, are consistently and steadfastly working to preserve world peace. The policy of the Soviet Government, the Soviet people, and the whole Socialist camp is a policy of peace. That is why the Soviet Union, which has the most perfect and powerful weapons, is the first to insist on general disarmament.

The preservation of peace, however, does not depend entirely on the good will of the Soviet people and all those who want peace. The black forces of imperialist reaction, ignoring the will of the peoples, the demands of common sense and the lessons of history, are once again prepared to plunge humanity into the maelstrom of war. These modern barbarians, proponents of the "strength policy" and "brinkmanship", refuse to see the important changes that have taken place in the world. Do they think they are still in the age of Napoleon?

It is fitting on this 150th anniversary of the battle of Borodino and the memorable heroic year of 1812 to recall the sober words recently spoken by Field-Marshal Lord Montgomery, the well-known British military figure. He emphasised that the lessons of Napoleon and Hitler should not be forgotten, that there should be no illusions about marching on Moscow. Although he bracketed two very different ages and two different wars, there is no doubt that his words contain a great historical truth.

THE BARONESS KRUDENER

By war's end, in 1814, Alexander's thought had taken a mystical and conservative bent. Historians have commonly considered him at this point to have been under the influence of a certain Baroness Krudener.

Source: J. H. Schnitzler, *Secret History of the Court and Government of Russia under the Emperors Alexander and Nicholas* (London, 1847), I, 401–4.

Barbara Juliana de Vietinghoff, born at Riga, on the 11th (23rd) of October, 1764, belonged to a family of consideration among the Lithuanian nobility. Her father was a Russian privy-councillor and senator; her mother, born countess of Munnich, was grand-daughter of the celebrated field marshal. She was educated for society, and was partly brought up in Paris, whither her father conducted her when nine years old. She was married before she attained her eighteenth year, to Baron Krudener, a diplomatist of ability and learning, who after being successively minister of Russia in Venice, Copenhagen, and Berlin, died in the latter city, on the 14th of June, 1802.

The marriage was far from being a happy one. Spoilt from her early years, by the homage of the world, which was captivated by the graces of her person, and by the vivacity of her mind, and possessing an unbridled imagination, she committed faults, which compelled her husband to send her back to her family, though she had borne him two children, a girl and a boy.

From that time Baroness Krudener led a wandering life; she excited attention in Paris by a romance called "Valerio," which she published in 1803. Her lively conversation procured her the favour of Queen Louise, at Berlin; at Geneva, whither she repaired in 1812, she began seriously to think of religion. Before that period she had from time to time listened to its voice, had a very decided tendency to mysticism, and during her stay in Prussia had formed a connection with the Moravian brethren, with whom she entertained much sympathy. But she had long been occupied with the allurements and pleasures of the world, and it was only as years crept on that she heeded the warnings of religion, and felt daily a greater want of its support. In 1813 she saw at Carlsruhe, Jung Stilling, the celebrated mystic visionary, who completed her conversion. From that time she thought she had a call to preach the gospel to the poor. At Heidelberg she undertook the mission of visiting prisons, and of conveying the word of God to prisoners condemned to death.

It was at Heilbronn, not far from Heidelberg, that the Baroness Krudener had her first interview with Alexander I., June, 1815. A letter which she had written to Mademoiselle Stourda, inspired the monarch with the wish to see her. Eloquent and sentimental, she gained ascendancy over his wandering imagination and fickle mind; her power over him became great as M. Empeytaz informs us,—a young priest of Geneva who joined her about this period, and became her zealous fellow-labourer. We shall soon see that the burning of Moscow had left a deep impression on the mind of the autocrat, and from that moment religion, that sweet comforter of man, found access to his heart.

According to the zealot of Geneva, he had lived up to that moment in sin, a result of the principles he had imbibed in the womb. "He became a religious man," says M. Emeytaz, "and one day told Madame Krudener, 'In my conferences with my ministers, who are far from having my principles, when we disagree, I pray inwardly, and see them by degrees come round to my principles of charity and justice.' "

Alexander entered Paris for the second time on the 11th of July, 1815. Madame Krudener followed him thither, held religious meetings, and owed undoubtedly to the distinguished protection of the emperor, the vogue which she enjoyed for some time, and which made her meetings the rendezvous of a select society, but which did not survive the absence of the monarch, upon whom all eyes were fixed.

He willingly yielded to the sympathy which attracted him toward a woman of sensibility formerly given up to sin, but now a zealous apostle in the faith of Christ. "Some days before his departure from Paris," says the priest of Geneva, "he told us,

I am about to quit France, but I wish before my departure to render a public act of thanksgiving to God the Father, Son, and Holy Ghost, for all we owe him for the protection he has accorded us, and to invite the people to act in obedience to the Gospel. I bring you a draft of the act, and wish you to examine it attentively, and if there be any expression you disapprove of, be pleased to let me know it. I wish the Emperor of Austria and the King of Prussia to join me in this act of adoration, that the people may see us, like the wise men of the East, acknowledging the superior authority of God the Saviour. Join yourselves to me to beg of God to dispose my allies to sign it.

"Next morning Alexander called for his deed, and heard most humbly the remarks submitted to him: the following day he took it to the allied sovereigns to sign, and had the satisfaction of seeing them adopt his views. In the evening he came to inform us what he had done, and to return thanks to God for his success."

This account has been published since Alexander's death; perhaps the words attributed to the emperor were written from memory, so that one must not scan them to the letter; but the fact so solemnly affirmed by a minister of the gospel, does not appear to us to admit of doubt; and nothing here stated contradicts the assertion personally used by the emperor, and quoted in the preceding pages. The idea of the Holy Alliance was not suggested by Madame Krudener, but this remarkable woman had evidently some share in drawing up the act, destined to put the idea in practice. We will briefly follow her to the close of her career.

Some time after the signing of the act, and the departure of the allied sovereigns from Paris, Madame Krudener, who had just described "Le Champ des Vertus," and the magnificent *fête* at which she had assisted on the plains of Chalon, finding she had ceased to attract attention, likewise quitted France.

She arrived at Basle at the close of 1815, and continued to preside over religious assemblies, occupying her time in attending the poor, the first of her duties. She became so followed, and her doctrines produced such sensation, that a minister felt compelled to denounce her from the pulpit, and the magistrates desired her to change her residence.

The same thing occurred at Baden as well as in many of the Swiss cantons, till at length no government would tolerate her presence. The police of one country handed her over to that of another; at last she decided to return to Russia, and reached the frontiers without ever having escaped *surveillance* for one instant. Even in Russia she found little favour. All her followers, numbering about twenty persons, were sent about their business, but the baroness having written the emperor a letter of complaint, the authorities were ordered to allow her to retain them. She tried to continue her preaching at Metau, but unsuccessfully; she met with no countenance at St. Petersburg, and the enthusiasm with which she pleaded the cause of the Greeks, displeased the emperor, at that time under Austrian influence. She retired to her estate of Kosse near Werro, in Livonia and led there an obscure life devoted to religion.

In June 1824, she accepted an invitation from her friend, the Princess Galitsin, to accompany her to her estates in the Crimea, and set out accompanied by her daughter, and son-in-law, the State Counsellor de Berkheim, but she had scarcely reached that distant country, when she fell sick and died, 12th December, the same year, at Karacoubasar, a city of 10,000 souls, the most populous of the peninsula.

"Her mind," says the Duke of Richelieu, "was the dupe of her heart." This criticism is very like eulogy. Madame Krudener had in reality a warm heart, ardent sensibility, and a vivid imagination; her reason though cultivated, and rather superior, had little part in guiding her conduct. Though a mark for criticism, she presents some luminous points, which will cause the memory of the zealous missionary to be respected. Her eloquence, which was captivating, was based upon sincere conviction; and if, abandoning her part of woman on the stage of private life, she appeared as a tribute in public, it was no doubt, as has been remarked, "because we cannot resist the longing to impart to others what we have deeply felt ourselves." She felt drawn onward by the "Spirit," and in these days of apathy, where miserable calculations predominate, we will not urge it as a crime that she yielded to a different impulse, that of enthusiasm carried to excess.

CHAPTER 5

Russia and Europe

THE DECEMBRIST REVOLT

In 1815 Russia enjoyed a predominance in Europe, the likes of which it could not match even in 1945. But the fruits of the victory over Napoleon were not long to be enjoyed. Russia could not keep pace in subsequent years with the economic development of western Europe, and therefore its relative military strength declined. Furthermore, the ideas of the French Revolution were not to be crushed by military conquest. When Alexander I died in 1825, the Imperial Guard attempted to win a constitution for Russia. The "Decembrist revolt" was a harbinger of further revolutionary developments, even as it, in method, represented a last attempt at a coup d'etat in the style of the 18th century. The new tsar, Nicholas I, took a personal hand in the investigation of the affair.

The arrests, which had been commenced in the night, were continued through the day of the 27th, and were facilitated by the indications found in the papers of Prince Troubetskoi and his associates. They included a large number of persons, and left grave suspicion attached to still more. The fortress was crowded with prisoners; amongst them were sons of generals, high functionaries, academicians, princes, superior officers, civil *tchinovinks*, literati, &c., &c. Ryleïeff, Rakhofski, Obolenski; several of the brothers Bestoujeff, and Iakoubovitch, were already, with Troubetskoi, in its dungeons.

Alexander Bestoujeff had, during the night, quitted his place of refuge in the suburbs, and hastened, as he himself expressed it, "to carry his guilty head to the emperor." Colonel Boulatoff has also voluntarily surrendered himself.

The young monarch himself conducted their first examination. It was

---

Source: J. H. Schnitzler, *Secret History of the Court and Government of Russia under the Emperors Alexander and Nicholas* (London, 1847), I, 256–64.

scarcely day when Bestoujeff found himself almost alone in his presence; he whose eloquent and persuasive words had led to revolt half a regiment, to which he was himself a personal stranger, stood petrified before the proud eye of the sovereign, as he addressed him with words, "General Bestoujeff was a faithful servant, but he has left behind him degenerate sons." When the emperor asked him, "Where were you on the day of the 26th?" he replied, "Near your person, sire, and if you had shewn any weakness I should have taken your life; but whilst your majesty exhibited such heroic bravery, I could not pursue my guilty purpose."

"But," pursued the emperor, "for such an enterprise as you undertook, large resources and much aid were requisite,—on what did you count?"

"Sire, things of this kind cannot be spoken of before witnesses."

Without heeding the danger he incurred, Nicholas led the conspirator into a private cabinet, where they conversed a long time.

We are not informed whether Bestoujeff descended to the meanness of denouncing his associates; but it is sure that he expressed himself with perfect frankness, to which his august auditor replied by expressions of regret that such a man was lost to society. The colonel departed with tears in his eyes; the conference had the effect of making him see the enormity of his crime.

The autocrat had listened to salutary truths, though painful to hear; he had, moreover, found the same truths dispersed through various papers of the conspirators which had been seized.

The impotence of the laws, the venality of the judges, the corruption of which the highest functionaries were guilty, the unparalleled injustice committed of late years, the punishments arbitrarily inflicted without sanction of law, were all at once revealed to him, and shewed him an abyss under which it seemed almost inevitable that social order should be submerged.

All relating to the plot was fully revealed by these papers; nothing remained hidden. Its ramifications, which extended over the whole empire, were exposed to view. From St. Petersburg general officers were sent to the army of the south, and to many points, to prevent a possible explosion. They were charged with the duty of hastily taking measures of security and precaution. Arrests were made; the captains of many regiments were changed; and several officers were charged to keep an eye upon their superiors, and to secure the obedience of the body of the army. Nicholas displayed extreme activity and vigilance. He was not eager to affix upon individuals imputations of guilt. Perhaps he had already discovered more than policy would permit him to avow. He manifested the upmost clemency, and pardoned, on the first sign of repentance, with a facility scarcely permitted to justice.

A young count, Zacharias Tchernycheff, captain in the chevalier guards, the joy and pride of an illustrious family, who had during the course of the 18th century numbered among them many ministers and field-marshals, was amongst those arrested. The emperor desired to save him, from consideration to his family and on account of his extreme youth. He had not been involved in the conflict, but he had been drawn into one of the secret societies by his brother-in-law, Captain Nikita Mouravieff, of whom we shall have to speak presently. He was brought before the monarch. "Is it possible," said the emperor, addressing him, "that you should rest under a stain of the heaviest guilt and infamy! you who belong to one of the best families in my empire! I hope not. Disavow the principles you have professed; tell me that you repent the mad acts you have committed, and I will grant you a pardon." (In Russia the sovereign can extend pardon by an act of his will either before or after judgment.) Tchernycheff refused. "I have acted according to my conscience," were the few words that formed his entire reply.

A veteran aide-de-camp general of the emperor, and commander of the first body of cavalry of reserve, himself brought his own son before his master, accusing him of being one of the conspirators. The monarch, touched by the fidelity of his servant, wishing to exercise clemency, said to his aide-de-camp that he left the punishment of his son in his hands. "If it be your majesty's pleasure to treat him favourably," replied the irritated father, "I pray you to put him under strict guard, else I shall kill him." Nicholas declared that he pardoned the offender, and interceded with his father to do so likewise. The inexorable old man replied, "Never."

In every case where the accused persons were not charged with serious guilt, the emperor followed equally the dictates of his own heart and of policy in granting a free pardon. On the 28th December, early in the morning, a grandson of the great Suwarrow, only son of the Prince Arcadius and of the gifted Helen, (née Naryschkin,) was brought before him. His father had been drowned in 1811 at Rymink in Wallachia, celebrated for the victory won on its banks. The youth was a cornet in the horse guards. Nicholas was still in bed. Whilst waiting his summons the young man was kept in a small room of the palace, under the eye of two sentinels. At eight in the morning he was sent for. The antechambers were occupied by a vast number of aides-de-camp, generals, and colonels, who all supposing him guilty, affected not to know him. He was introduced to the emperor.

"Suwarrow, Suwarrow," cried he, as he stood before him, "is it thus you dishonour a name which all Russia reveres?" He was moved, and hardly gained courage to ask, "How have I merited such a reproach?" In fact, in his youth and inexperience, he had drawn upon himself suspicion, but no grave fact stood against him. The emperor pointed out the complaints that were made, and questioned him concerning his intimacy with the Prince Odoïefski. Suwarrow avowed that he had been on intimate terms with the prince; that at his house the discourse was very free, too free perhaps; but that never in his presence had anything been said disrespectful or hostile concerning his imperial majesty, for he avowed, "Never would I have suffered that." The monarch replied in a tone of triumph, "I should indeed say that a Suwarrow was incapable of betraying his sovereign!" He pardoned him his indiscretions, embraced him, and sent him away an attached subject. As he passed again through the ranks of those who a few moments before had shewn him such cold countenances, each individual had suddenly become a friend; felicitations and embraces were proffered, but he stood aloof: he had learned a bitter lesson, and he proudly rejected the insincere homage. The following day he was named lieutenant, and soon after was promoted to the rank of *Flighel adioudant* (flying adjutant) to the emperor. His promotion was rapid. Since the year 1839 he has been major-general in the suite of his imperial majesty.

Strict investigation was immediately instituted; at a later page we shall arrive at its results; the commission appointed by the ukase of the 29th of December, to proceed with it, had only been two days sitting, when the emperor published his manifesto of the 31st, with the design of reassuring the public, with regard to the disposition of the army, that very important wheel in the social mechanism.

"Two classes of men," he declared, "have taken part in the insurrection of the 14th (26th) December, an event which, little important in itself, is highly so in its principle and consequences. The one class, misled, ignorant men, knew not what they did; the other, composed of rank conspirators, desired to annihilate the throne and the laws, to overturn the empire, and to introduce anarchy." "Drawn away in the tumult," continued the emperor, "the soldiers of the companies seduced have neither participated in the crime by deed, nor by intention; strict investigation has given me the proof of this, and I regard it as a first act of justice, and as my highest consolation, to declare them innocent; the same justice forbids me to spare the guilty."

The paragraph which follows, deserves to be read with most serious attention. Coupled with some insinuations, not very flattering to foreigners, Russia might regard as a consoling promise, the passage, some words of which we quote in italics:

The measures which have been already taken, together with the examinations, the judgments, and the steps which are yet to follow, will pursue to their full extent, and through all their ramifications—evils, the germs of which have existed for years within our country; and I am confident that they will destroy them to the very roots; they will purge the holy soil of Russia from foreign contagion; they will annihilate some *melancholy truths* and odious suspicions, which have estranged and afflicted noble souls; they will draw forever a line of demarcation between the love of country, and revolutionary passions; between *the desire for improvement and the fury of radicalism;* they will shew to the world, that the Russian nation, always faithful to the sovereign and the laws, repulses the secret efforts of anarchy, as she repulses the attack of open foes; they will shew how she purifies herself from such an evil; and will prove that it is not everywhere indestructible.

Notwithstanding the comparison, so little flattering to foreign countries, between the *sacred soil* of Russia, and their less hallowed ground,—the seat of an indestructible plague, which they have transmitted by contagion; countries, however, where, we venture to believe, the rightous power of law is not less firmly established than it is under the regime of ukase:— notwithstanding this little flattering comparison, we are bound to do justice to the calm and dignified language of this manifesto, and to its almost liberal spirit; since it recognizes the desire of progress as a legitimate sentiment. It does honour to the pen of the wise Karamzin, if it is true, as has been said, that it is to be attributed to him. Calculated at once to inspire agitators with salutary terror, to re-assure the peaceable populations of the empire, and to weaken abroad, the unhappy effect which the events of the last week might have produced, in regard to the political consideration of Russia; it is incontestably the production of a clever man, and a true statesman.

UNIVERSITY REFORMS

Nicholas was by nature an extreme conservative. He sought to keep Russia just as he had received it, and, as quoted in the selection above, he distrusted western influences, possibly the more because he could not control them. Despite his efforts, Russian universities became hotbeds of liberal and radical thought. Although Russia remained relatively quiet in 1848, as revolution swept through most of Europe, Nicholas decided that the time had finally come for more drastic action against the institutions of higher learning.

It is just thirty years ago that the Emperor Nicholas, frightened by the events of 1848, and under the influence of his intimate adviser, General Buturlin, conceived the plan of abolishing all the Russian universities, long suspected as the homes of liberal ideas, and of replacing them with special schools for the various branches of learning, to be formed on a military

Source: Julius von Eckardt, *Russia Before and After the War* (New York, 1880), 27–28, 29–30.

model and removed to different provincial cities. This plan was never fully realized; but the Czar was bent on giving it partial effect. Uvaroff, the Minister of Instruction, gave place to Prince Schirinski-Schichmatoff, and the restriction of academical freedom began. A Ukase was issued which deprived the universities of the right of electing their rector, abolished the professorships of European international law, placed the teaching of philosophy in the hands of Greek-Orthodox priests, made the supervision both of teachers and students considerably more stringent, limited the number of students to 300 for each university, and virtually excluded the lower classes from academical study. The number of medical students alone remained undiminished, on account of the deficiency of army surgeons; and the Universities of Dorpat and Helsingfors were allowed to retain the chair of Philosophy, which was necessary for the study of Protestant theology, and to educate as many Lutheran ministers as they pleased.

This Ukase, notwithstanding the short period of its operation (from 1849 to 1856), produced very lasting results. It has largely determined the development of the entire system of higher education in Russia, and has been the source of all the difficulties and complications now existing at St. Petersburg, Moscow, Kieff, and Charkoff.

The Russian Empire, including Poland, Finland, and the Baltic provinces, possessed at that time seven universities and several departmental schools, on a like footing, among which the Medico-Chirurgical Academy, the School of Law, and the Lyceum at St. Petersburg, the Richelieu at Odessa, and the Besborodko Lyceum at Nekin, were the most important. Two of the universities, Dorpat and Helsingfors, were not taken into account, when the means of educating sixty millions of people came to be considered. Dorpat was purely German in character, Helsingfors was exclusively Swedish. Both of them were outside of Old Russia; both were subject to special regulations, and prided themselves on representing the culture of Protestantism and Western Europe. Dorpat, after its restoration in 1802, became the distinctive University of Livonia; but the few Russians, belonging mostly to the higher ranks of society, who studied there, looked upon it as a foreign university, and adopted the usages of German student-life so completely, that for several years they formed a body of their own, the "Ruthenia." Polish students went to Dorpat for two reasons; first, because it was not a Russian university; and, secondly, because they found there the spirit of *Burschenschaft*, which in Russian universities was then unknown. At Helsingfors the only students were Swedish Finns, since the study of Protestant theology formed the introduction to all other departments of learning. The only Russian professor at Dorpat or Helsingfors was a lecturer on Russian language and literature, whose ample fees consoled him for the paucity of employment.

Among the Russian universities proper, that of Moscow undoubtedly occupied the first place, not only from its age (it had been founded in 1755), but from its superior number of students, and the greater liberty they enjoyed. Even in the days when university study was looked upon in court and military circles as *mesquin* and dangerous, there were always among the students at Moscow a large number of the sons of good families, who went thither for real study, "living in lodgings in the town, but being regularly matriculated—not mere pupils of the university "boarding-houses for young nobles," or attending only such lectures as they chose. Among the professors there were always some men of independent thought and genuine culture, and impressed with the dignity of their calling—men who treated the students as comrades, not as mere subordinates; who recognized as their duty the nurture of knowledge, not the mere preparation of the students for their examination as servants of the State; and who sought to promote with all their power the freedom of academical life. All those who, between 1830 and 1850, desired a higher and more liberal cultivation than they could find elsewhere, went to Moscow University, where the chairs of Philosophy and Natural Science in particular were filled by really able men. Well-nigh all the most conspicuous representatives of modern Liberal and National Russia, such as Herzen, Belinski, Granovski, Ivan Turgenieff, the two Aksakoffs, Prince Tcherkasski, M. N. Katkoff, and others, have belonged to this university, which was broad enough to embrace parties as widely different as the Nationalists, the European-Liberals, and the Socialists, while maintaining its position at the centre of national and intellectual life at Moscow.

The University of St. Petersburg, founded in 1819, ranks second in importance; it has not yet succeeded in becoming a real *Universitas litterarum*. It has never possessed a medical faculty (theological faculties do not exist in Russia proper). Students of philology were "interned" in the pedagogic Institute, affiliated to the university, and a place of strict discipline. The juristic faculty was of minor esteem, the sons of grandees being usually put into the Law School, which was endowed with exceptional privileges, or else into the Lyceum—to each of which establishments separate gymnasia were attached. The university students consisted of men who could find no other place to go; or whose parents, at the risk of incurring the displeasure of society, gave them the advantage of greater liberty and a wider intellectual culture than could be met with in the other "institutions of the Crown." At St. Petersburg, as at Moscow, the majority of the students were the sons of nobles, officials, or learned men—all of independent mind, who thought of something beyond securing a "grand career;" who possessed a genuine desire for culture, and regarded an academical degree as an honorable distinction. Most of the students belonged to the Faculty of Law and Politics, in which the German element at times was pretty strongly represented. To study at the German University at Dorpat was for many years considered too dangerous for a young man to risk who aimed at high office.

The Medico-Chirurgical Academy was an institution of a peculiar kind. It was separated from the university, being subject to the Minister of War, and was relegated to a distant suburb of the capital. Three-fourths of the students, who numbered altogether from 1200 to 1500, were "Crown students." They lived in a large barrack; they were not allowed to appear abroad except in the regular uniform with red facings, and with helmet and sword; and they were under strict military discipline. They were supposed to have a certain *penchant* for Radical ideas, even in the days of a merciless severity toward everything that had a tinge of Liberalism; nor was it strange that young medical students of the nineteenth century, and living in the metropolis, should parade their materialism with a certain air of cynical affectation. They were recruited exclusively from the poorer families of the middle classes and the Jews; the few men of higher rank who wished to study medicine went regularly to Moscow.

* * * * *

At St. Petersburg, Moscow, Kieff, and other universities, every kind of learned or social gathering was interdicted. The students there were told precisely what lectures they were to attend. The notes of the professors and the text-books in use were subject to strict control, and if not approved of, cashiered. Every year the student had to attend a prescribed "course" of lectures, any deviation from which was an act of high-treason. At the end of the first course he had to pass an examination before he was qualified to commence the next, and so on until the entire course of studies was completed. If the professor ever noticed any irregulartiy of attendance at his lectures and reported it to the Inspector, the delinquents were punished in disciplinary fashion. Professors who clung to the old traditions of student liberty, both personally and in respect of their choice of studies, had to expect to be excluded from all promotion or reward, and, if re-elected when their term of office expired, to have their re-election annulled. No wonder that from year to year these academical professorships, with their moderate salaries in the bargain, became less attractive; that learned men of any independent spirit declined to accept them, and preferred a more modest but less irksome position in life; and that, notwithstanding the offers of new stipends and special courses of lectures, numbers of chairs either remained empty, or were filled provisionally by ungraduated *dilettanti*. In the faculties of Medicine and Natural Science a remedy, if needed, was at hand, by calling in Germans from Dorpat or foreign countries, who in course of time learned to express themselves, however imperfectly, in Russian, and supplied by their knowledge of the subject their defective power of communication.

Half the professorships of Russian law, Russian history, philology and archaeology, were either not filled up at all, or filled by lecturers and *adjoints*, appointed as stop-gaps, and only waiting for the first opportunity to accept other employment.

This paucity of competent professors was due, to a certain extent, to the difficulty in Russia of obtaining the degree of Doctor, indispensable for the higher educational posts. No one, except a medical man, can be made a doctor, unless he has first been a "candidate," and then a "magister." To be a candidate he must have completed his courses at a university, passed a somewhat difficult State examination with a certificate of "very good," and composed a learned essay to the approval of the faculty. To be a magister, he must have been a candidate for a whole year, have passed an examination in all the chief subjects embraced by the particular faculty, have written another dissertation, and defended it in public. These proceedings, as expensive as they are tedious, are repeated a third time before the degree of doctor is conferred. Naturally, the number of those who possess both the inclination and the talent for fulfilling these complicated conditions is extremely small. Among the Slav race, whose tendencies are decidedly realistic, idealism and devotion to the cause of learning are far more rare than in other races; and even now, when the requirements for a university appointment are reduced to a reasonable standard, and the salaries considerably improved, the number of Russians who embrace an academical career is still extremely small.

In the days of the Emperor Nicholas, indeed, nothing but an actual fanaticism for the cause of learning would have induced any man to spend either time or money on preparing for a career which stamped the candidate as a suspicious character, which he could only pursue at the price of a life-long subjection to the whims of uneducated officials and the mistrust of a suspicious government; and which, moreover, brought a very moderate pecuniary gain. Those who filled the chair of Natural Science had at least the opportunity of doing service to their branch of learning, and of acquiring reputation and honor; but for the historian, the jurist, or the political economist such a prospect was hopeless. If he stooped to conform to the ruling system, he rendered himself useless for scientific knowledge; if he attempted to follow his own bent, he was sure to fall into the snares of the secret police. Hence, as a matter of course, professors of eminence, especially those who had risen under the *régime* of the old liberal statute of 1804, learned to regard the later system with aversion, and in this sense became "political malcontents;" while their younger successors fell off every year both in numbers and ability. It gradually became more common for professors, out of sheer disgust at their position, to accept inferior posts in the administration, while young men, educated at the expense of the Government, were forcibly made to accept professorships assigned to them. Thus the real power fell into the hands of inferior men of routine, who owed their promotion to the favor of Curators and Inspectors. Accordingly, patronage and corruption began to regulate the matriculation and graduation of students; and the more independent among the teachers were daily made to feel the suspicious surveillance not only of the Inspectors, but of servile colleagues who hungered for promotion. The case of the smaller universities was the worst in this respect. Here the influence of the Curator was all-powerful, and academical life degenerated into a system of the most miserable adulation and petty intrigue. Added to these evils came the constant jealousy and national hatred shown by the Russian professors toward their foreign colleagues, who were treated as interlopers and heretics, though, from the dearth of native learning, their services could not be dispensed with.

Great, however, as was the discontent among the professors and tutors with the system prevailing from 1840 to 1860, and with those who supported it, this discontent was still more deeply implanted in the students. Everything seemed to have been purposely designed to make these young men, the future mainstays of intellectual culture, feel that they were the mere stepchildren of the government and the ruling caste. It was understood that a university student ranked socially beneath an officer, in many cases even beneath the pupils in the Page corps and the schools for young nobles, and he was treated no better than a mere school-boy. With regard to future service in the State, the pupils of the Lyceum and the Law School enjoyed a double advantage over them. Not only were their examinations notoriously far easier than those at the universities, but they had also the privilege of receiving the titular rank of councillor after the termination of their course of study, and were qualified at once to enter any of the ministries. The student, on the contrary, even after he had gained the degree of "candidate," became merely a "college secretary." Only after serving for three years in the province could he obtain any ministerial employment; and even then he knew well that any former pupil of the Law School would be preferred before him. The special favor shown to the latter was publicly accepted fact, the reason being that they were looked upon in higher quarters as particularly pliable and, moreover, not open to "corruption."

To this neglect of university students as a class were added the most humiliating distinctions made among the students themselves. Those who were poor and educated at the expense of the Crown, either at the universities or the Medico-Chirurgical Academy, were subject to restraints of liberty and measures of control unknown to their more favored comrades. If they failed to pass the examinations, they ran the risk of being made barber-surgeons in the army, or even common soldiers. Rank and property were rewarded in all respects with an indulgence as invidious as unjust. Nothing was more provoking and vexatious than the constant interference of the Inspectors with the social conduct of the students. Bitter experience had amply taught these victims of official tyranny that any derelictions of duty on their part were more severely punished and more harshly judged, in consequence of the emperor's distrust of the universities, than the excesses of young men in other classes.

So intolerable was the rigor of discipline at some of the universities, that numbers of young men, fully qualified in other respects to take their place as students, preferred to enter as "voluntary scholars," and, though exposed to the satire of their comrades, imitated the example of the officials and persons advanced in life, who attended the lectures without being matriculated. These restraints grew doubly unbearable, when compared with other countries. Little as any one cared, in general, to know about Western Europe, or the difference between Russian and foreign institutions, still at times even the students at Kasan or Charkoff got to hear of the greater freedom and higher social position enjoyed by their brethren at Dorpat and Helsingfors, of the more favorable treatment accorded to French and German students by their governments, and of the advantages of the old Liberal Statute of 1804, compared with the hateful regulations of 1835. The more enlightened and humane of the professors did not conceal their own and the students' opinion that such treatment was unworthy. The government, on the other hand, took good care to let the universities know the reason for these oppressive restrictions, and it was no secret to any one after 1848 that the emperor had been most reluctant to abandon his intention of closing every university in the empire. All the world knew, moreover, that the limitation of the number of students to 300 at each university had originated with Nicholas, and that Uvaroff, his Minister of Instruction, notoriously a pliant statesman, had resigned because he considered it inconsistent with his honor to agree either to this measure or to the abolition (decreed at the same time) of instruction in the Greek language at most of the gymnasia. It appeared, indeed, as if every one connected with the universities was intended to be brought up in systematic hatred toward the government, which treated the highest institutions of science and culture as so many necessary evils, and more than once seemed ready to turn into bitter earnest the words put by Griboyedoff into the mouth of the military blusterer Skalosub:

> Had I my way, I'd shut up the schools,
> Turn out professors and such learned fools.
> Plague on their teaching! for their A B C
> I'd have drill-sergeants with their 'One, two, three.'
> Books should be kept to please an idle crew
> On feast-days, when there's nothing else to do!

THE CRIMEAN WAR

Russia's failure to develop at the same pace as western Europe was made obvious to all in the Crimean war of the 1850s. The Russian state was humiliated by the outcome, the neutralization of the Black Sea. This defeat could not but have wide repercussions.

Since the great Napoleonic invasion of 1812, the foreign wars carried on by Russian monarchs have never failed to exercise a permanent and penetrating influence upon the internal policy of the State and the development of national life. Until then, and in fact ever since the days of Peter the Great, the external affairs of the empire had passed by without leaving any trace among the mass of the nation. But, in 1812, what Alexander Herzen aptly calls the "St. Petersburg period" of Russian history came at length to an end; and Moscow, the "first city of Holy Russia," became for a short but eventful epoch the centre of the national life, awakened from its long sleep. The firebrands of Rostoptchin kindled for awhile the slumbering sparks of Russian patriotism, and made Russians feel proud of their country. This sentiment, however, was short-lived, and changed into a cosmopolitan enthusiasm for freedom and the welfare of peoples, when the officers of 1814 and 1815 returned from Germany and France. "It was impossible, after the excitement of the national war and the glorious march through a liberated Europe, to go back at once to the dull monotony of despotism at St. Petersburg." Rash attempts to import institutions of Western Europe into Russia, such as those of the military conspirators of the "North" and "South" under Pestel and Rylejeff, and the foolish insurrectionists of December, 1825, had to pay, it is true, the full penalties of defeat. But the seeds of change, then scattered, were not lost; the soil they fell on was unbroken, but was all the more fertile for that reason. While outwardly, for full thirty years, there reigned the perfect stillness of the tomb, and the government, discarding altogether the civilizing traditions of Peter the Great, ruled more absolutely than ever, a revolution was preparing in the heart of Russian society—a revolution which was silently maturing and developing the impressions received between 1812 and 1815, and aspiring in every sphere of life to reverse the objects of the Emperor Nicholas.

Toward the end of this period it seemed, indeed, as if the government would hold their own against the Liberals at home as they had done with

Source: *Ibid.*, 42–43.

Europe abroad. The absolutism of the Czar reached its climax with the Hungarian campaign of 1849. Henceforth, those in the Imperial camp looked upon it as a settled thing that Russia had only to continue in the path she had taken to become the mistress of the world, and to lay Europe prostrate "at the feet of his Majesty," just as, in the language of Prince Paskevitch, she had done with conquered Hungary. The Emperor's hatred of everything savoring of reform or freedom of initiative rendered him incapable at length of discerning his own responsibilities. The three several projects for relieving the oppressed condition of the peasantry were "shelved" among the public archives. The most absurd abuses of military and civil administration were pronounced sacred, and declared to be integral parts of the conservatism system which was supposed to have accomplished such "grand results."

The days of these "results" were numbered, however, even before the Eastern complications after 1850 culminated in the Crimean War. Was not the gigantic collapse of Russia in this contest mainly due to the fatal influence which the apparent triumph of the Hungarian campaign had exercised upon the mind of the Autocrat and the views of his myrmidons? They had talked themselves into a state of self-complacency and an arrogance of infallibility which excluded any serious preparation for the war. If only the Czar remained firm, they said, Europe would once more have to submit to the will of Russia. On the other hand, the small but influential number of cultivated Russians who clung firmly to the traditions of 1812 and 1825, entertained very different thoughts at the prospect of the coming struggle. At the very outset of the war they maintained that the real salvation of Russia depended on the failure of an enterprise undertaken in such immeasurable ignorance of their own and foreign resources. In spite of their genuine patriotic grief at the fall of Sebastopol and the misfortunes of its heroic garrison, they held quietly but unyieldingly to their conviction that the true welfare of the Russian nation had nothing to fear from the victories of the allies at Inkermann and the Tchernaya, and that the capture of the Russian Saragossa would prove of greater service to Russia herself than to those who had stormed the Malakoff.

The succeeding twenty years of Russian history have been so indissolubly connected with the experiences of the Crimean War, that it is unnecessary to enlarge further on this point. With the humiliation of national defeat came an awakening from the dreams of optimism, and a sense of dissatisfaction with the past. Up to the Polish insurrection of 1863 nothing passed for any value in official as well as non-official circles but what was opposed to the old system, and recommended itself, or appeared to recommend itself, as a protest against its errors and vices. But after 1863 the fashion of reform began to pall, and a certain reaction again set in. The system of centralization, pursued by the government of Nicholas, was condoned, and even patronized to some extent, by the prominent leaders of public opinion as the means best fitted for the establishment and furtherance of "true national development." With a view to eliminate as speedily as possible the Polish, German, Swedo-Finnish, and other foreign elements of the western half of the empire, the government, which from 1858 to 1863 had been watched with constant suspicion and thwarted at every step, was once more intrusted for a time with absolute power, and allowed to exercise it without limit in the department of foreign policy. Not, indeed, that this absolute power was granted irrevocably, or intended as unconditional. Young Russia, standing, as it were, upon the ruins of Nicholas's system and the disastrous experiences of 1854–55, still claimed the right of determining her own destinies, and of having a voice in the foreign policy of the government, so far, at least, as seemed necessary in the interests of her internal development. This claim had been dormant for a time and for a definite purpose, but it had not been finally renounced; and the strongest proof of its vitality was afforded by the events which accompanied the recent reopening of difficulties in the East. The declaration of war against Turkey, on April 24, 1877, was the act not of the government of St. Petersburg but of the Russian nation. It was essentially the product of the internal policy pursued by Alexander II. since 1863 and 1864. Domestic considerations had at least quite as large a share in unchaining the anti-Turkish passions of the Russian people as the ancient ambition to raise the Greek cross upon the Mosque of St. Sophia, or the modern Panslavistic theories of concentrating all Slavonic power in the hands of Russia.

THE ADVANCE IN CENTRAL ASIA

The previous selection mentioned the Polish rebellion of 1863 as a turning point in Russian thoughts on reform. The Polish question in fact had both internal and external significance for the Russian state. Since the Poles enjoyed strong sympathy in London and Paris, the rebellion also provoked new international tension between East and West. On March 2, 1863, the British government vainly sought to intervene.

Her Majesty's Government view with the deepest concern the state of things now existing in the Kingdom of Poland. They see there, on the one

Source: Tytus Filipowicz, *Confidential Correspondence of the British Government Respecting the Insurrection in Poland: 1863* (Paris, 1914), pp. 103–5.

side, a large mass of the population in open insurrection against the Government; and, on the other, a vast military force employed in putting that insurrection down. The natural and probable result of such a contest must be expected to be the success of the military forces. But that success, if it is to be achieved by a series of bloody conflicts, must be attended by a lamentable effusion of blood, by a deplorable sacrifice of life, by widespread desolation, and by impoverishment and ruin, which it would take a long course of years to repair.

Moreover, the acts of violence and destruction on both sides, which are sure to accompany such a struggle, must engender mutual hatreds and resentments, which will embitter, for generations to come, the relations between the Russian Government and the Polish race.

Yet, however much Her Majesty's Government might lament the existence of such a miserable state of things in a foreign country, they would not, perhaps, deem it expedient to give formal expression of their sentiments, were it not that there are peculiarities in the present state of things in Poland which take them out of the usual and ordinary condition of such affairs.

The Kingdom of Poland was constituted, and placed in connection with the Russian Empire by the Treaty of 1815, to which Great Britain was a Contracting Party. The present disastrous state of things is to be traced to the fact that Poland is not in the condition in which the stipulations of that Treaty require that it should be placed.

Neither is Poland in the condition in which it was placed by the Emperor Alexander I, by whom that Treaty was made.

During his reign a National Diet sat at Warsaw, and the Poles of the Kingdom of Poland enjoyed privileges fitted to secure their political welfare.

Since 1832, however, a state of uneasiness and discontent has been succeeded from time to time by violent commotion and a useless effusion of blood.

Her Majesty's Government are aware that the immediate cause of the present insurrection was the conscription lately enforced upon the Polish population; but that measure itself is understood to have been levelled at the deeply-rooted discontent prevailing among the Poles in consequence of the political condition of the Kingdom of Poland.

The proprietors of land and the middle classes in the towns bore that condition with impatience; and if the peasantry were not equally disaffected they gave little support or strength to the Russian Government.

Great Britain, therefore, as a Party to the Treaty of 1815, and as a Power deeply interested in the tranquility of Europe, deems itself entitled to express its opinion upon the events now taking place, and is anxious to do so in the most friendly spirit towards Russia, and with a sincere desire to promote the interest of all the parties concerned. Why should not His Imperial Majesty, whose benevolence is generally and cheerfully acknowledged, put an end at once to this bloody conflict by proclaiming mercifully an immediate and unconditional amnesty to his revolted Polish subjects, and at the same time announce his intention to replace without delay his Kingdom of Poland in possession of the political and civil privileges which were granted to it by the Emperor Alexander I, in execution of the stipulations of the Treaty of 1815?

If this were done, a National Diet and a National Administration would, in all probability, content the Poles, and satisfy European opinion.

THE ADVANCE IN CENTRAL ASIA

Russia rejected the British move. Russo-British relations were further complicated by imperial rivalries. Russia participated actively in Europe's empire building of the latter half of the 19th century, even though its empire was distinctive in being a land, rather than an overseas, expansion. The following is Foreign Minister Gorchakov's explanation of the Russian advance in Central Asia, contained in a circular memorandum to the Russian foreign service, November 9, 1864.

Russian journals have reported the latest military operations in Central Asia executed with remarkable success and important results by a detachment of our troops.

It was to be expected that these events would excite the foreign public, the more so as they take place in lands hardly known.

Our August Master has directed me to lay out for you, succinctly but with clarity and precision, the posture which is forced upon us in Central Asia, the interests which motivate our action, and the final goal which we pursue there.

Russia's position in Central Asia is that of all civilized States which find themselves in contact with semi-savage, wandering peoples who have no fixed social organization.

As always happens in such cases, the demands of security of the frontiers and those of commercial relations require that the more civilized State exercise a certain ascendancy over such neighbors as are made very troublesome by their turbulent and nomadic ways.

Source: *British and Foreign State Papers*, LVIII, 635–39.

First of all, one has to curb raids and pillaging. In order to put these at an end, one is forced to bring the neighboring peoples under more or less direct submission.

Once this is done, these people take on more sedate ways, but they find themselves in turn exposed to aggressions from tribes further away.

The State is obliged to defend them against these depradations and to punish those who commit them. Hence the necessity of periodic, far off, expensive expeditions against an enemy whose social organization renders him undistrainable. If one limits oneself to punishing the plunderers and then withdrawing, the lesson is soon lost; the withdrawal is attributed to weakness; the Asiatic peoples in particular respect only visible and palpable force. The moral force of reason and of the interests of civilization has no influence on them. The task always has to be repeated.

In order to put an end to these permanent disorders, either one has to establish some fortified points among the enemy populations, or one gains over them an ascendancy which little by little reduces them to a more or less forced submission.

But beyond this second line, other peoples, farther removed, soon provoke the same dangers and the same repressions.

The State finds itself confronted with the dilemma of either abandoning this incessant work and surrendering its frontier to perpetual disorders, which make impossible any prosperity, any security, any civilization, or else of advancing deeper and deeper into the savage countries where at each step the distances only increase the difficulties and the burdens to which it exposes itself.

Such has been the fate of all those countries which have been placed in the same situation. The United States of America, France in Algeria, Holland in its colonies, England in India—all have inevitably been forced to follow this progressive march where ambition plays a lesser role than imperative necessity and where the greatest difficulty consists in knowing when to stop.

This is also the reason which has led the Imperial Government to establish itself on the one hand on the Syr Daria and on the other on the Lake Issyk-Kaul, and to consolidate these two lines by advanced forts which little by little have penetrated to the heart of these remote regions, still without being able to establish there the tranquillity indispensable for the security of our frontiers.

The cause of this instability lies first in the fact that between the extreme points of this double line there is an immense unoccupied space, where invasions of the pillaging tribes continue to paralyze all colonization and all commerce by caravans; secondly, in the perpetual fluctuations of the political situation of the areas, where Turkestan and Kokand, now united and now separated, always at war either between themselves or with Bokhara, offered no possibility of stable relations or of any regular transactions.

Therefore the Imperial Government finds itself confronted with the dilemma which we have noted—that is to say, either to allow a state of permanent disorder to continue, a state which paralyzes all security and progress, or to condemn itself to expensive and remote expeditions without any practical result, and which must be continually renewed, or else, finally, to embark on the undefined path of conquests and annexations which has led England to the Empire of India as she was seeking to subjugate, one after another by force of arms, the small independent states whose robbing and turbulent ways and perpetual revolts left their neighbors neither truce nor peace.

None of these alternatives corresponded to the aims of the policy of our August Master, which is not to increase out of all reasonable proportion the countries under his sceptre, but to found his dominion on solid bases, to guarantee security and to develop the social organization, the trade, the well-being and civilization.

Our task, therefore, was to find a suitable system to attain this three fold aim.

In this respect, the following principles have been posed:

1. It has been judged indispensable that our two fortified frontier lines— one running from China to Lake Issyk-Kaul, the other from the Aral Sea along the Syra Daria—be joined by fortifications so that all our posts could provide mutual support and leave no interval through which the nomadic tribes could freely carry on invasions and depradations.

2. It was essential that the line thus completed be situated in a rather fertile region, not only to assure their provisions, but also to facilitate the regular colonization which alone can give an occupied land a future of stability and prosperity, by winning the neighboring peoples to a civilized life.

3. Finally, it was urgent to fix this line in a definitive manner so as to escape the dangerous and almost inevitable enticements which could lead, from repression and reprisals, to a limitless expansion.

To this end it was necessary to lay the bases of a system founded not only on reason, which could be elastic, but on geographic and political conditions which are fixed and permanent.

This system was suggested to us by a very simple fact, based on our long experience; that is to say, that the nomadic tribes, which one cannot distrain, punish, or effectively contain, are the most inconvenient neighbors for us, and that on the contrary, agricultural and commercial populations, settled on the soil and endowed with a more developed social organism, offer us the chance of tolerable neighbors and perfectible relations.

The line of our frontiers ought to include the first and it ought to stop at the border of the second.

These three principles give a clear, natural, and logical explanation of the recent military operations in Central Asia.

In effect, the first line of our frontiers, along the Syr Daria to Fort Perovsky on the one hand, and on the other to Lake Issyk-Kaul, had the disadvantage of being almost at the edge of the desert. It was broken by an immense gap between the two extreme points. It did not give our troops enough resources and it left out tribes without cohesion, with whom no stable relations were possible.

Despite our repugnance to extend our frontiers much farther, these reasons have nevertheless been strong enough to force the Imperial Government to establish a line between Lake Issyk-Kaul and the Syr Daria, by fortifying the village of Chemkend which we recently occupied.

In adopting this line we achieved a double result. On the one hand, the region included is fertile, forested, well supplied with water; it is inhabited in part by Kirghiz tribes who have already recognized our domination; it offers therefore favorable circumstances for colonization and for the maintenance of our garrisons. On the other hand, it gives us the agricultural and commercial population of Kokand as our immediate neighbors.

We have before us a more stable social structure, more compact, less mobile, better organized. This consideration marks with geographic precision the limit where interest and reason tell us to go and command us to stop, since on the one hand, any further extension of our domination will no longer meet unstable elements such as nomadic tribes, but instead states more regularly constituted, and this would demand considerable effort and would drag us from annexation to annexation with incalculable complications. On the other hand, we have henceforth for neighbors such states with which, despite their retarded civilization and the instability of their political conditions, we can nevertheless hope that regular relations will one day replace the permanent disorders which have up to now paralyzed the development of these regions.

Such are, Monsieur, the interests underlying the policy of our August Master in Central Asia; such is the limit which the orders of our August Master have posed for this cabinet's action.

You are invited to draw from these considerations the sense of the explanation which you will furnish to the government to which you are accredited, if you are asked or if you see false assumptions being spread about our action in these remote regions.

I need not emphasize the obvious interest which Russia has not to enlarge its territory and above all not to create at its borders complications which could only retard and paralyze its internal development.

THE TRANSIBERIAN RAILROAD

One of the major factors in Russia's Asiatic expansion was railroad building. Just as the lack of railroads in southern Russia during the 1850s had hampered defense efforts in the Crimean War, the building of the Transiberian railroad at the end of the 19th century strengthened Russia's position in the Far East.

The results of Russian railway advance were, in 1901, by far the most general and absorbing subjects of conversation among non-Russian foreigners in the Far East. Indeed, from the beginning of the Siberian road, the consequences of this extraordinary enterprise have occasioned anxious thought in the minds of every careful student of the world's material activities. And, as will be seen, Russia's Manchurian railroad is only another step in her railway extension to the Orient, of which the Siberian railway was the first step. The purposes of the Manchurian railway, as given by Engineer-in-Chief Tugovitch, have already been set out, as have the comments of Administrator Girshmann. But, perhaps, an independent analysis, illustrated by various observations made on the ground, may also be helpful to an understanding of the meaning and effect of this greatest agency of civilization which the Czar has employed in the Russian advance upon the Pacific.

To what, then, will this railroad which Russia is building through Manchuria lead? What results will follow its completion and operation? He is a daring reasoner who would attempt to deduce all the consequences. The man would be called an immoderate dreamer who should suggest to the world, which looks upon this industrial phenomena from afar, what appear to be certainties to those who survey the ground itself. No one but two or three prophets of empire, such as Russia, with all her deficiencies, is so fortunate as always to have about the Czar at St. Petersburg, understood the sure results of the great Siberian railroad. Most men regarded it as a military enterprise only; although why Russia should exhaust herself in military enterprises which in themselves would bear no fruit seems not to have suggested itself to most non-Russian thinkers.

But the Siberian railway was no sooner completed to Irkutsk than a steadily swelling volume of Russian emigrants began to pour all over the agricultural portions of western and central Siberia, irrigating that neglected land with the fertilizing fluid of human effort. No sooner was the railroad

Source: Albert J. Beveridge, *The Russian Advance* (New York, 1904), 68–80.

extended to Stretensk, at the head of the navigation of the Shilka and Amur rivers (hundreds of miles east of Irkutsk, and yet almost thousands of miles from the Pacific), than this current of Slav peasantry ran still farther eastward, spreading itself to right and left, until finally the Russian agriculturist and miner were slothfully at work, even to the very shores of the ocean.

Trade, which had been nothing but barter, rapidly increased to the dignity of commerce. Fields which for centuries had been only pasture-lands grew golden with grain, even under the negligent and wasteful methods of the Russian farmer. Mines which, since the days of Ivan the Terrible, had been little more than rumor became richly productive, notwithstanding the stupid legal restrictions and the sleepy Muscovite inertia which exploited them. Cities with beautiful homes, astonishing public buildings, commercial houses so considerable that you must see them to believe that they exist, and temples of worship magnificent in size, decoration, and design, sprang into being where not so long ago the nomad camped or the Chinaman revelled in his village dirt. Such had been the practical results of the building of the Siberian railroad. Such were the results of the building of our own transcontinental lines, except, of course, that the greater intelligence, greater energy, and higher general sum of modern qualities which distinguish the American from every other people produced along our transcontinental lines consequences larger, higher, more miracle-like.

But, without entering into speculation which might be disputed, what are the obvious consequences, the small and immediate effects, which will be produced by the Manchurian railway? It is one of the few defects of our race and our present system that we look only to immediate results. We are intent only upon "the instant need of things," as Kipling puts it. It is one of our shortcomings, which many a temporary set-back must remedy, that we do not take thought for the morrow. The English look farther ahead in foreign matters than do we as a nation, but even the English do not have so much concern for distant results of her policies as do the Russians. A keen English observer records of an English Oriental merchant who, in response to the pointing out of the decline of British commerce in the Far East, unless improvement occurred in the out-of-date methods of English trade conditions, said: "What do I care for the future? We are not here for the benefit of posterity." But we Americans are already improving in this, and our foreign commercial necessity will some day make our foreign commercial policy rational, continuous, and far-sighted.

But we are examining the railway features of the Russian advance towards the Pacific. Let us, then, look at the immediate aspects of this railway, which is by far the greatest single work of construction recently accomplished anywhere in the world.

First of all, the road branches off from the Siberian railroad about one thousand miles from Vladivostock and takes a practically straight course, a little to the north of the middle of Manchuria, to Vladivostock. Thus the port of Vladivostock, on the Pacific, is directly connected with Moscow, St. Petersburg, Berlin, and Paris, without varying the mode of transportation, or even changing cars.

In the second place, this road, on its way to Vladivostock, cuts a great artery of Manchuria, the Sungari River, several hundred miles south of the point where this principal commercial tributary of the Amur empties into the larger stream. Thus, water communication is secured with the rich mining and agricultural Russian provinces north of the Amur River (for the Amur, impracticable for most of its course on account of sand-bars and rocks, is profitably navigable for several hundred miles from where this Manchurian river empties into it).

But the harbor at Vladivostock is frozen part of the year, and so, in the third place, the Russians were building, at the time of the author's investigations, and have now completed, another branch of this road from Harbin, the point where the Sungari River is crossed, almost due south to Port Arthur and Dalni, on the never-frozen sea. This branch passes through the most populous and productive portions of Manchuria, and connects Russia and all of Europe with splendid ports, on Oriental waters, open all the year round. Changed conditions have changed Russia's plans, and this new branch now becomes itself the principal line.

First of all, then, Oriental passenger travel to Europe is turned westward through the Russian Empire. A quick, comparatively pleasant, and comparatively cheap method of transportation is provided for all European business-men who want to reach Asia, and for all Asiatic business-men who want to visit Europe. Personal communication is established between the civilization of Europe, on the one hand, and the chaos of vital humanity and disintegrating institutions in the Orient, on the other hand. Think of the Oriental, for ages separated from the rest of the world, travelling from Pekin to Paris in a fortnight. A true *Arabian Nights* tale this, and more astonishing. The profound significance of this circumstance was probably not foreseen by its Russian creators. It is one of those larger meanings which always accompany any really great work of man; the achievement of that work always has results so vast and momentous as to startle those who undertook the original enterprise. Witness the immediate purpose and final results of Bismarck's plan of German federation; witness the original intention and the ultimate result of our late war with Spain; witness the development of all large and permanent national policies; witness the original purpose and final results of any of the great movements of history.

So of these Russian railways in Asia. Already passenger-trains running westward are well filled with European business-men returning home; and among them, even now, is a sprinkling of Chinese merchants on their way to the capitals of Europe. Even in 1901 the passenger-trains travelling eastward on the Siberian road were well filled with Russians, Germans, Frenchmen, an occasional Englishman, and sometimes an American journeying towards the Orient—this, too, when the road was uncompleted, and with days and weeks of vexatious discomfort on forest-fringed rivers. For remember that, until last year, a hard journey of many days on the Amur and Shilka rivers was necessary before you could board the Siberian train at Stretensk.

With the Manchurian line finished, nearly all the business-men of Europe and China will travel by this route. They can go from Pekin to Moscow in three weeks, in trains equipped with most modern conveniences and luxuries. Where, until now, one Chinese merchant visited European markets in person, hereafter one hundred will do so. Where, formerly, one European businessman investigated commercial conditions in China in person, a hundred will do so hereafter; and all of them who take this trip will pass through Russian dominion, breathe Russian atmosphere, be impressed with Russian influence and power.

A branch of the Manchurian railway has been built to the port of New-Chwang, hitherto the commercial door through which most imports into Manchuria were admitted. From this port a well-constructed railroad runs to the very gates of Pekin itself. This line was built by English engineers, under authority of the Chinese government, and its bonds were held by a British syndicate under a contract between the Chinese government and the Hong-Kong and Shankhai Banking Corporation, the great English financial institution of the Orient. Rumors were current in 1901 that this English syndicate was ready to sell its investments to the highest bidder, just as the owners of English ship-lines in the Orient seem to be willing to sell out to the highest bidder. We all know who that highest bidder will ultimately prove to be. It will be Russia.

The Chinese Emperor has a richly constructed special car on this railroad to Pekin. Immediately after the Boxer troubles the administration of this road was taken over by the allies, and its active operations intrusted by agreement to the English military forces. This military operation of the road by the English was still effective in the summer of 1901. In company with the English general in command of the British forces in China, a trip was made on this car from Tien-Tsin to Pekin. Recent from a journey over the Siberian railway from Moscow, fresh from the scenes attending the building of grades, the bridging of rivers, the laying of rails, and other incidents of the construction of the Manchurian railway, it was difficult not to associate this continued journey to Pekin with those great lines. Other passenger-cars were filled with English officers on leave of absence, going to Pekin from posts at which they had been recently stationed near Manchuria.

One could not help remembering that at the World's Fair in Paris a rolling panorama of the Siberian railway was exhibited by the Russian government, taking the travellers from Moscow directly by rail to the very gates of the Chinese capital. And it is not unreasonable to foresee a journey of the Chinese ruler to the courts and capitals of Europe. When this imperial journey takes place—indeed, when any man takes this trip—the first flag that greets his vision when he passes the Great Wall will be the colors of Russia. As he speeds upon his journey he will behold at every station the uniform of Russia, every hour he will hear the speech of Russia. For days and nights and nights and days he will pass through the unending territories of Russia. As he rolls rapidly westward, Russian conditions increase; Russian flag multiply; Russian atmosphere thickens, until finally, when he steps from his train in Moscow, he feels the very beat of the heart of the Russian nation.

It will be hard for that man ever to get away from the feeling that the great power of the future is Russia. No ordinary Oriental mind will be able to overcome the impression that the other nations of Europe are but inferior states compared with Russia and that the bearded Slav, notwithstanding his defects, is nevertheless the coming autocrat of all the Asia. And if that conviction is once fixed in the Eastern mind it will have an important if not determining influence not only upon the commercial conditions, but upon the destiny of the world. The first thing, then, that is the plain result of the Manchurian road is that the quickest—and in any case the only—overland business route to China is through the dominions under the protection and surrounded by the influences of the Czar.

An English merchant, a German investigator, and an American traveller were sitting under the tree before the English Club, looking out upon the charming bay of Chefoo. What were they discussing? Russia, of course. In the Far East everybody is discussing Russia wherever you go, and the Manchurian-Siberian railway as the most conspicuous illustration of her activity. The Englishman closed an intemperate assault on Russia as follows:

"She will flood Oriental markets with goods from Moscow and Tver, Smolensk and Lodz, and her other manufacturing centres, as she will flood China with her soldiers."

"That opinion seems absurd to me," said the German. "It is unprofitable for freight to be shipped to the Orient over the Siberian-Manchurian road. The distance is too great, and freight charges, if based on nothing more than operating expenses only, would be too heavy. The world's trade with the Orient, so far as European exports to China or any other parts of the Far East are concerned, must long continue to be by water."

The careful student of traffic who goes over the ground will be inclined to agree with this German opinion. The Siberian-Manchurian road will bring very little European merchandise into the Orient for some time to come. It is too long a haul. At lowest possible rates, the freight charge is so heavy that any thought of competition with ship-lines for that class of business does not appear possible, for the present at least. Large Oriental shipments of freight will go westward by the road to Europe, but not the reverse. For example, all of the finer brands of tea, which are so much injured by moisture when transported by ship, will hereafter be shipped very largely by this railroad. Indeed, heretofore a considerable part of this traffic has been by camel caravan across the desert for many weeks, until the Siberian railroad was reached, and then by rail.

As elsewhere, Oriental exports to Europe, and all kinds of freight requiring quick despatch, will also go by the Siberian railroad; but European exports to the Orient, in whose markets cheapness is an element of such moment, must for the present continue to be by water. This is a fact of first-class importance to America. We are less than five thousand miles from Oriental markets, and our competitors—Germany, England, Russia, and France— are, practically, eight or nine thousand miles away by water. Comparatively, Oriental markets are right at our door; and very far away, indeed, from our European rivals. And, for purposes of freight traffic, the Siberian-Manchurian railroad does not bring our European competitors any closer to the markets for which we are mutually contending.

"Why, then," said the Englishman, "is Russia building this road? Not for fun, I think!"

"Oh no, not for fun—certainly not!" responded the German, "but for very far-seeing, long-headed reasons, in which Russia surpasses us all. In the first place, Russia considers nothing hers which she does not control in a visible, tangible, material way; in the second place, she is always looking one or two centuries ahead; in the third place, the Russian people are hardly a people yet—they are still in the process of being compounded. Our children's children may find themselves worn out when these thick-skulled, hairy, no-nerved Slavs are just coming into their prime; and, similarly, our posterity may find themselves without markets when the future Russian may find himself in the actual possession of the only markets of the world now capable of seizure."

This bit of commercial philosophy is given for what it is worth. But, confining ourselves to the Manchurian road at present, it appears that it and the Siberian road will serve as highways for the introduction of European and American products into the very shops of the merchants and homes of the people in the interior of Manchuria, and into the markets of Siberia itself, until a point is reached where American merchants cannot afford to ship farther westward and where Moscow merchants can afford to pay the railway freights. And since America is thousands of miles nearer to the Orient by water than any European rival, including Russia itself, these Russian railways through Manchuria and Siberia would naturally become the principal distributing agencies for American goods.

But two circumstances can prevent this result: First, the placing of Port Arthur, Dalni, and New-Chwang under a Russian tariff so that American importers will have to pay heavy duties, whereas Russian importers will have to pay nothing at all on landing their goods at these Russian-Asiatic ports; or, second, a system of differential railroad rates by which, even if the ports remain open, the goods of every other nation except Russia will have to pay such extravagant freight charges that none but Russian merchandise can penetrate the interior along the line of the road. But if railway rates remain uniform and ports remain open, American commerce along the lines of these roads will not only be considerably increased, but actually multiplied manyfold.

"Do you not think that the long-hoped-for reform of internal communication in China will begin as a natural result of the railroad through Manchuria?" was a question asked of one of the deepest students of Oriental commerce. (The greatest practical difficulty, you know, in extending commerce among China's four hundred millions is to get the goods into the interior; an internal transportation tax on foreign goods—sometimes irregular, exorbitant, and corrupt—consumes all the profits before imports penetrate two hundred miles from any port.)

"Yes," was the reply, "I have thought of that myself, and, Englishman though I am, I will admit that if the Manchurian railway would break up the ruinous, foolish, and villainous obstruction to foreign commerce in the interior, the world should accept it as a blessing, notwithstanding its menace to the supremacy of other powers in the Orient; and no possible help to the Chinese could be of such far-reaching benefit."

Let us see just what this means. The Manchurian railway runs through about seventeen hundred miles of Chinese provinces, mostly populated. Over this region has spread that net-work of commercial obstruction which prevents internal foreign commerce all over China—that is to say, that heretofore the Chinese merchant who wanted to transport foreign goods from one point to another in China, has had to do it by carts over unimaginable roads (let us rather say immaginary roads), or by boats, or, what is more usual, on the backs of coolies; and he has been, and still is, literally "held up," every few stages, by collectors of transportation tax. (This is the famous "likin" tax.) This tax, even if it were legally charged and honestly collected, would be a serious enough burden on commerce to discourage trade for any great distance in the interior; but the "likin" tax serves as an excuse for numerous irregular collectors to still further burden all transportation of merchandise into the interior by exacting, under the guise of the tax, arbitrary, illegal, and corrupt charges.

But the irregular collector of corrupt transportation tax does not "hold up" the train of the Manchurian railroad; it thunders by him unheeding. Indeed, the traffic over the road is free from the regular "likin," as will be seen when we come to the railway agreement. The merchant gets his goods as quickly as possible to the railway, and, for a fixed and definite price, his merchandise is transported to distant points. Not by any other law, therefore, than the irresistible operation of practical progress, the reform of this ancient abuse of the whole Empire of China has begun. And when you reflect that, if transportation of imports were free throughout the Chinese Empire, foreign imports to the Chinese people would increase almost immediately, with little effort, from two hundred and fifty million dollars a year (the present amount) to a thousand million dollars a year (and this is the conservative estimate of the most conservative minds), you will understand what the working out of such reform would mean to the producers of America, who are many thousand miles nearer these markets than any of their competitors.

Think of America with a Chinese export trade of one hundred millions a year—of two hundred millions a year! And yet, unless our statesmanship is unequal to our opportunity, we shall ultimately have a greater commerce than that.

The stimulus to the commercial spirit of the people, on the one hand, and the deadening effect upon governmental obstruction on the other, which the railroad is producing already in Manchuria, are astonishing only because we do not think of these things till we are brought face to face with them. The local merchant who thought no market possible to him except that within the reach of his cart suddenly finds commercial limitations lifted, and a demand for his merchandise hundreds, even thousands, of miles away. The agriculturist or other producer who sold through his little merchant to this little market at no price at all, and with no demand, suddenly finds that his products are sought for, and at comparatively better prices. It would be a low order of mind which did not see the cause for this, and the Chinaman has not a low order of mind; commercially, he has a very keen mind. He finds the cause of this in a steel railway; from this it becomes clear to him that to get to that railway is the best thing for him.

Therefore he sees for the first time in his life the necessity for good roads. And although in 1901 the railroad was only in process of construction, and although freight was as yet hauled along the southern divisions only, and then merely as a matter of obliging merchants, and not as a matter of business, little branches of highway were already springing up and out from this steel spinal column of commerce like growing trade-nerves. As yet, of course, the improvement on these roads amounts to little. You would not notice it unless you were looking for it; but it is a safe prophecy that within ten years from the completion of the Manchurian railway fairly passable roads will lead from every station for distances into the interior; and from these roads others will gradually branch off. And so a people hitherto segregated from their fellow-men will be brought into contact with the other inhabitants of the earth.

Good roads in China! Free transportation of exports through the interior of China! Five years ago no serious thinker upon the development of commerce in the Orient would have even talked to you about those subjects, so impossible would he have declared them; for the roads of China (and Manchuria is a part of China) are impassable sloughs of mire in the rainy season and almost impassable rivers of dust when the weather is dry. Only in winter is transportation in Manchuria practicable, except by boats. In winter the solidly frozen earth makes a firm road bed, and the snow gives possibility of speed. In this respect Manchurian roads are like Russian roads, but in all other seasons—well, an attempt was made to drive to a Chinese town three miles from the point where the Russians were building a railway grade, but it had been raining for two days, and the cart sank to its bed and the ponies to their bellies before the start was fairly made. The road was impracticable, and that town was cut off from the world.

"The theory of the Chinese government concerning roads has been that if there were no roads insurrection would be less probable and each community would be more firmly rooted to its own village," explained a gentleman of forty years' acquaintance with China and Manchuria. And the following patriotic reason was given by the Governor of one of the Manchurian provinces:

"If we had good roads, the Russians or any other invader could march right down into the very heart of our country. To build a fine road through Manchuria or any other part of China would be to invite invasion by our foreign enemies."

"So you see," said a European traveller in the Orient, "Chinese logic makes the building of fine highways the very substance of treason."

CHAPTER 6

The Russian Peasant

PEASANT LIFE

The Crimean War brought the whole Russian system into crisis. In foreign policy, in internal politics, in its intellectual life, Russia entered a period of self-reevaluation. The Russian peasant gained the first fruits of this development in 1861 when Tsar Alexander II issued his Emancipation decree. The peasant, however, was still not completely free. The following selection from Mackenzie Wallace's account of his travels in Russia illustrates the problems of Russian peasant life in the latter part of the 19th century.

My illness had at least one good result. It brought me into contact with the Feldsher, and through him after my recovery I made the acquaintance of several peasants living in the village. Of these by far the most interesting was an old man called Ivan Petroff.

Ivan must have been about sixty years of age, but was still robust and strong, and had the reputation of being able to mow more hay in a given time than any other peasant in the village. His head would have made a fine study for a portrait-painter. Like Russian peasants in general, he wore his hair parted in the middle—a custom which perhaps owes its origin to the religious pictures. The reverend appearance given to his face by his long fair beard, slightly tinged with gray, was in part counteracted by his eyes, which had a strange twinkle in them—whether of humor or of roguery, it was difficult to say. Under all circumstances—whether in his light, nondescript summer costume, or in his warm sheep-skin, or in the long, glossy, dark-blue, double-breasted coat which he put on occasionally on Sundays and holidays—he always looked a well-fed, respectable, well-to-do member of society; whilst his imperturbable composure, and the entire absence of obsequiousness or truculence in his manner, indicated plainly that he possessed no small amount of calm, deep-rooted self-respect. A stranger, on

Source: D. Mackenzie Wallace, *Russia* (New York, 1881), 83–116.

seeing him, might readily have leaped to the conclusion that he must be the Village Elder, but in reality he was a simple member of the Commune, like his neighbor, poor Zakhar Leshkof, who never let slip an opportunity of getting drunk, was always in debt and difficulties, and, on the whole, possessed a more than dubious reputation. Ivan had, it is true, been Village Elder some years before. When elected by the Village Assembly against his own wishes, he had said quietly, "Very well, children; I will serve my three years;" and at the end of that period, when the Assembly wished to re-elect him, he had answered firmly, "No, children; I have served my time. It is now the turn of some one who is younger, and has more time. There's Peter Alekseyef, a good fellow and an honest: you may choose him." And the Assembly chose the peasant indicated; for Ivan, though a simple member of the Commune, had more influence in Communal affairs than any other half-dozen members put together. No grave matter was decided without his being consulted, and there was at least one instance on record of the Village Assembly postponing deliberations for a week because he happened to be absent in St. Petersburg.

No stranger casually meeting Ivan would ever for a moment have suspected that that big man, of calm, commanding aspect, had been during a greater part of his life a serf. And yet a serf he had been, from his birth till he was about forty years of age—not merely a serf of the State, but the serf of a proprietor who had lived habitually on his property. For forty years of his life he had been dependent on the arbitrary will of a master, who had the legal power to flog him as often and as severely as he considered desirable. In reality, however, he had never been subjected to corporal punishment, for the proprietor to whom he had belonged had been, though in some respects severe, a just and intelligent master.

Ivan's bright and intelligent face had early attracted the master's attention, and it was accordingly decided that he should learn a trade. For this purpose he was sent to Moscow, and apprenticed there to a carpenter. After four years of apprenticeship he was able not only to earn his own bread, but to help the household in the payment of their taxes, and to pay annually to his master a fixed yearly sum—first ten, then twenty, then thirty, and ultimately, for some years immediately before the Emancipation in 1861, seventy roubles—that is to say, seventy of the old paper roubles, or about twenty "roubles silver," as the new paper roubles are commonly termed. In return for this annual sum he was free to work and wander about as he pleased, and for some years he had made ample use of his conditional liberty. I never succeeded in extracting from him a chronological account of his travels, but I could gather from his occasional remarks that he had wandered over a great part of European Russia. Evidently he had been in his youth what is colloquially termed "a roving blade," and had by no means confined himself to the trade which he had learned during his four years of apprenticeship. At one time he had helped to navigate a raft from Vetluga to Astrakhan, a distance of about two thousand miles. At another time he had been at Arkangel and Onega, on the shores of the White Sea. St. Petersburg and Moscow were both well known to him, and once at least he had visited Odessa. The precise nature of his occupations during these wanderings I could not ascertain; for, with all his openness of manner, he was extremely reticent regarding his commercial affairs. To all my inquiries on this topic he replied vaguely, "Lesnoe dyelo"—that is to say, "A wood affair;" and from this I concluded that his chief occupation had been that of a timber merchant. Indeed, when I knew him, though he was no longer a regular trader, it was well known that he was always ready to buy any bit of forest that could be bought in the vicinity for a reasonable price. His reticence regarding his commercial transactions was probably learned from the regular traders, who are always very reluctant to communicate anything regarding their mercantile affairs.

During all this nomadic period of his life, Ivan had never entirely severed his connection with his home or with agricultural life. When about the age of twenty he had spent several months at home, taking part in the field labor, and had married a wife—a strong, healthy young woman, who had been selected for him by his mother, and strongly recommended in consideration of her good character and her physical strength. In the opinion of Ivan's mother, beauty was a kind of luxury which only nobles and rich merchants could afford, and ordinary comeliness was a very secondary consideration— so secondary as to be left almost entirely out of sight. This was likewise the opinion of Ivan's wife. She had never been comely herself, she used to say, but she had been a good wife to her husband. He had never complained about her want of good looks, and had never gone after those who were considered good-looking. In expressing this opinion she always first bent forward, then drew herself up to her full length, and finally gave a little jerky nod sideways, so as to clench the statement. Then Ivan's bright eye would twinkle more brightly than usual, and he would ask her how she knew that—reminding her that he was not always at home. This was Ivan's stereotyped mode of teasing his wife, and every time he employed it he was called an "old scarecrow," or something of the kind.

Perhaps, however, Ivan's jocular remark had more significance in it than his wife cared to admit, for during the first years of their married life they had seen very little of each other. A few days after the marriage, when according to our notions the honeymoon should be at its height, Ivan had gone to Moscow for several months, leaving his young bride to the care of his father and mother. The young bride did not consider this an extraordinary hardship, for many of her companions had been treated in the same way, and according to public opinion in that part of the country there was nothing abnormal in the proceeding. Indeed, it may be said in general that there is very little romance or sentimentality about Russian peasant marriages. The wife is taken as a helpmate, or in plain language a worker, rather than as a companion, and the mother-in-law leaves her very little time to indulge in useless regrets and fruitless dreaming.

As time wore on, and his father became older and frailer, Ivan's visits to his native place became longer and more frequent, and when the old man was at last incapable of work, Ivan settled down permanently and undertook the direction of the household. In the meantime his own children had been growing up. When I knew the family it comprised—besides two daughters who had married early and gone to live with their parents-in-law—Ivan and his wife, two sons, three daughters-in-law, and an indefinite and frequently varying number of grandchildren. The fact that there were three daughters-in-law and only two sons was the result of the Conscription, which had taken away the youngest son shortly after his marriage. The two who remained spent only a small part of the year at home. The one was a carpenter and the other a bricklayer, and both wandered about the country in search of employment as their father had done in his younger days. There was, however, one difference. The father had always shown a leaning towards commercial transactions, rather than the simple practice of his handicraft, and consequently he had usually lived and traveled alone. The sons, on the contrary, confined themselves to their handicrafts, and were always during the working season members of *artels*.

The artel in its various forms is a curious institution. Those to which Ivan's sons belonged were simply temporary, itinerant associations of workmen, who during the summer lived together, fed together, worked together, and on the termination of each bit of work divided amongst themselves the profits. This is the primitive form of the institution, and is now not very often met with. Here, as elsewhere, capital has made itself felt, and destroyed that equality which exists among the members of an artel in the above sense of the word. Instead of forming themselves into a temporary association, the workmen now generally make an engagement with a contractor who has a little capital, and receive from him fixed monthly wages. According to this arrangement the risk is less and the wages are smaller, and if any exceptional profit accrues from the undertaking it goes into the pocket of the contractor, in compensation for the exceptional losses which he may have to bear. The only association which exists in this case is for the purchase and preparation of provisions, and even these duties are very often left to the contractor.

In some of the larger towns there are artels of a much more complex kind —permanent associations, possessing a large capital, and pecuniarily responsible for the acts of the individual members. Of these, by far the most celebrated is that of the Bank Porters. These men have unlimited opportunities of stealing, and are often intrusted with the guarding or transporting of enormous sums; but the banker has no cause for anxiety, because he knows that if any defalcations occur they will be made good to him by the artel. Such accidents, however, rarely if ever happen, and the fact is by no means so extraordinary as many people suppose. The artel, being responsible for the individuals of which it is composed is very careful in admitting new members, and a man when admitted is closely watched, not only by the regularly constituted office-bearers, but also by all his fellow-members who have an opportunity of observing him. If he begins to spend money too freely or to neglect his duties, though his employer may know nothing of the fact, suspicions are at once aroused among his fellow-members, and an investigation ensues—ending in summary expulsion if the suspicions prove to have been well-founded. Mutual responsibility, in short, creates naturally a very effective system of mutual supervision. Might not some of our employers of labor, who complain loudly of the carelessness and dishonesty of their servants, make some practical use of this principle?

Of Ivan's two sons, the one who was a carpenter by trade visited his family only occasionally, and at irregular intervals; the other, on the contrary, as building is impossible in Russia during the cold weather, spent the greater part of the winter at home. Both of them paid a large part of their earnings into the family treasury, over which their father exercised uncontrolled authority. If he wished to make any considerable outlay, he always consulted his sons on the subject, but as he was a prudent, intelligent man, and enjoyed the respect and confidence of the family, he never met with any decided opposition. All the field work was performed by him with the assistance of his daughters-in-law; only at harvest time he hired one or two laborers to help him.

Ivan's household was a good specimen of the Russian peasant family of the old type. Previous to the Emancipation in 1861, there were many households of this kind, containing the representatives of three generations. All the members, young and old, lived together in patriarchal fashion under the direction and authority of the Head of the House, called usually *Khozain*, that is to say, the Administrator; or, in some districts, *Bolshak*, which means literally "the Big One." Generally speaking, this important position was occupied by the grandfather, or, if he was dead, by the eldest brother, but this rule was not very strictly observed. If, for instance, the grandfather became infirm, or if the eldest brother was incapacitated by disorderly habits or other cause, the place of authority was taken by some other member—it might be by a woman—who was a good manager, and possessed the greatest moral influence. The relations between the Head of the Household and the other members depended on custom and personal character, and they consequently varied greatly in different families. If the Big One was an intelligent man, of decided, energetic character, like my friend Ivan, there was probably perfect discipline in the house, except perhaps in the matter of female tongues, which do not readily submit to the authority even of their owners; but very often it happened that the Big One was not thoroughly well filled for his post, and in that case endless quarrels and bickerings inevitably took place. Those quarrels were generally caused and fomented by the female members of the household—a fact which will not seem strange if we try to realize how difficult it must be for several sisters-in-law, within the narrow limits of a peasant's house. The complaints of the young bride, who finds that her mother-in-law puts all the hard work on her shoulders, form a favorite motive in the popular poetry.

The house, with its appurtenances, the cattle, the agricultural implements, the grain and other products, the money gained from the sale of these products—in a word, the house and nearly everything it contained—was the joint-property of the family. Hence, nothing was bought or sold by any member—not even by the Big One himself, unless he possessed an unusual amount of authority—without the express or tacit consent of the other grown-up males, and all the money that was earned was put into the common purse. When one of the sons left home to work elsewhere, he was expected to bring or send home all his earnings, except what he required for food, lodgings, and other *necessary* expenses; and if he understood the word "necessary" in too lax a sense, he had to listen to very plain-spoken reproaches when he returned. During his absence, which might last for a whole year or several years, his wife and children remained in the house as before, and the money which he earned was probably devoted to the payment of the family taxes.

The peasant household of the old type is thus a primitive labor association, of which the members have all things in common, and it is not a little remarkable that the peasant conceives it as such rather than as a family. This is shown by the customary terminology and by the law of inheritance. The Head of the Household is not called by any word corresponding to Paterfamilias, but is termed, as I have said, Khozain, or Administrator—a word that is applied equally to a farmer, a shopkeeper, or the head of an industrial undertaking, and does not at all convey the idea of blood-relationship.

The law of inheritance is likewise based on this conception. When a household is broken up, the degree of blood-relationship is not taken into consideration in the distribution of the property. All the adult male members share equally. Illegitimate and adopted sons, if they have contributed their share of labor, have the same rights as the sons born in lawful wedlock. The married daughter, on the contrary—being regarded as belonging to her husband's family—and the son who has previously separated himself from the household, are excluded from the succession. Strictly speaking, there is no succession or inheritance whatever, except as regards the wearing apparel and any little personal effects of a similar kind. The house and all that it contains belong not to the Khozain, but to the little household community; and consequently, when the Khozain dies and the community is broken up, the members do not inherit, but merely appropriate individually what they had hitherto possessed collectively. Thus there is properly no inheritance or succession, but simply liquidation and distribution of the property among the members. The written law of inheritance, founded on the conception of personal property, is quite unknown to the peasantry, and quite inapplicable to their mode of life. In this way a large and most important section of the Code remains a dead letter for about four-fifths of the population!

This predominance of practical economic considerations is likewise exemplified by the way in which marriages are arranged in these large families.

In all respects the Russian peasantry are, as a class, extremely practical and matter-of-fact in their conceptions and habits, and are not at all prone to indulge in sublime, ethereal sentiments of any kind. They have little or nothing of what may be roughly termed the Hermann-and-Dorothea element in their composition, and consequently they know very little about those sentimental, romantic ideas which we habitually associate with the preliminary steps to matrimony. This fact is so patent to all who have studied the Russian peasantry, that even those who have endeavored to idealize peasant life have rarely ventured to make their story turn on a sentimental love affair. These general remarks I insert here parenthetically, in order that the reader may more clearly understand what I have to say regarding peasant marriages.

In the primitive system of agriculture usually practiced in Russia, the natural labor-unit—if it be allowed to use such a term—comprises a man, a woman, and a horse. As soon, therefore, as a boy becomes an able-bodied laborer he ought to be provided with the two accessories necessary for the completion of the labor-unit. To procure a horse, either by purchase or by rearing a foal, is the duty of the Head of the House; to procure a wife for the youth is the duty of "the female Big One" (*bolshukha*). And the chief consideration in determining the choice is in both cases the same. Prudent domestic administrators are not to be tempted by showy horses or beautiful brides; what they seek is not beauty, but physical strength and capacity for work. When the youth reaches the age of eighteen he is informed that he ought to marry at once, and as soon as he gives his consent negotiations are opened with the parents of some eligible young person. In the larger villages the negotiations are sometimes facilitated by certain old women called *svakhi*, who occupy themselves specially with this kind of mediation; but very often the affair is arranged directly by, or through the agency of, some common friend of the two houses. Care must of course be taken that there is no legal obstacle to the marriage, and these obstacles are not always easily avoided in a small village, the inhabitants of which have been long in the habit of intermarrying. According to Russian ecclesiastical law, not only is marriage between first-cousins illegal, but affinity is considered as equivalent to consanguinity—that is to say, a mother-in-law and a sister-in-law are regarded as a mother and a sister—and even the fictitious relationship created by standing together at the baptismal font as godfather and godmother is legally recognized. If all the preliminary negotiations are successful, the marriage takes place, and the bridegroom brings his bride home to the house of which he is a member. She brings nothing with her as a dowry except her trousseau, but she brings a pair of good strong arms, and thereby enriches her adopted family. Of course it happens occasionally—for human nature is everywhere essentially the same—that a young peasant falls in love with one of his former playmates, and brings his little romance to a happy conclusion at the altar; but such cases are very rare, and as a rule it may be said that the marriages of the Russian peasantry are arranged under the influence of economic rather than sentimental considerations.

The custom of living in large families has many decided economic advantages. We all know the edifying fable of the dying man who showed to his sons by means of a piece of wickerwork the advantages of living together and mutually assisting each other. In ordinary times the necessary expenses of a large household of ten members are considerably less than the combined expenses of two households comprising five members each, and when a "black day" comes, a large family can bear temporary adversity much more successfully than a small one. These are principles of world-wide application, and in the life of the Russian peasantry they have a peculiar force. Each adult peasant possesses, as I shall hereafter explain, a share of the Communal land, but this share is not sufficient to occupy all his time and working power. One married pair can easily cultivate two shares—at least in all provinces where land is not very abundant. Now if a family is composed of two married couples, one of the men can go elsewhere and earn money, whilst the other, with his wife and sister-in-law, can cultivate the two combined shares of land. If, on the contrary, a family consists merely of one pair with their children, the man must either remain at home, in which case he may have difficulty in finding work for the whole of his time, or he must leave home, and intrust the cultivation of his share of the land to his wife, whose time must be in great part devoted to domestic affairs.

In the time of serfage the proprietors clearly perceived these and similar advantages, and compelled their serfs to live together in large families. No family could be broken up without the proprietor's consent, and this consent was not easily obtained unless the family had assumed quite abnormal proportions, and was permanently disturbed by domestic dissension. In the matrimonial affairs of the serfs, too, the majority of the proprietors systematically exercised a certain supervision, not necessarily from any paltry, meddling spirit, but because their material interests were thereby affected. A proprietor would not, for instance, allow the daughter of one of his serfs to marry a serf belonging to another proprietor—because he would thereby lose a female laborer—unless some compensation were offered. The compensation might be a sum of money, or the affair might be arranged on the principle of reciprocity, by the master of the bridegroom allowing one of his female serfs to marry a serf belonging to the master of the bride.

However advantageous the custom of living in large families may appear when regarded from the economic point of view, it has very serious defects, both theoretical and practical.

That families connected by the ties of blood-relationship and marriage can easily live together in harmony is one of those social axioms which are accepted universally and believed by nobody. We all know by our own experience, or by that of others, that the friendly relations of two such families are greatly endangered by proximity of habitation. To live in the same street is not advisable; to occupy adjoining houses is positively dangerous; and to live under the same roof is certainly fatal to prolonged amity. There may be the very best intentions on both sides, and the arrangement may be inaugurated by the most gushing expressions of undying affection and by the discovery of innumerable secret affinities, but neither affinities, affection, nor good intentions can withstand the constant friction and occasional jerks which inevitably ensue. Now the reader must endeavor to realize that Russian peasants, even when clad in sheep-skins, are human beings like ourselves. Though they are often represented as abstract entities—as figures in a table of statistics or dots on a diagram—they have in reality "organs, dimensions, senses, affections, passions." If not exactly "fed with the same food," they are at least "hurt with the same weapons, subject to the same diseases, healed by the same means," and liable to be irritated by the same annoyances as we are. And those of them who live in large families are subjected to a kind of probation that most of us have never dreamed of. The families comprising a large household not only live together, but have nearly all things in common. Each member works not for himself, but for the household, and all that he earns is expected to go into the family treasury. The arrangement almost inevitably leads to one of two results—either there are continual dissensions or order is preserved by a powerful domestic tyranny infinitely worse than serfage.

It was quite natural, therefore, that when the authority of the landed proprietors was abolished in 1861, the large peasant families almost all fell to pieces. The arbitrary rule of the Khozain was based on, and maintained by the arbitrary proprietor, and both naturally fell together. Households like that of our friend Ivan have been preserved only in exceptional cases, where the Head of the House happened to possess an unusual amount of moral influence over the other members. This change has unquestionably had a prejudicial influence on the material welfare of the peasantry, but it must have added considerably to their domestic comfort, and can scarcely fail to produce good moral results. For the present, however, the evil consequences are by far the most prominent. Every married peasant strives to have a house of his own, and many of them, in order to defray the necessary expenses, have been obliged to contract debts. This is a very serious matter. Even if the peasants could obtain money at five or six per cent, the position of the debtors would be bad enough, but it is in reality much worse, for the village usurers consider twenty or twenty-five per cent a by no means exorbitant rate of interest. Thus the peasant who contracts debts has a hard struggle to pay the interest in ordinary times, and when some misfortune overtakes him—when, for instance, the harvest is bad or his horse is stolen— he probably falls hopelessly into pecuniary embarrassments. I have seen peasants not specially addicted to drunkenness or other ruinous habits sink to a helpless state of insolvency. Fortunately for such insolvent debtors, they are treated by the law with extreme leniency. Their house, their share of the common land, their agricultural implements, their horse—in a word, all that is necessary for their subsistence, is exempt from sequestration. The Commune may, however, subject them to corporal punishment if they do not pay their taxes, and in many other respects the position of a peasant who is protected against utter destitution merely by the law is very far from being enviable.

Ivanofka may be taken as a fair specimen of the villages in the northern half of the country, and a brief description of its inhabitants will convey a tolerably correct notion of the northern peasantry in general.

Nearly the whole of the female population, and about one-half of the male inhabitants, are habitually engaged in cultivating the Communal land, which comprises about two thousand acres of a light sandy soil. The arable part of this land is divided into three large fields, each of which is cut up into long narrow strips. The first field is reserved for the winter grain—that is to say, rye, which forms, in the shape of black bread, the principal food of the peasantry. In the second are raised oats for the horses, and buckwheat, which is largely used for food. The third lies fallow, and is used in the summer as pasturage for the cattle.

All the villagers in this part of the country divide the arable land in this way, in order to suit the triennial rotation of crops. This triennial system is extremely simple. The field which is used this year for raising winter grain will be used next year for raising summer grain, and in the following year will lie fallow. Before being sown with winter grain it ought to receive a certain amount of manure. Every family possesses in each of the two fields under cultivation one or more of the long, narrow strips or belts into which they are divided.

The annual life of the peasantry is that of simple husbandmen inhabiting a country where the winter is long and severe. The agricultural year begins in April with the melting of the snow. Nature has been lying dormant for some months. Awaking now from her long sleep, and throwing off her white mantle, she strives to make up for lost time. No sooner has the snow disappeared than the fresh young grass begins to shoot up, and very soon afterwards the shrubs and trees begin to bud. The rapidity of this transition from winter to spring astonishes the inhabitants of more temperate climes.

On St. George's Day (April 23rd), the cattle are brought out for the first time and sprinkled with holy water by the priest. The cattle of the Russian peasantry are never very fat, but at this period of the year their appearance is truly lamentable. During the winter they have been cooped up in small unventilated cowhouses, and fed almost exclusively on straw; now, when they are released from their imprisonment, they look like the ghosts of their former emaciated selves. All are lean and weak, many are lame, and some cannot rise to their feet without assistance.

Meanwhile the peasants are impatient to begin the field labor. An old proverb which they all know says: "Sow in mud and you will be a prince;" and they always act in accordance with this dictate of traditional wisdom. As soon as it is possible to plow they begin to prepare the land for the summer grain, and this labor occupies them probably till the end of May. Then comes the work of carting out manure and preparing the fallow field for the winter grain, which will last probably till about St. Peter's Day (June 29th), when the hay-making generally begins. After the hay-making comes the harvest, by far the busiest time of the year. From the middle of July—especially from St. Elijah's Day (July 20th), when the saint is usually heard rumbling along the heavens in his chariot of fire—until the end of August, the peasant may work day and night, and yet will find that he has barely time to get all his work done. In little more than a month he has to reap and stack his grain—rye, oats, and whatever else he may have sown either in spring or in the preceding autumn—and to sow the winter grain for next year. To add to his troubles, it sometimes happens that the rye and the oats ripen almost simultaneously and his position is then still more difficult than usual.

Whether the seasons favor him or not, the peasant has at this time a hard task, for he can rarely afford to hire the requisite number of laborers, and has generally the assistance merely of his wife and family; but he can at this season work for a short time at high pressure, for he has the prospect of soon obtaining a good rest and an abundance of food. About the end of September the field labor is finished, and on the first day of October the harvest festival begins—a joyous season, during which the parish fêtes are commonly celebrated.

To celebrate a parish fête in true orthodox fashion it is necessary to prepare beforehand a large quantity of *braga*—a kind of home-brewed small beer—and to bake a plentiful supply of *piroghi* or pies. Oil, too, has to be procured, and vodka (rye spirit) in goodly quantity. At the same time the big room of the *izba*, as the peasant's house is called, has to be cleared, the floor washed, and the table and benches scrubbed. The evening before the fête, while the piroghi are being baked, a little lamp burns before the Icon in the corner of the room, and perhaps one or two guests from a distance arrive in order that they may have on the morrow a full day's enjoyment.

On the morning of the fête the proceedings begin by a long service in the church, at which all the inhabitants are present in their best holiday costumes, except those matrons and young women who remain at home to prepare the dinner. About midday dinner is served in each izba for the family and their friends. In general the Russian peasant's fare is of the simplest kind, and rarely comprises animal food of any sort—not from any vegetarian proclivities, but merely because beef, mutton, and pork are too expensive; but on a holiday, such as a parish fête, there is alway on the dinner-table a considerable variety of dishes. In the house of a well-to-do peasant there will be not only greasy cabbage-soup and *kasha*—a dish made from buckwheat—but also pork, mutton, and perhaps even beef. Braga will be supplied in unlimited quantities, and more than once vodka will be handed round. When the repast is finished, all rise together, and, turning towards the Icon in the corner, bow and cross themselves repeatedly. The guests then say to their host, *"Spasibo za khleb za sol"*—that is to say, "Thanks for your hospitality," or more literally, "Thanks for bread and salt;" and the host replies, "Do not be displeased, sit down once more for good luck"—or perhaps he puts the last part of his request into the form of a rhyming couplet to the following effect: "Sit down, that the hens may brood, and that the chickens and bees may multiply!" All obey this request, and there is another round of vodka.

After dinner some stroll about, chatting with their friends, or go to sleep in some shady nook, whilst those who wish to make merry go to the spot where the young people are singing, playing, and amusing themselves in various ways. As the sun sinks towards the horizon, the more grave, staid guests wend their way homewards, but many remain for supper; and as evening advances the effects of the vodka become more and more apparent. Sounds of revelry are heard more frequently from the houses, and a large proportion of the inhabitants and guests appear on the road in various degrees of intoxication. Some of these vow eternal affection to their friends, or with flaccid gestures and in incoherent tones harangue invisible audiences; others stagger about aimlessly in besotted self-contentment, till they drop down in a state of complete unconsciousness. There they will lie tranquilly till they are picked up by their less intoxicated friends, or more probably till they awake of their own accord on the next morning.

As a whole, a village fête in Russia is one of the most saddening spectacles I have ever witnessed. It affords a new proof—where, alas! no new proof was required—that we northern nations, who know so well how to work, are utterly incapable of amusing ourselves. In France or Italy a popular holiday is a pleasing sight, and may easily make us regret that life has so few holidays. Not only in the morning, but also in the evening, after a long day, there is a bright, joyous expression on every face, and a hum of genuine merriment rises continually from the crowd. In northern countries, on the contrary, the people do not know how to enjoy themselves in a harmless, rational way, and seek a refuge in intoxication, so that the sight of a popular holiday may make us regret that life has any holidays at all.

If the Russian peasant's food were always as good and plentiful as at this season of the year, he would have little reason to complain; but this is by no means the case. Gradually as the harvest-time recedes, it deteriorates in quality, and sometimes diminishes in quantity. Besides this, during a great part of the year the peasant is prevented from using much that he possesses by the rules of the Church.

In southern climes, where these rules were elaborated and first practiced, the prescribed fasts are perhaps useful not only in a religious, but also in a sanitary sense. Having abundance of fruit and vegetables, the inhabitants do well, perhaps, in abstaining occasionally from animal food. But in countries like Northern and Central Russia, the influence of these rules is very different. The Russian peasant cannot obtain as much animal food as he requires, whilst sour cabbage and cucumbers are probably the only vegetables he can procure, and fruit of any kind is for him an unattainable luxury. Under these circumstances, abstinence from eggs and milk in all their forms during several months of the year seems to the secular mind a superfluous bit of asceticism. If the Church would direct her maternal solicitude to the peasant's drinking, and leave him to eat what he pleases, she might exercise a beneficial influence on his material and moral welfare. Unfortunately she has a great deal too much inherent immobility to do anything of the kind, and there is no reasonable probability of her ever arriving at the simple truth, for which there is very high authority, that rules and ordinances were made for man, and not man for the rules and ordinances. Meanwhile, the Russian peasant must fast during the seven weeks of Lent, during two or three weeks in June, from the beginning of November till Christmas, and on all Wednesdays and Fridays during the remainder of the year.

From the festival time till the following spring there is no possibility of doing any agricultural work, for the ground is hard as iron, and covered with a deep layer of snow. The male peasants, therefore, who remain in the villages, have very little to do, and may spend the greater part of their time in lying idly on the stove unless they happen to have learned some handicraft that can be practiced at home. Formerly, many of them were employed in transporting the grain to the market town, which might be several hundred miles distant; but now this species of occupation has been greatly diminished by the extension of railways.

Another winter occupation which was formerly practiced, and has now almost fallen into disuse, was that of stealing wood in the forest. This was, according to peasant morality, no sin, or at most a very venial offense, for God planted and watered the trees, and therefore forests belong properly to no one. So thought the peasantry, but the landed proprietors and the Administration of the Demesnes held a different theory of property, and consequently precautions had to be taken to avoid detection. In order to insure success it was necessary to choose a night when there was a violent snowstorm, which would immediately obliterate all traces of the expedition; and when such a night was found, the operation was commonly performed with success. During the hours of darkness a tree would be felled, stripped of its branches, dragged into the village, and cut up into firewood, and at sunrise the actors would be tranquilly sleeping on the stove as if they had spent the night at home. In recent years the justices of the peace have done much towards putting down this practice and eradicating the loose conceptions of property with which it was connected.

For the female part of the population winter is a busy time, for it is during these four or five months that the spinning and weaving have to be done.

In many of the northern villages the tedium of the long winter evenings is relieved by so-called Besyedy, a work which signifies literally conversazioni. A Besyeda, however, is not exactly a conversazione as we understand the term, but resembles rather what is by some ladies called a Dorcas meeting, with this essential difference, that those present work for themselves and not for any benevolent purpose. In some villages as many as three Besyedy regularly assemble about sunset: one for the children, the second for the young people, and the third for the matrons. Each of the three has its peculiar character. In the first, the children work and amuse themselves under the superintendence of an old woman, who trims the torch and endeavors to keep order. The little girls spin flax in a primitive way without the aid of a "jenny," and the boys, who are, on the whole, much less industrious, make lapti— rude shoes of plaited bark—or simple bits of wicker-work. These occupations do not prevent an almost incessant hum of talk, frequent discordant attempts to sing in chorus, and occasional quarrels requiring the energetic interference of the old woman who sits by the torch. To amuse her noisy flock she sometimes relates to them, for the hundreth time, one of those wonderful old stories that lose nothing by repetition, and all listen to her attentively, as if they had never heard the story before. The second Besyeda is held in another house by the young people of a riper age. Here the workers are naturally more staid, less given to quarreling, sing more in harmony, and require no one to look after them. Some people, however, might think that a chaperon or inspector of some kind would be by no means out of place, for a good deal of flirtation goes on, and, if village scandal is to be trusted, strict propriety in thought, word, and deed is not always observed. How far these reports are true I cannot pretend to say, for the presence of a stranger always acts on the company like the presence of a severe inspector. In the third Besyeda there is always at least strict decorum. Here the married women work together and talk about their domestic concerns, enlivening the conversation occasionally by the introduction of little bits of village scandal.

Such is the ordinary life of the peasants who live by agriculture; but many of the villagers live occasionally or permanently in the towns. Probably the majority of the peasants in this part of Russia have at some period of their lives gained a living in some other part of the country. Many of the absentees spend regularly a part of the year at home, whilst others visit their families only occasionally, and, it may be, at long intervals. In no case, however, do they sever their connection with their native village. The artisan who goes to work in a distant town never takes his wife and family with him, and even the man who becomes a rich merchant in Moscow or St. Petersburg remains probably a member of the Village Commune, and pays his share of the taxes, though he does not enjoy any of the corresponding privileges. Once I remember asking a rich man of this kind, the proprietor of several large valuable houses in St. Petersburg, why he did not free himself from all connection with his native Commune, with which he had no longer any common interests. His answer was, "It is all very well to be free, and I don't want anything from the Commune now; but my old father lives there, my mother is buried there, and I like to go back to the old place sometimes. Besides, I have children, and our affairs are commercial (*nashe dyelo torgovoe*). Who knows but my children may be very glad some day to have a share of the Communal land?"

In respect to these non-agricultural occupations, each district has its specialty. The province of Yaroslaff, for instance, supplies the large towns with waiters for the Traktirs, or lower class of restaurants, whilst the best hotels in Petersburg are supplied by the Tartars of Kasimof, celebrated for their sobriety and honesty. One part of the province of Kostromá has a special reputation for producing carpenters and stove-builders, whilst another part, as I once discovered to my surprise, send yearly to Siberia—not as convicts, but as free laborers—a large contingent of tailors and workers in felt! On questioning some youngsters who were accompanying as apprentices one of these bands, I was informed by a bright-eyed youth of about sixteen that he had already made the journey twice, and intended to go every winter. "And you always bring home a big pile of money with you?" I inquired. "Nitchevo!" replied the little fellow, gayly, with an air of pride and self-confidence; "last year I brought home three roubles!" This answer was, at the moment, not at all welcome, for I had just been discussing with a Russian fellow-traveler as to whether the peasantry can fairly be called industrious, and the boy's reply enabled my antagonist to make a point against me. "You hear that!" he said, triumphantly. "A Russian peasant goes all the way to Siberia and back for three roubles! Could you get an Englishman to work at that rate?" "Perhaps not," I replied, evasively, thinking at the same time that if a youth were sent several times from Land's End to John o' Groat's House, and obliged to make the greater part of the journey in carts or on foot, he would probably expect, by way of remuneration for the time and labor expended, rather more than seven and sixpence!

Very often the peasants find industrial occupations without leaving home, for various industries which do not require complicated machinery are practiced in the villages by the peasants and their families. Textile fabrics, wooden vessels, wrought iron, pottery, leather, rush-matting, and numerous other articles are thus produced in enormous quantities. Occasionally we find not only a whole village, but even a whole district occupied almost exclusively with some one kind of manual industry. In the province of Vladimir, for example, a large group of villages live by Icon-painting; in one locality near Nizhni, nineteen villages are occupied with the manufacture of axes; round about Pavlovo, in the same province, eighty villages produce almost nothing but cutlery; and in a locality called Ouloma, on the borders of Novgorod and Tver, no less than two hundred villages live by nail-making.

These domestic industries have long existed, and have hitherto been an abundant source of revenue—providing a certain compensation for the poverty of the soil. But at present they are in a very critical position. They belong to the primitive period of economic development, and that period in Russia is now rapidly drawing to a close. Formerly the Head of a Household bought the raw material, and sold with a reasonable profit the manufactured articles at the "Bazaars," as the local fairs are called, or perhaps at the great annual *Yarmarka* of Nizhni-Novgorod. This primitive system is now rapidly becoming obsolete. Great factories on the West-European model are quickly multiplying, and it is difficult for manual labor, unassisted by machinery, to compete with them. Besides this, the periodical Bazaars and Yarmarki, at which producers and consumers transacted their affairs without mediation, are being gradually replaced by permanent stores and various classes of middle-men, who facilitate the relations between consumers and producers. In a word, capital and wholesale enterprise have come into the field, and are revolutionizing the old methods of production and trade. Many of those who formerly worked at home on their own account are now forced to enter the great factories and work for fixed weekly or monthly wages; and nearly all who still work at home now receive the raw material on credit, and deliver the manufactured articles to wholesale merchants at a stipulated price.

To the orthodox political economist this important change must afford great satisfaction. According to his theories it is a gigantic step in the right direction, and must necessarily redound to the advantage of all parties concerned. The producer now receives a regular supply of the raw material, and regularly disposes of the articles manufactured; and the time and trouble which he formerly devoted to wandering about in search of customers he can now employ more profitably in productive work. The creation of a class between the producers and consumers is an important step towards that division and specialization of labor, without which great industrial and commercial enterprises are impossible. The consumer no longer requires to go on a fixed day to some distant point, on the chance of finding there what he requires, but can always buy what he pleases in the permanent stores. Above all, the production is greatly increased in amount, and the price of manufactured goods is proportionally lessened.

All this seems clear enough in theory, and any one who values intellectual tranquillity will feel disposed to accept this view of the case without questioning its accuracy; but the unfortunate traveler, who is obliged to use his eyes as well as his logical faculties, will probably find some little difficulty in making the objective facts fit into the à priori formula. Far be it from me to question the wisdom of political economists, but I cannot refrain from remarking that of the three classes concerned—producers, middle-men, and consumers—two fail to perceive and appreciate the benefits which have been conferred upon them. The producers complain that on the new system they work more and gain less; and the consumers complain that the manufactured articles are far inferior in quality. The middle-men, who are popularly supposed to take for themselves the lion's share of the profits alone seem satisfied with the new arrangement. However this may be, one thing is certain: the great factories have not hitherto contributed to the material or moral welfare of the population among which they have been established. Nowhere is there so much disease, drunkenness, demoralization, and misery, as in the manufacturing districts.

The reader must not imagine that in making these statements I have any wish to calumniate the spirit of modern enterprise, or to advocate a return to primitive barbarism. All great changes produce a mixture of good and evil, and at first the evil is pretty sure to come prominently forward. Russia is at this moment in a state of transition, and the new condition of things is not yet properly organized. In general there is no proper accommodation for the workmen in the neighborhood of the factories, and in the smaller works no attention is paid to sanitary considerations. Thus, for instance, in the province of Novgorod there was in 1870 a lucifer-match manufactory, in which all the hands employed worked habitually in an atmosphere impregnated with the fumes of phosphorus; and the natural consequence of this was that a large number of the workers were suffering from disease of the jaw-bone and other complaints. Similar imperfections are seen in the commercial world. As very many branches of industry and commerce are still in their infancy, it often happens that some enterprising trader acquires practically a monopoly, and uses his influence in reckless fashion. Not a few industrial villages have thus fallen under the power of the *Kulaki*—literally Fists— as these monopolists are called. By advancing money the Kulak may succeed in acquiring over a group of villages a power almost as unlimited as that of the proprietor in the time of serfage.

Attempts are frequently made to break the power of the *Kulaki* by means of association. The favorite form of association is that recommended by Schulze-Delitsch, which has had so much success in Germany. What the ultimate result of this movement will be it would be hazardous to predict, but I may say that already some of these associations work remarkably well.

During all my travels in Russia, one of the objects which I constantly kept in view was the collection of materials for a History of the Emancipation of the Serfs—a great reform, which has always seemed to me one of the most interesting events of modern history. It was natural, therefore, that I should gather in this northern region as much information as possible regarding the life of the peasantry and their relation to the landed proprietors during the time of serfage; and I think that a little of this information will be not unacceptable to the reader.

In this, as in other parts of Russia, a very large portion of the land— perhaps as much as one-half—belonged to the State. The peasants living on this land had no masters, and were governed by a special branch of the Imperial Administration. In a certain sense they were serfs, for they were not allowed to change their official domicile, but practically they enjoyed a very large amount of liberty. By paying a small sum for a passport they could leave their villages for an indefinite length of time, and so long as they regularly paid their taxes and dues they were in little danger of being molested. Many of them, though officially inscribed in their native villages, lived permanently in the towns, and not a few of them succeeded in amassing large fortunes.

Of the remaining land, a considerable portion belonged to rich nobles, who rarely or never visited their estates, and left the management of them either to the serfs themselves or to a steward, who acted according to a code of instructions. On these estates the position of the serfs was very similar to that of the State peasants. They had their Communal land, which they distributed among themselves as they thought fit, and enjoyed the remainder of the arable land in return for a fixed yearly rent.

Some proprietors, however, lived on their estates and farmed on their own account, and here the condition of the serfs was somewhat different. A considerable number of these, perhaps as many as ten per cent, were, properly speaking, not serfs at all, but rather domestic slaves, who fulfilled the functions of coachmen, grooms, gardeners, gamekeepers, cooks, lackeys, and the like. Their wives and daughters acted as nurses, domestic servants, ladies maids, and seamstresses. If the master organized a private theatre or orchestra, the actors or musicians were drawn from this class. These serfs lived in the mansion or the immediate vicinity, possessed no land, except perhaps a little plot for a kitchen-garden, and were fed and clothed by the master. Their number was generally out of all proportion to the amount of work they had to perform, and consequently they were always imbued with an hereditary spirit of indolence, and performed lazily and carelessly what they had to do. On the other hand, they were often sincerely attached to the family they served, and occasionally proved by acts their fidelity and attachment. Here is an instance out of the many for which I can vouch. An old nurse, whose mistress was dangerously ill, vowed that, in the event of the patient's recovery, she would make a pilgrimage first to Kief, the Holy City on the Dnieper, and afterwards to Solovetsk, a much-revered monastery on an island in the White Sea. The patient recovered, and the old woman walked in fulfillment of her vow more than two thousand miles!

I have called this class of serfs "domestic slaves," because I cannot find any more appropriate term, but I must warn the reader that he ought not to use this phrase in presence of a Russian. On this point Russians are extremely sensitive. Serfage, they say indignantly, was something quite different from slavery; and slavery never existed in Russia!

This assertion, which I have heard scores of times from educated Russians, cannot be accepted unreservedly. The first part of it is perfectly true; the second, perfectly false. In old times slavery was a recognized institution in Russia, as in other countries. It is almost impossible to read a few pages of the old native chronicles without stumbling on references to slaves; and I distinctly remember—though I cannot at this moment give chapter and verse—that there was one Russian Prince who was so valiant and so successful in his wars, that during his reign a slave might be bought for a few coppers. How the distinction between serfs and slaves gradually disappeared, and how the latter term fell into disuse, I need not here relate; but I must assert, in the interests of truth, that the class of serfs above mentioned, though they were officially and popularly called *dvorovuiye lyudi*—that is to say, court-yard people—were to all intents and purposes domestic slaves. Down to the commencement of the present century the Russian newspapers contained advertisements of this kind—I take the examples almost at random from the *Moscow Gazette* of 1801: "TO BE SOLD, three coachmen, well-trained and handsome; and two girls, the one eighteen and the other fifteen years of age, both of them good-looking and well acquainted with various kinds of handiwork. In the same house there are for sale two hair-dressers: the one twenty-one years of age can read, write, play on a musical instrument, and act as huntsman; the other can dress ladies' and gentlemen's hair. In the same house are sold pianos and organs." A little further on, a first-rate clerk, a carver, and a lackey are offered for sale, and the reason assigned is superabundance of the articles in question (*za izlisheston*). In some instances it seems as if the serfs and the cattle were intentionally put in the same category, as in the following: "In this house one can buy a coachman, and a Dutch cow about to calve." The style of these advertisements and the frequent recurrence of the same address show plainly that there was at that time a regular class of slave-dealers.

The humane Alexander I. prohibited public advertisements of this kind, but he did not put down the custom which they represented; and his successor, Nicholas, took no active measures for its repression. Thus until the commencement of the present reign—that is to say, until about twenty years ago—the practice was continued under a more or less disguised form. Middle-aged people have often told me that in their youth they knew proprietors who habitually caused young domestic serfs to be taught trades, in order afterwards to sell them or let them out for hire. It was from such proprietors that the theaters obtained a large number of their best actors.

Very different was the position of the serfs properly so-called. They lived in villages, possessed houses and gardens of their own, tilled the Communal land for their own benefit, enjoyed a certain amount of self-government, of which I shall speak presently, and were rarely sold except as part of the estate. They might, indeed, be sold to a landed proprietor, and transferred to his estates; but such transactions rarely took place. The ordinary relations which existed between serfs and the proprietor may be best explained by one or two examples. Let us take first Ivánofka.

Though the proprietor's house was situated, as I have said, close to the village, the manor land and the Communal land had always been kept clearly separate, and might almost be said to form two independent estates. The proprietor who reigned in Ivánofka during the last years of serfage was keenly alive to his own interest, and always desirous of increasing his revenue; but he was, at the same time, a just and intelligent man, who was never guilty of extortion or cruelty. Though he had the welfare of his serfs really at heart, he rarely interfered in their domestic or Communal arrangements, because he believed that men in general, and Russian peasants in particular, are the best administrators of their own affairs. He did not, indeed, always carry out this principle to its logical consequences, for he was not by any means a thorough doctrinaire. Thus, for example, he insisted on being consulted when a Village Elder was to be elected, or any important matter decided; and when circumstances seemed to demand his interference, he usually showed the peasants that he could be dictator if he chose. These were, however, exceptional incidents. In the ordinary course of affairs he treated the Commune almost as a respected farmer or trusted steward. In return for the land which he ceded to it, and which it was free to distribute among its members as it thought fit, he demanded a certain amount of labor and dues; but he never determined what particular laborers should be sent to him, or in what way the dues should be levied.

The amount of labor-dues was determined in this way. The *tyagló*, or labor-unit, was composed of a man, a woman, and a horse; and each *tyagló* owed to the proprietor three days' labor every week. If a household contained two *tyágla*, one of them might work for the proprietor six days in the week, and thereby liberate the other from its obligation. In this way one-half of a large family could labor constantly for the household, whilst the other half fulfilled all the obligations towards the proprietor. The other dues consisted of lambs, chickens, eggs, and linen-cloth, together with a certain sum of money, which was contributed by those peasants who were allowed to go away and work in the towns.

At a short distance from Ivánofka was an estate, which had been managed in the time of serfage on entirely different principles. The proprietor was a man who had likewise the welfare of his serfs at heart, because he knew that on their welfare depended his own revenues, but he did not believe in the principle of allowing them to manage their own affairs. The Russian peasant, he was wont to say, is a child—a foolish, imprudent, indolent child, who inevitably ruins himself when not properly looked after. In accordance with this principle the proprietor sought to regulate not merely the Communal, but also the domestic concerns of his serfs. Not only did he always nominate the Village Elder and decide all matters touching the Communal welfare, but he at the same time arranged the marriages, decided who was to seek work in the towns and who was to stay at home, paid frequent visits of inspection to the peasants' houses, prohibited the heads of families from selling their grain without his permission, and exercised in various other ways a system of minute supervision. In return for all this paternal solicitude he was able to extract a wonderfully large revenue from his estate, though his fields were by no means more fertile or better cultivated than those of his neighbors. The additional revenue was derived not from the land, but from the serfs. Knowing intimately the domestic affairs of each family, he could lay on them the heaviest possible burdens without adding that last

hair which is said to break the camel's back. And many of the expedients
he employed did more credit to his ingenuity than to his moral character.
Thus, for instance, if he discovered that a family had saved a little money,
he would propose that one of the daughters should marry some one of whom
he knew, her father would certainly disapprove, or he would express his
intention of giving one of the sons as a recruit. In either case a ransom was
pretty sure to be paid in order to ward off the threatened danger.

All the proprietors who lived on their estates approached more or less
nearly to one of these two types; but here in the northern regions the latter
type was not very often met with. Partly from the prevailing absenteeism
among the landlords, and partly from the peasants' old-established habit of
wandering about the country and going to the towns in search of work,
these peasants of the north are more energetic, more intelligent, more independent, and consequently less docile and pliable than those of the fertile
central provinces. They have, too, more education. A large proportion of
them can read and write, and occasionally one meets among them men who
have a keen desire for knowledge. Several times I encountered peasants in
this region who had a small collection of books, and twice I found in such
collections, much to my astonishment, a Russian translation of Buckle's
"History of Civilization"!

How, it may be asked, did a work of this sort find its way to such a place?
If the reader will pardon a short digression, I shall explain the fact.

At the commencement of the present reign there was a curious intellectual
movement—of which I shall have more to say hereafter—among the Russian
educated classes. The movement assumed various forms, of which two of
the most prominent were a desire for encyclopædic knowledge, and an attempt to reduce all knowledge to a scientific form. For men in this state of
mind, Buckle's great work had naturally a powerful fascination. It seemed
at first sight to reduce the multifarious, conflicting facts of human history to
a few simple principles, and to evolve order out of chaos. Its success, therefore, was great. In the course of a few years no less than four independent
translations—so at least I have been informed by a good authority—were
published and sold. Every one read, or at least professed to have read, the
wonderful book, and many believed that its author was the great genius of
the present generation. During the first year of my residence in Russia, I
rarely had a serious conversation without hearing Buckle's name mentioned;
and my friends almost always assumed that he had succeeded in creating a
genuine science of history on the inductive method. In vain I pointed out
that Buckle had merely thrown out some hints in his introductory chapter
as to how such a science ought to be constructed, and that he had himself
made no serious attempt to use the method which he commended. My ob-
jections had little or no effect: the belief was too deep-rooted to be so easily

eradicated. In books, periodicals, newspapers, and professional lectures, the name of Buckle was constantly cited—often violently dragged in without the slightest reason—and the cheap translations of his work were sold in enormous quantities. It is not, then, so very wonderful after all that the book should have found its way to two villages in the province of Yaroslaff.

The enterprising, self-reliant, independent spirit which is often to be found among those peasants of the north, appears occasionally in the young generation. Often in this part of the country I have encountered boys who recalled young America rather than young Russia. One of these young hopefuls I remembered well. I was waiting at a post-station for the horses to be changed, when he appeared before me in a sheep-skin, fur cap, and gigantic double-soled boots—all of which articles had been made on a scale adapted to future rather than actual requirements. He must have stood in his boots about three feet eight inches, and he could not have been more than twelve years of age; but he had already learned to look upon life as a serious business, wore a commanding air, and knitted his innocent little brows as if the cares of an empire weighed on his diminutive shoulders. Though he was to act as Yemstchik, he had to leave the putting in of the horses to larger specimens of the human species, but he observed carefully that all was done properly. Putting one of his big boots a little in advance, and drawing himself up to his full shortness, he watched the operation attentively, as if the smallness of his stature had nothing to do with his inactivity. When all was ready, he climbed up to his seat, and at a signal from the stationkeeper, who watched with paternal pride all the movements of the little prodigy, we dashed off at a pace rarely attained by post-horses. He had the faculty of emitting a peculiar sound—something between a whirr and a whistle—that appeared to have a magical effect on the team, and every few minutes he employed this incentive. The road was rough, and at every jolt he was shot upwards into the air, but he always fell into his proper position, and never lost for a moment his self-possession or his balance. At the end of the journey I found we had made about fourteen miles within the hour.

Unfortunately, this energetic, enterprising spirit sometimes takes an illegitimate direction. Not only whole villages, but even whole districts have in this way acquired a bad reputation for robbery, the manufacture of paper-money, and similar offenses against the criminal law. In popular parlance, these localities are said to contain "people who play pranks" (*narod shalit*). I must, however, remark that, if I may judge by my own experience, these so-called "playful" tendencies are greatly exaggerated. Though I have traveled hundreds of miles at night on lonely roads, I have never been robbed or in any way molested. Once, indeed, when traveling at night in a tarantass, I discovered on awaking that my driver was bending over me, and had introduced his hand into one of my pockets; but the incident ended without serious consequences. When I caught the delinquent hand, and demanded an explanation from the owner, he replied, in an apologetic, caressing tone, that the night was cold, and he wished to warm his fingers; and when I advised him to use for that purpose his own pockets rather than mine, he promised to act in future according to my advice. More than once, it is true, I believed that I was in danger of being attacked, but on every occasion my fears turned out to be unfounded, and sometimes the catastrophe was ludicrous rather than tragical. Let the following serve as an illustration.

I had occasion to traverse, in company with a Russian friend, the country lying to the east of the river Vetluga—a land of forest and morass, with here and there a patch of cultivation. The majority of the population are Tcheremiss, a Finnish tribe; but near the banks of the river there are villages of Russian peasants, and these latter have the reputation of "playing pranks." When we were on the point of starting from Kozmodemiansk, a town on the right bank of the Volga, we received a visit from an officer of rural police, who painted in very somber colors the habits and moral character—or, more properly, immoral character—of the people whose acquaintance we were about to make. He related with excited, melodramatic gesticulation his deadly encounters and hair-breadth escapes in the villages through which we had to pass, and ended the interview with a strong recommendation to us not to travel at night, and to keep at all times our eyes open and our revolver ready. The effect of his narrative, like the effect of so many stories that appear in print, was considerably diminished by the prominence of the moral, which was to the effect that there never had been a police-officer, either in Russia or any other country, who had shown so much zeal, energy, and courage in the discharge of his duty as the worthy man before us. We considered it, however, advisable to remember his hint about keeping our eyes open.

In spite of our intention of being very cautious, it was already dark when we arrived at the village which was to be our halting-place for the night, and it seemed at first as if we should be obliged to spend the night in the open air. The inhabitants had already retired to rest, and refused to open their doors to unknown travelers. At length one woman, more hospitable than her neighbors, consented to let us pass the night in an outer apartment (*seni*), and this permission we gladly accepted. My friend, who had not forgotten the graphic descriptions of the police-officer at Kezmodemiansk, made a careful inspection of the place, and declared that the room, though densely populated, contained no bipeds but ourselves. Still, in view of a curious opening in the roof, he thought that we ought to mount a guard alternatively during the night and proposed to take the first watch. This was at once agreed to. When we had carefully fastened the windows by ingenious, extemporized contrivances, I gave him my revolver, for self-defense or for raising an alarm, as circumstances might dictate, and lay down to rest. Our precautions had not been unnecessary. First there was an attempt to open the outer door; then an attempt to open the door from the inner apartment; and, lastly, an attempt to open the door from the inner apartment; and, lastly, an attempt to open the window. All these attempts were duly frustrated, and at length I fell asleep; but shortly afterwards I was suddenly aroused by some one tightly grasping my arm. As the light had been in the meantime extinguished, I could see nothing, but I instinctively sprang up, and endeavored to close with my invisible assailant. In vain! He dexterously eluded my grasp, and I stumbled over my portmanteau, which was lying on the floor; but my prompt action revealed who the intruder was, by producing a wild flutter and a frantic cackling! Before my companion could strike a light, the mysterious attack was fully explained. The supposed midnight robber and possible assassin was simply a peaceable hen that had gone to roost on my arm, and, on finding her position unsteady, had dug her claws into what she mistook for a roosting-pole!

Though I have not yet visited the extreme north of Russia, perhaps I ought to insert here some information, which I collected from various sources, concerning the life of the peasantry in that region.

If we draw a wavy line eastward from a point a little to the north of St. Petersburg, as is shown in the map, we shall have between that line and the Polar Ocean what may be regarded as a distinct, peculiar region, differing in many respects from the rest of Russia. Throughout the whole of it the climate is very severe. For about half of the year the ground is covered by deep snow, and the rivers covered with ice. By far the greater part of the surface is occupied by forests of pine, fir, larch, and birch, or by vast, unfathomable morasses. The arable land and pasturage taken together form only about one and a half per cent of the area. The population is scarce—little more than one to the English square mile—and settled chiefly along the banks of the rivers. The peasantry support themselves by fishing, hunting, felling and floating timber, preparing tar and charcoal, cattle-breeding, and, in the extreme north, by breeding reindeer.

These are their chief occupations, but they do not entirely neglect agriculture. Their summer is short, but they make the most of it by means of a peculiar and ingenious mode of farming, which, though it may seem strange, not to say absurd, to the English farmer, is well adapted to the peculiar local conditions. The peasant knows of course nothing about agronomical chemistry, but he, as well as his forefathers, have observed that if wood be burnt on a field, and the ashes be mixed with the soil, the probable result is a good harvest. On this simple principle his system of farming is based. When spring comes round and the leaves begin to appear on the trees, a band of peasants, armed with their hatchets, proceed to some spot in the woods previously fixed upon. Here they begin to make a clearing. This is no easy matter, for tree-felling is hard and tedious work; but the process does not take so much time as might be expected, for the workmen have been brought up to the trade, and wield their axes with marvelous dexterity. Besides this, they contrive, it is said, to use fire as an assistant. When they have felled all the trees, great and small, they return to their homes, and think no more about their clearing till the autumn, when they return, in order to strip the fallen trees of their branches, to pick out what they require for building purposes or firewood, and to pile up the remainder in heaps. The logs for building or firewood are dragged away by horses as soon as the first fall of snow has made a good slippery road, but the piles are allowed to remain till the following spring, when they are stirred up with long poles and ignited. The flames first appear at several points, and then, with the help of the dry grass and chips, rapidly spread in all directions till they join together, and form a gigantic bonfire, such as is never seen in more densely-populated countries. If the fire does its work properly, the whole of the space is covered with a layer of ashes; and when these have been slightly mixed with soil by means of a light plow, the seed is sown.

On the field prepared in this original fashion is sown barley, rye, or flax; and the harvest, nearly always good, sometimes borders on the miraculous. Barley or rye may be expected to produce thirtyfold under peculiarly favorable circumstances. The fertility is, however, short-lived. If the soil is poor and stony, not more than two crops can be raised; but if it is of a better quality, it may give tolerable harvests for six or seven years. In most countries this would be an absurdly expensive way of manuring, for wood is much too valuable a commodity to be used for such a purpose; but in this northern region the forests are boundless, and in the districts where there is no river or stream by which timber may be floated, the trees not used in this way rot from old age. Under these circumstances the system is reasonable, but it must be admitted that it does not give a very large return for the amount of labor expended, and in bad seasons it gives almost no return at all.

The other sources of revenue are scarcely less precarious. With his gun and a little parcel of provisions, the peasant wanders about in the trackless forests, and too often returns after many days with a very light bag; or he starts in autumn for some distant lake, and comes back after five or six weeks with nothing better than perch and pike. Sometimes he tries his luck at deep-sea fishing. In this case he starts in February—probably on foot—for Kem, situated on the shore of the White Sea, or perhaps for the more distant Kola, situated on a small river which falls into the Arctic Ocean. There, in company with three or four others, he starts on a fishing cruise along the Murman coast, or, it may be, off the coast of Spitzbergen. His gains will depend on the amount caught, for it is a joint-venture; but in no case can they be very great, for three-fourths of the fish brought into port belong to the owner of the craft and tackle. Of the sum realized, he brings home perhaps only a small part, for he has a strong temptation to buy rum, tea, and other luxuries, which are very dear in those northern latitudes. If the fishing is good and he resists temptation, he may save as much as 100 roubles—about £ 12—and thereby live comfortably all winter; but if the fishing season is bad, he may find himself at the end of it not only with empty pockets, but in debt to the owner of the boat. This debt he may pay off, if he has a horse, by transporting the dried fish to Kargopol, St. Petersburg, or some other market.

CHAPTER 7

The Crisis of the Old Order

THE AGRICULTURAL QUESTION

The emancipation of the peasants offered the Tsarist regime the opportunity to find new support in Russian society. Eventually Stolypin was in fact to place his "wager" on the "strong," on the independent land holder. But once social change was introduced into Russia, there was no time to tarry. Russia became the object of a race between social reform and social revolution. The problems of Russia's economic and political development were summarized by the noted Russian historian Paul Miliukov in a series of lectures which he delivered at the University of Chicago in 1903.

We now know what the social forces are, and the political schemes and theories, that condition the coming reform in Russia. Some of these social forces—namely, those of the higher social strata—we have seen to be too weak to force reforms upon the government through their social influence. The other forces—namely, those inherent in the lower social strata—we have found to be as yet too little organized. Therefore, should any reform commend itself by virtue of its intrinsic usefulness and urgency, there would be imminent danger of its being indefinitely postponed—as has actually been the case up to the present time. The chances for the immediate realization of reform being too small, it was only natural for us to find the very schemes for reform unsuited for such immediate realization, either because they were not definite enough for practical purposes—which was generally the case with the liberal programs—or because they were too definite; i.e., abstract and extreme. Of course, this would be changed at once, if some impelling force could be found to bring the lethargic social elements and the torpid political schemes into action. It now remains for us to investigate whether some such force really exists; and, if it does, to weigh its possible consequences.

Source: P. N. Miliukov, *Russia and its Crisis* (Chicago, 1905), 433–71.

There are two chief agencies which will make political action effective—the growth of material want and the growth of political disaffection; and these will render reform unavoidable. Material want, growing more and more acute, finally takes the shape of a general crisis—agricultural, industrial, and financial. Political disaffection, becoming permanent, forms an atmosphere of social unrest which finds expression in individual or combined violent action. A political condition which has not only proved to be powerless against the crisis and the social unrest, but which has even notoriously contributed to the former and fostered the latter, has by this shown itself to be incompatible with the gratification of the most elementary social needs. This order of things is thenceforth doomed. And it writes its own sentence when, in the very midst of a crisis and a state of social unrest, it is driven, by no one's fault but its own, into an unsuccessful war.

These agencies, not unmentioned in our previous exposition, must now be studied more closely. What is the Russian crisis? And what is the Russian social unrest? An attempt to elucidate these questions is not an act of indiscretion toward my countrymen. The crisis is now being chirped about even by the sparrows on the roofs, and is being studied by government committees and discussed in hundreds of publications. The social unrest cannot be too strongly emphasized before an audience that enjoys the privilege of being well informed by a free press, and of thus knowing much more about it than many an average citizen of my own country can ever hope to know. Unhappily, it is not from knowing too much, but from knowing too little, that we suffer in Russia: and the danger is not for those who know that a position is untenable, but for those who hesitate to surrender an untenable position in time to prevent their own destruction.

. . . .

The situation was rendered particularly acute by the increased rapidity of this transition from the agricultural to the industrial stage. The causes of this increased rapidity of transition from the so-called "domestic economy" or "natural" stage to that of "exchange economy" in Russia are many, and they are pretty complicated. The most important causes are the demands of the rapidly growing state, and the situation of Russia among the economically more developed nations with which she has had to compete in the international market.

Briefly stated, the agrarian crisis in Russia is the necessary consequence of two agents: the elementary state of public economy, and the increased strain exerted on it by the demands of the state and by the changed conditions of life. As a result, private expenditures have greatly increased, while private incomes have remained the same as before, or have even diminished, owing to the exhaustion of the natural resources, the increase of population, the condition of the foreign market, etc. Hence the balance between revenue and expense has been quite disturbed. This is the crisis reduced to its simplest terms. Let us proceed to a more detailed explanation.

Prior to the emancipation of the peasants, forty years ago, economic life in Russia still preserved its medieval character. It was based on home production for home consumption—at least so far as peasant life was concerned. The outlay for food, lodging, clothing, fuel, and light—in short, for all the chief items of the family budget—was practically naught. A man paid nothing for his own hovel; he fed on the products of his own field and garden; he was amply supplied with homespun clothing made of the wool of his own sheep and of the fiber of his own flax; he did not spare the wood to keep hot the old-fashioned, enormous oven which filled a quarter of the house, and which during the long winter months turned it into a bathhouse; nor did he spare his eyes, for he lit the interior of the hut with thin chips constantly renewed in a stand of prehistoric shape, during the long winter evenings while the women spun threads on their distaffs and spindles. Now, however, all this has changed. Wooden chips have given way to a kerosene "smoker"; homespun linen has been superseded by calicoes, while woolen stuffs have disappeared without a substitute; fuel has become very scarce and expensive. Food—which consists of vegetable products alone—is insufficiently supplied; too often it has to be bought by the grain-producers themselves; in fact, so often that the question has seriously been raised, and has been answered in the affirmative by a body of learned economists, whether it is not better for the Russian producers to have low grain prices.

Why have the conditions of life thus changed? In Russia you may sometimes hear the explanation, on the part of the former landlords, that it is because the Russian peasant has become lazy; that he is now a spendthrift, since nobody is there to take care of him. This is adduced as a reason why the peasant prefers the factory products to those of his own making. The fact is that the peasant now is too poor to utilize his and his family's work for himself; and, at the same time, he has no more raw material for his home industry. He can no longer have his clothes prepared by the women of his own family, because he has no more wool or linen to spare. His new expenses for the factory calico are certainly not inspired by any taste for fancy articles, but by mere necessity; and his purchases are generally cheap and of inferior quality. He can hardly be accused of lavishness on the ground that he has to buy some food in the market, since the fact is that on an average his yearly consumption is still below the necessary minimum. He gets only about twenty-three to twenty-six Russian *poods* [a *pood* equals thirty-six pounds] of grain, and sometimes even as little as fifteen, while the soldiers are entitled to not less than twenty-nine *poods*. Moreover, the Russian peasant does not eat wheat, which he produces for sale only, but rye or, more frequently, potatoes. While the production of grain in general is now only

88 per cent. of what it was forty years ago, the potato crop is more than three times as large. Thus, his buying of grain in the market only shows that the Russian peasant is obliged to sell the better sorts to cover other necessary expenses; or that he is compelled to sell at one time in order to buy at another (and this at a loss, as we shall soon see); or that upon his holdings he is unable to produce even the necessary minimum of food. To be sure, he will not be found buying meat, because on the average he eats meat only four times a year. If he still finds money to buy alcohol—the famous vodka—it is not because he is a drunkard, but because vodka is considered by the Russian to be as necessary for social entertainment as soda and whisky in the American clubs. And yet the consumption of alcohol is lower in Russia than in any other civilized country, and, as we have seen, is still decreasing.

Thus, such purchases in the market as we have enumerated are absolutely compulsory. The increase in the peasant's cash expenditure for food, clothing, light, etc., does not at all signify any rise in his standard of life or any enhancement of his material well-being; on the contrary, it is a symptom of the deterioration of his condition. This will become still more evident upon a closer examination of that most important item of the peasant's expenditure, the one which conditions all others; namely, his payment of taxes.

If the Russian peasant has no time to work for himself; if he is fatally underfed and underclothed; if he needs money badly, it is, first and foremost, because he is compelled to perform his functions as a taxpayer. He does his best to pay his taxes; and if, in spite of all his exertions, he accumulates arrears upon arrears, it is not because he will not, but because he cannot, pay. In the decade 1883–92, while the population increased 16 per cent., taxation increased 29 per cent.; i.e., nearly twice as much; and in the following decade, 1893–1902, while the growth of the exhausted population still further fell off, the increase being only 13 per cent., taxation took an unheard-of upward leap, showing an increase of 49 per cent., or nearly four times as much. No wonder then that, while in 1871–80 every *dessyatin* (2.7 acres) of the land owned by the peasant owed to the state 19 cents in arrears, in 1881–90 this debt had increased to 24 cents, and in 1891–1900 to 54 cents. We must add that ordinarily the authorities collect the taxes by compulsory sales before allowing the arrears to accumulate. Thus the peasantry is reduced to a state of chronic insolvency, and finally grows quite apathetic.

*   *   *   *   *

The unsatisfactory state of rural economy was acknowledged as early as 1873, by a government commission. Ten years later, at the initiative of a liberal minister of finance, Mr. Bunge, an attempt was made to alleviate the burden of direct taxation. First of all, the heavy redemption tax (for land bought from the landlords by the peasants, with the pecuniary help of the state) was somewhat reduced; the northern half of Russia profited most by the reform. Then the antiquated capitation tax, introduced by Peter the Great, was abolished. The general decrease of the direct taxation from 1882 to 1885, caused by these reforms of Mr. Bunge, was about 50 millions, or from 150 to 100 millions. Thus, at present the amount of direct taxes forms only two-thirds of what it was before Mr. Bunge's reform. But under Mr. Bunge's successor, Mr. Vishnegradski, the policy of the government was abruptly reversed. To meet the deficit in the budget, a large increase in indirect taxation was resorted to, which took back from the peasantry more than had just been granted them. The excises and customs paid into the treasury (1885–95) a valuable yearly addition of 309.8 millions; i.e., six times as much as had been taken from it by Mr. Bunge's reform. The successor of Mr. Vishnegradski, Mr. Witte, went still farther. He not only retained and enlarged the system of indirect taxes, which he found to be paid "voluntarily" and "fairly to correspond to the paying powers" of the population, but he made it his leading maxim "not only to satisfy the current demands of the state out of the yearly income, but to collect a certain free surplus." Mr. Witte indeed succeeded in collecting as "free surplus" more than one billion rubles in eight years (1893–1900), which he brilliantly spent in the protection of the large industries and the introduction of the gold standard, while at the same time he was obliged to feed the starving rural population and to deal with the enormously increasing arrears. For the first purpose 275 millions have been spent by the treasury, and 314 millions more were lost through the remission of unpaid arrears. The population, though unable to pay direct taxes, still contributed to the treasury by buying liquors, tea, sugar, matches, kerosene, and the products of the protected industries: iron, cotton manufactures, etc. The real, the financial, crisis was to begin only when that buying power was exhausted and the Russian peasants had to curtail their expenses. Unhappily, this is now the case.

. . . .

All the foregoing leads to one unavoidable conclusion: that the necessity of buying and spending has greatly increased, while at the same time the prices of products and the rates of taxes have likewise risen enormously. Thus a large portion of the peasant's expenses has to be met with money. On the other hand, we know that he is short of money and cannot meet this increased demand. But we cannot realize how great his distress is until we inquire into the sources of his income, as we have already done in the case of his expenditures.

The chief, if not the only, product which can be raised and sold is grain; and thus we return to the condition of Russian agriculture. We shall soon see that, while the expenditure has increased, this basis of the peasant's income has materially weakened. The only question is as to what extent agriculture and the sale of grain constitute the sole basis of the peasant's budget. And this question, as we have already seen, is differently answered in the case of northern and southern Russia.

In the northern half of Russia the peasant long ago learned how to derive from additional sources what his unfruitful soil refused to yield him. As early as the eighteenth century, and even earlier, he began to find subsidiary employment in transportation, in the building and home industries, or in petty trade. Thus, before the emancipation, a Russian peasant from the middle Volga out of every dollar earned did not receive more than 12.37 cents from husbandry. For the remaining 87.63 cents he had to depend on subsidiary industries. That is why, after the liberation, he did not find himself entirely lost under the new conditions of life, but, in spite of the enormously increased demand for money, still found means to cover his expenses.

With the peasant of the southern half of Russia it turned out quite differently. He did not know so well how to earn money and relied entirely on tilling the land, which was much more fertile here, in the "black-soil" region, than in the northern country of clay and sand. His landlord, even in olden times, did not permit him to go to town or abroad in search of employment. As a rule, he kept him upon the manor, not even giving him any allotment for private tilling, as was the general practice in northern Russia. Thus the peasant was obliged to pay his lord in kind, by manual labor, much more than he might have had to pay in specie.

Now, when the hour struck for liberation, the northern landlord was ready to sell to his peasant as much of his unproductive soil as the latter might desire, provided that the peasant redeemed himself by paying for his holding more than the soil was worth. At the same time, the southern landlord withheld from his field laborers as much black-soil land as he could, doling out to him as small a lot as possible, for which, however, the peasant had to pay a very high price. Thus poorly equipped, the southern peasant went out to meet the new era. The demands on him were the same as on his northern brother. He had to get money—as much as he could—since there was no landlord to pay his taxes. But, unlike his northern brother, he had nothing to sell besides his grain. And the conditions for producing and selling grain had grown decidedly worse.

In the first place, the per capita area on which grain may be sown had greatly diminished throughout Russia. The average peasant allotment in 1860 was 6.21 acres, while forty years later, owing to the increase of population, it was only 3.51 acres. Yet even this amount would not have been entirely insufficient, if an intensive system of agriculture could have been resorted to. But with the three-field system in use—one-third of the arable land always lying fallow, while the other two-thirds are badly tilled and worse manured—the productivity of this small lot is not, on the average, sufficient to yield enough food for the laborer and his horse. The average crop is 16.6 *poods* of grain per inhabitant, while not less than 20 *poods* are necessary to feed him; and the average yield of oats is 23.6 *poods* per horse, while not less than 40 *poods* are needed. The returns are thus 17 and 41 per cent., respectively, less than they should be in order that men and animals may not be underfed, let alone the possibility of sale and export. At the same time, on this small lot, under the system of tillage in vogue, the working power of man and horse cannot be used to its full extent. Every laborer can till about 39 acres, yet he actually does till only 8—i.e., nearly five times less; and thus 79 per cent. of his working capacity remains unemployed upon his plot of land. A horse can till 10–11 acres; yet its labor is generally employed on an area one-third of that.

The insufficiency of food is thus in a strange way associated with an abundance of working power. To find additional food and to spend additional work in producing it, two methods are possible: either to increase the productivity of the given plot, or to increase the plot itself. But the productivity of the soil cannot be increased without new investment of capital, if even we admit, what many writers do not grant, that such increase is possible at all on lands in communal ownership and in precarious possession of the single cultivator. Now the peasant in distress does not possess any capital, and rural credit for improving land does not exist in Russia. The other, and, under existing conditions, the only possible, method, is to buy or rent additional plots of land. This has always been the most ardent desire of the peasants, and a real struggle for buying or renting land has been going on during the whole period under consideration.

*   *   *   *   *

The face is that the production of grain for export is on the verge of becoming unprofitable in Russia, as it cannot stand foreign competition, first, because the productivity of the soil under the given conditions of tillage is too small, and, secondly, because the prices of grain have fallen too low to cover the expense of production, and particularly the cost of transportation, which in Russia is very badly organized.

*   *   *   *   *

For a better understanding of this question, we must pass to the consideration of another side of the crisis; the crisis in the industries which are more especially protected by the government, and which now follow agriculture in the general collapse.

We have seen that the protection of industries proved one of the most important causes of the agricultural crisis, since it considerably increased the prices of commodities without creating a corresponding increase in the purchasing power of the customers. So long as this purchasing power was thought to be practically unlimited, the Russian government was always on the side of protection, in order to secure for itself a favorable balance and large custom revenues. Of course, the theoretical argument—of "developing the productive forces" and "organizing production upon a national basis"—has never been wanting. As a result, many branches of industry have been fostered which were unable to exist—or to thrive—without artificial help from the state. Claims for the protection of manufactures have been very strongly supported by the influential circles, and protectionist legislation has gone on increasing since time immemorial. It began with the foundation of Russian factories by Peter the Great, and, with the two temporary interruptions of 1819 and 1857 (the "free trade" tariffs having been immediately repealed), it reached the present phase of enforced protection beginning with the "gold customs" of 1876 and culminating in the prohibitive tariff of 1891. The following figures . . . indicate . . . the average yearly increase of manufactures:

1878–87	26.1 millions of rubles,
1888–92	41.6
1893–97	161.2

Thus it is under the administration of Mr. Witte that the development of Russian industry has reached its climax. The mighty leap to the last figure of 161 millions—four times as much as the average yearly increase of the preceding decade—could not have been performed by the efforts of the Russian capitalists alone. To achieve that, Mr. Witte had recourse to foreign capital . . .

Some people may have cherished the hope that foreign capital would introduce with it the European regime of competition, thus lowering the prices of commodities for the benefit of the Russian customer, and by and by accustoming the Russian capitalist to be satisfied with smaller profits. But foreign capital was attracted to Russia by the opposite hope of profiting by the existing high rates, and it adapted itself admirably to the Russian conditions of production protected by prohibitive customs. The Russian customer, who was already paying a tariff on imported merchandise . . . had also to pay all the dividends of the new enterprises. For instance, the cost of cotton manufactures amounted to about 123 million rubles yearly over and above what they would have cost without protection; that is, an increase of 28.5 per cent. In another branch of manufacture which particularly attracted foreign capital, the metal industry, the output was intended to cover the direct orders of the government. Here the dividends were not less than 40 per cent. To support the new enterprises in that branch, government railways were built on a large scale. The population again had to pay—this time in the form of increased taxes. The minister of finance then argued that "one must not be hindered by a temporary strain on the paying power of the population, which would be amply rewarded by the respective accretion of means for the further increase and development of this very power." The phrase may sound well in a handbook of political economy; unfortunately, it was used in a report to the Tsar, and it served to cover the fiasco of the whole system—which had become too evident, even to the naked eye.

Just then, at the close of the nineties, the "paying" and the "purchasing" power of the population proved to be so exhausted that the protected industries themselves began sorely to feel the consequences. The crisis had come; industry had to face (relative) over-production. Even government orders for rails and rolling-stock could not be secured indefinitely. . . .

Under these conditions, the government found it difficult to support, on the former large scale, metallurgic enterprises started under its auspices. The comptroller-general, in his confidential report to the Tsar for the year 1902, stated that, besides facilitating the conditions of loan and discount to meet the crisis, the National Bank had been obliged to advance funds to support the metal industries, though by its statutes it was not permitted to do so. . . .

In countries enjoying a higher degree of industrial development the device would have been to look for foreign markets. But this is not possible for the Russian manufacturers, for the reasons noted above. Russian industry is conditioned by that regime of protection which brought it into existence. With its high cost of production, its still higher profits, and an inferior organization of the whole mechanism of exchange it cannot bear competition, and thrives only behind "closed doors." No commercial conquests have been possible for it—except some neighboring markets in central Asia, where Russian trade has been at home for two centuries.

The "foreign market" thus afforded no outlet for Russian industry in times of crisis. In the end, the idea of mastering their home market must dawn upon the Russian manufacturers, since protection alone has proved insufficient to secure for them the domestic customer. Up to this moment the interests of agriculture and industry have been supposed to be antagonistic. Now that the purchasing power of the Russian customer has been exhausted, the mutual interdependence of the two has for the first time become clear. The question of expanding the home market by other means than a constant increase of the prices of commodities forces itself upon our attention.

*   *   *   *   *

The gold standard was definitely introduced in 1895. While introducing it, the ministry of finance scarcely foresaw the many exertions and sacrifices required to keep the machinery of the new currency in perfect operation. It was not sufficient to hoard up an enormous mass of gold in the treasury. It proved necessary constantly to be on guard lest the country be drained of the much-coveted metal. Keeping up the gold reserve became thenceforth the chief object of financial solicitude; all other aims were made subservient to it; and the administration thus became slave to its own reform.

The task was by no means easy. With a favorable balance of foreign payments a gold reserve is easily kept up; but this condition has never existed in Russia. It is true that our balance of trade, owing to the prohibitive duties, is generally in our favor; i.e., the exports exceed the imports. But even this surplus has become noticeably smaller during the last decade—just after the prohibitive tariff of 1891. It seems, indeed, that protection has already done what it could, and that no further increase of duties can diminish the demand for foreign merchandise. Thus, in the five years following the introduction of the new currency the average surplus of exports was no more than $48,000,000. This could by no means cover the Russian expenses abroad. Twice this amount of gold, or about $93,000,000, is wanted merely to pay the interest upon foreign loans. And then the annual expenses of Russian tourists reach $30,000,000 as a minimum. Some $10,000,000, at least, must be paid to the foreign investors. The expenses of the government abroad cannot be less than $8,000,000. These items—though certainly attenuated—raise the excess of Russian expenses abroad beyond the profits from foreign imports to the considerable sum of $93,000,000 a year. To pay this balance out of the gold reserve of the treasury would be impossible without compromising the currency. The only sound means would be to increase the exports. But that would mean protection for agriculture, which alone does the exporting. Any other remedies would be mere palliatives, or worse: they would be very much like wasting funds to pay interest—temporary stop-gaps inefficient in the long run.

The government first tried to attract foreign gold by inviting investments; and it was successful, as we have seen; but only for a short time, and only by offering exceptionally good terms and securing high dividends to the investors. That this meant increased taxation has already been pointed out. Increased taxation, however, had its limit. This limit was reached, when any further increase proved impossible. Even if taxation should have proved more efficient than it actually did, it would have been unable to procure gold; and it was gold that was wanted. The only means available for getting gold was to contract foreign loans, and to sell Russian bonds and securities abroad. The government was obliged to resort to these means, if for no other reason than to clear the balance. But this was moving in a circle, since every new loan, by inflating the public debt and the interest to be paid on it—in gold—increased the balance to be cleared. The Russian public debt has already reached the unheard-of figure of more than three billions, with an interest of more than a hundred and twenty-five million dollars. Our budget in the ten years 1893–1903 has doubled (from $500,000,000 to $1,000,000,000).

Taxation has doubled, too, with the result that, after having eaten up the net profit of the population, it is eating into the very core of its subsistence. The question has naturally arisen: Where is this going to end?

MINORITY PROBLEMS

One major factor blocking the realization of liberal hopes in Russia was the nationalities question. Could the minority nationalities, if given the vote, be trusted to respect Russia's unity? We have already noted the role of the Polish rising of 1863 in Russian thought. Miliukov in 1924 addressed himself to this question in a way which demonstrated the liberals' distrust of the exuberance and the direction of the various national movements in Russia.

Not so long ago it was possible to compare Russia with an ethnographic museum, in which the remains of nationalities, numbering about 100, were being conserved, were dying out and finally were being assimilated, as part of a historic process on the east-European plain. Now it is rather necessary to speak of a sociological laboratory in which mass and systematic tests, with experimental methods, are being carried out in the vivification, rebirth and awakening of national consciousness even among nationalities which have died out, not to speak of those among whom there developed a proper internal process of the realization of nationality.

. . .[Our] relationship [to these nationalities] is positive insofar as we generally act positively toward the healthy sides of the development of national feeling and consciousness. This relationship can be negative when we here or there speak about the negative sides of "nationalism." It is impossible to act positively or negatively to a spontaneous process (the "creation" of nationalities); one can only look at this objectively. But an ambiguous attitude is unavoidable to a voluntaristic process, as we know the process of the "realization" of nationalities. That same factor which constitutes the strength of this voluntaristic process, constitutes also its negative side, namely the hypertrophy of national feeling, expressing itself in a number of deviations and dissemination of a national consciousness from above, from the upper intellectual stratum, which also gives the material for imitation to the lower classes. In a great number of cases the hypertrophy of national feeling can be inutile, and even harmful for that very nationality which suffers from this illness. Some examples:

Source: P. N. Miliukov, *Natsional'nyi vopros* (Prague, 1924), 150–56.

1. When national feeling is born in an effort for conquests in foreign policy. This is usually the case with so called "ruling" nationalities. But now we know also a number of cases when an "oppressed" nationality, suddenly transformed into a triumphant one, either by its own doing or by a confluence of external circumstances, quickly begins itself the presecution of other nationalities which fall into dependence on it, and it does this in the name of a new "great power" national ideal.

2. When national feeling adheres to forms of the past, and, ignoring the conditions in which this past developed and existed, makes of the past an ideal for the present and the future, posing thereby an obstacle to a free creative process.

3. When a feeling of national pride or national injury pushes aside other feelings and necessities of contemporary normal man: namely, (a) when nationalism posits itself before the state and begins a struggle against the government; (b) when nationalism ignores the social side of life and sacrifices the material interests of the national masses; (c) when nationalism ignores the higher interests of moral life and creativity (in religion, art, science, etc.), which are beyond the bounds of the interests of a given nationality and comprise the general cultural heritage of mankind, etc.

All these negative aspects of the process of national self-consciousness we designate under the general term "nationalism," and it should make no difference whether this refers to this or that side of the frontier, to "ruling" or to "oppressed" nationalities. We must likewise recognize the positive sides of national self-consciousness, whether they are our own or beside us.

In speaking about the various degrees of national consciousness of the hundreds of peoples inhabiting the territory of the former Russian Empire, we must first of all differentiate the different categories of these peoples.

1. A significant part of them took part in the very process of the formation of the Russian nationality, in its different variations, the result of the process of many centuries of the settling of this nationality on the territory of the eastern plain. . . . A complicated anthropological amalgam was formed on the basis of which arose a unity of a social-psychological type, called national. We determined above the chronology of this process. The stage of the "creation of the nationality" came in the 7th to 11th centuries A.D., and the stage of primary "consciousness" in the 12th to 15th centuries. The amalgamation with other national types (themselves still not having reached their "consciousness") continued, apparently, almost to the end of these two periods. In the Russian north and in the basin of the Volga and Oka this process stopped, it seems, between the end of the 14th and the middle of the 16th centuries. Studying a contemporary ethnographic map of north central and eastern Russia, we find non-Russian nationalities in those very places where Russian colonization stopped in the 14th to 16th centuries. Thereafter the

assimilation process went much more slowly in the lower regions of the Oka and Volga and along the Siberian rivers to the Pacific Ocean. Directly south, in the southern steppes, Russian colonization proceeded from the middle of the 16th century without mixing with anyone, for here was a wilderness, abandoned by nomads and inherited by the higher Muscovite culture. . . .

2. The second category is made up of nationalities unassimilated by the Russian type but themselves not as yet come to the stage of national "consciousness," when the Russian government, in its rapid growth, included them as an "enclave" in its territory and thus, involuntarily, actually drew them into the Russian historical process of the last three or four centuries. The coexistence of these nationalities with the "ruling" one was peaceful and their national inventory remained in a passive state up to the time when nationalism, having awoken in other regions, brought here its seeds and called to life, even among the weak nationalities, its own however small and weak, intelligentsia (teachers, clergy, bureaucrats and university students). . . .

3. Somewhat different is the case of the third category of nationalities, which entered into Russia relatively recently, in the 18th and 19th centuries, for the most part on the western frontier and in the Caucasus. In part we find here relatively unselfconscious nationalities, whose process of "consciousness" begins after their incorporation into Russia. But here we have also old national cultures (Polish) or even very ancient ones now temporarily slumbering (Georgian and Armenian). A general characteristic of this category of nationalities is that the awakening of their national consciousness is independent of the Russian. In the case of Poland this is not so much an awakening—since in Poland national consciousness had not fallen asleep—as a reinforcement of national consciousness, and it took place in contradiction to and struggle with the Russian national-voluntaristic process. The fact is that Polish nationalism competed with Russian on a broad strip of border territories inhabited by Belorussians and Ukranians. This was a struggle of two centers of imitation and since the 17th century it has taken very violent forms which continue to the present day. The return of Russian territories as a result of the partitions of Poland in Catherine II's time was one of the stages of this struggle. Russia then received no Polish population; Polish territory was taken under Alexander I in 1815, as a result of the Congress of Vienna, and in 1917 it was returned by the Provisional Government which proclaimed the independence of Poland, made up of three parts. A second stage, a contrary one, again sharpening the conflict, was the transfer to Poland, by the Riga peace of 1921, of Russian lands with a population of 3½ million.

In all other cases the Russian government itself, naturally not out of high-minded considerations but rather for reasons of state, supported the national consciousness of a given group of nationalities. The goal of this support was to posit the beginnings of a local national culture against the influence of a second neighboring culture, stronger and inimical to Russia. Here it is necessary to note that this stronger culture, as everywhere, had first conquered and subordinated to its own influence the social elite of the given nationality. Russian governmental support was given to the lower social classes, taking the form of Russia's participation in the local social struggle on the side of the democratic elements. Thus, in Finland, where Swedish culture ruled, comprising a privilege of the upper social stratum, an effort at liberation from Swedish domination was made already in the 18th century with the aid of Russia. And after the annexation of Finland in 1809, which took the form of a voluntary agreement, a Finnish literary language was developed with Russian participation. A Finnish intelligentsia appeared, and a consciousness of Finnish nationality developed. Traces of the old sympathies of Finnish agricultural population for Russian authority long remained in the views of the "Old Finn" party, formerly very numerous. In the Baltic Provinces, Russian authority also stood on the side of the exploited peasantry—the Ests and the Letts—against the dominant class of German "barons" (landlords). And these nationalities to a definite degree were indebted to Russian official protection for the beginnings of their new national culture, literature and intelligentsia. The Lithuanians, in the history of their rebirth, also cannot avoid one factor: the liberation by Russian authority of the peasants from the Poland landlords. When the Poles organized their risings of 1830 and 1863 against Russian authority in the territories annexed by Russia after the partitions of Poland, they learned that the peasant population of these lands—Lithuanian, Belorussian and Ukrainian—joined the Russian forces and turned their resentments against the Polish landlords.

Going on to the Caucasus, we find here too the traces of positive influence of Russian rule on local national development. Above all, only this governmental authority could bring peace between three nationalities standing at different degrees of existence and constantly fighting among themselves: the semi-industrialized Georgians, the agricultural Armenians and the semi-nomadic Tatars. Russian authority brought a certain well-being and material development to these lands. We find under Russian rule a tremendous growth of production—grain, oil, wine, tobacco, tea, cotton, manganese. In 45 years, 1868–1913, export and import grew 50 times, the population of the cities grew in Tiflis from 64,000 to 350,000, in Baku from 12 to 250,000, in Kutais from 8 to 58,000, in Erivan from 14 to 29,000, etc. On the soil of this well-being arose national feeling among these ancient tribes and a new flowering of national literature was achieved. In particular among the Georgians, since the time of cultural-national flowering in the 13th century, in a condition of tribal separation and rivalry, national unity came about only under Russian rule. . . . Only in the last quarter of the 19th century did the idea of national unity appear among the Georgians and a new literature develop. Earlier, the noble upper layers of Georgian society underwent an unconscious denationalization. Among the Armenians, the impetus to national unification was given by the annexation of Echmiadzin in 1929. Since their nobility had been swept away and replaced by the Tatars and their clergy was weak, the national ideal here was from its very beginning worldly and democratic: its sources were the ideals of "young Germany," brought from Derpt University, and also the French literature carried over by the Turkish Armenians.

THE TERRORISTS

There were also those in Russia who put no trust in the hope of peaceful evolution. Revolution offered the only solution. The revolutionaries, however, long lacked unity and purpose. The fate of the movement "to the people," in 1876–77, illustrates their problems.

The years 1876 and 1877 were the darkest and most mournful for the Russian Socialists. The propagandist movement cost immense sacrifices. An entire generation was mown down by Despotism in a fit of delirious fear. The prisons were crammed with propagandists. New prisons were built. And the result of so much sacrifice? Oh, how petty it was compared with the immense effort!

What could the few working men and peasants do who were inflamed by Socialist ideas? What could the "colonies" do, dispersed here and there?

The past was sad; the future, gloomy and obscure. But the movement could not stop. The public mind, overstimulated and eager to act, only sought some other means of attaining the same end.

But to find one was very difficult under the conditions in which Russia was placed. Long and arduous was this work; many were its victims; for it was like endeavouring to issue from some gloomy cavern, full of dangers and pitfalls, in which every step costs many lives, and the cries of fallen brethren are the sole indications for the survivors, of the path to be followed.

The propagandist movement was a sublime test of the power of Words. By a natural reaction the opposite course was now to be tried, that of Acts.

"We did not succeed because we were mere talkers, incapable of real work." Such was the bitter reproach of the survivors of the great movement, con-

Source: Stepniak (S. Kravchinskii), *Underground Russia* (New York, 1883), 30–42.

fronted with the new revolutionary generation which had arisen to occupy the place of the preceding; and the cry of "Let us act" became as general as that of "among the people" had been a few years before.

But what kind of action was to be taken?

Impelled by their generous desire to do everything for the people, and for the people only, the Revolutionists endeavoured, above all things, to organise some insurrectionary movement among the people. The first societies of the so-called "buntari" (fanatics) of Kieff, Odessa, and Karkoff, the fixed object of which was an immediate rising, date from the year 1875. But a revolution, like a popular movement, is of spontaneous growth, and cannot be forced. One attempt alone—that of Stefanovic—very skillfully based upon local agitation and aspirations, succeeded in making some few steps, at least, towards the object. The others had not even this success. They were discovered and dissolved before giving effect to their sanguinary projects. In the towns the same tendency manifested itself in another form; the Revolutionists made their first essays in street demonstrations.

The years 1876, 1877, and the early months of 1878, were periods of "demonstrations" more or less energetic; such as the funeral of Cernisceff and Padlevsky, the demonstration of Kazan, which had such a tragical ending, and, finally, that of Odessa, on the day of the condemnation of Kovalsky, which was a veritable battle, with dead and wounded on both sides, and several hundred arrests.

It was evident that by this path there could be no advance. The disproportion between the material forces at the disposition of the revolutionary party and those of the Government was too great for these demonstrations to be other than voluntary sacrifices of the flower of the Russian youth to the Imperial Moloch. With us a revolution, or even a rising of any importance, like those in Paris, is absolutely impossible. Our towns constitute only a tenth of the entire population; and most of them are only large villages, miles and miles apart. The real towns, those for instance of 10,000 or 15,000 inhabitants, form only four or five per cent. of the entire population, that is about three or four millions in all. And the Government, which has under its orders the military contingent of the entire population, that is 1,200,000 soldiers, can transform the five or six principal towns, the only places where any movement whatever is possible, into veritable military camps, as indeed they are.

This is a consideration which should always be borne in mind, in order to understand the cause of everything that has since happened.

Demonstrations of every kind were abandoned, and from the year 1878 entirely disappeared.

But a noteworthy change in the revolutionary type dates from this period. The Revolutionist was no longer what he had been five years before. He had not yet revealed himself by any daring acts; but by dint of constantly meditating upon them, by repeating that bullets were better than words, by nourishing sanguinary projects in his mind, something of their spirit entered into his disposition. Thus the man was formed. And the Government did everything it could to develop still more these nascent tendencies of his and force him to translate them into acts.

The merest suspicion led to arrest. An address; a letter from a friend who had gone "among the people;" a word let fall by a lad of twelve who, from excess of fear, knew not what to reply, were sufficient to cast the suspected person into prison, where he languished for years and years, subjected to all the rigour of the Russian cellular system. To give an idea of this it need only be mentioned that, in the course of the investigations in the trial of the 193, which lasted four years, the number of the prisoners who committed suicide, or went mad, or died, reached 75.

The sentences of the exceptional tribunal, which was simply a docile instrument in the hands of the Government, were of an incredible cruelty. Ten, twelve, fifteen years of hard labour were inflicted, for two or three speeches, made in private to a handful of working men, or for a single book read or lent. Thus what is freely done in every country in Europe was punished among us like murder.

But not satisfied with these judicial atrocities, the Government, by infamous secret orders, augmented still more the sufferings of the political prisoners, so that in the House of Horrors—the central prison of Karkoff—several 'revolts' took place among them in order to obtain equality of treatment with those condemned for common crimes. Such was their condition! And from time to time, by ways which only prisoners know how to find out, there came from these men buried alive some letter, written on a scrap of paper in which tobacco or a candle had been wrapped up, describing the infamous treatment, the vile and useless cruelty, which their gaolers had inflicted upon them, in order to curry favour with superiors; and these letters passed from hand to hand, and this information passed from mouth to mouth, causing tears of grief and rage, and arousing in the most gentle and tender minds thoughts of blood, of hatred, and of vengeance.

The first sanguinary events took place a year before the Terrorism was erected into a system. They were isolated cases, without any political importance, but they clearly showed that the effects of the Government had begun to bear fruit, and that the 'milk of love' of the Socialists of the previous lustre was already becoming changed, little by little, into the gall of hatred. Sprung from personal resentment, it was directed against the more immediate enemies, the spies, and in various parts of Russia some half-dozen of them were killed.

These first acts of bloodshed evidently could not stop there. If time were consumed in killing a vile spy, why allow the gendarme to live on with impunity who sent him forth, or the procurator who from the information of the spy obtained materials for ordering the arrest, or the head of the police who directed everything? The logic of life could not but compel the Revolutionaries to mount these steps by degrees, and it cannot be doubted that they would have done so, for the Russian may be wanting in many things, but not in the courage to be logical. Nay, one of the most striking peculiarities of the Russian character is that it never hesitates before the practical consequences of chains of reasoning.

There was, however, a fact of primary importance which gave such a strong impetus to the movement, that this step, which otherwise would perhaps have required several years, was taken at a single bound.

On January 24 of the year 1878, the memorable shot was fired by the revolver of Vera Zassulic against General Trepoff, who had ordered a political prisoner named Bogoluiboff to be flogged. Two months afterwards she was acquitted by the jury.

I need not narrate the details of the occurrence, nor those of the trial, nor insist upon their importance. Everyone understood them, and even now, four years afterwards, everyone remembers that wave of admiration which invaded every hearer, without distinction of party, of class, or of age. It is easy to imagine what it must have been in Russia.

Zassulic was not a terrorist. She was the angel of vengeance, and not of terror. She was a victim who voluntarily threw herself into the jaws of the monster in order to cleanse the honour of the party from a moral outrage. It was evident that if every infamous act had to await its Zassulic, he who committed it might sleep in peace, and die hoary-headed.

Yet this occurrence gave to the Terrorism a most powerful impulse. It illuminated it with its divine aureola, and gave to it the sanction of sacrifice and of public opinion.

The acquittal of Zassulic was a solemn condemnation of the entire arbitrary system which had impelled her to raise her avenging hand against the bully. The press and the public were unanimous in confirming the sentence of the jury.

And how did the Government receive the judgment of the nation?

The Emperor Alexander II. went in person to pay a visit to Trepoff, covered with so much ignominy, and ransacked the whole city in search of the acquitted Zassulic, in order to put her again in prison.

It was impossible to show a more impudent contempt for justice, and the universal feeling.

The general discontent grew beyond measure, for to the sting of the outrage was added the pang of deception.

Here I ought to stop for a moment to analyse the purely Liberal movement which germinated among the cultivated and privileged classes of Russian society at the commencement of the reign. Being unable to do this even briefly, I will merely say, that the event which imparted to it the greatest intensity was the war with Turkey, because it laid bare, like that of the Crimea, the shameful abuses of our social system, and awakened hopes of a new reorganization of the State, especially after the Constitution which Alexander II. gave to Bulgaria.

The return of the Emperor to his capital exactly coincided with the trial of Zassulic.

The Liberals awoke from their dreams. It was then that they turned in despair to the only party which was struggling against despotism, the Socialist party. The first efforts of the Liberal Party to approach the Revolutionaries in order to form an alliance with them date from 1878.

The government, however, seemed bent on exasperating not only the Liberals but also the Revolutionists. With a vile desire for vengeance, it redoubled its cruelty against the Socialists, whom it had in its power. The Emperor Alexander II. even went so far as to annul the sentence of his own Senate, which, under the form of a petition for pardon, acquitted most of the accused in the trial of the 193.

What government, therefore, was this which acted so insolently against all the laws of the country, which was not supported, and did not wish to be supported, by the nation, or by any class, or by the laws which it had made itself? What did it represent except brute force?

Against such a Government everything is permitted. It is no longer a guardian of the will of the people, or of the majority of the people. It is organised injustice. A citizen is no more bound to respect it, than to respect a band of highwaymen who employ the force at their command in rifling travellers.

But how shake off this *camarilla* before it could avail itself of its forces, thus rendered useless in their impregnable positions?

Thus arose the Terrorism.

Conceived in hatred, nurtured by patriotism and by hope, it grew up in the electrical atmosphere, impregnated with the enthusiasm awakened by an act of heroism.

On August 16, 1878, that is five months after the acquittal of Zassulic, the Terrorism, by putting to death General Mesentzeff, the head of the police and of the entire *camarilla,* boldly threw down its glove in the face of autocracy. From that day forth it advanced with giant strides, acquiring strength and position, and culminating in the tremendous duel with the man who was the personification of despotism.

I will not relate its achievements, for they are written in letters of fire upon the records of history.

Three times the adversaries met face to face. Three times the Terrorist by the will of fate was overthrown, but after each defeat he arose more threatening and powerful than before. To the attempt of Solovieff succeeded that of Hartman, which was followed by the frightful explosion at the Winter Palace, the infernal character of which seemed to surpass everything the imagination could conceive. But it was surpassed on March 13. Once more the adversaries grappled with each other, and this time the omnipotent Emperor fell half dead to the ground.

The Terrorist had won the victory in his tremendous duel, which had cost so many sacrifices. With a whole nation prostrate he alone held high his head, which throughout so many tempests he had never bent.

He is noble, terrible, irresistibly fascinating, for he combines in himself the two sublimities of human grandeur: the martyr and the hero.

He is a martyr. From the day when he swears in the depths of his heart to free the people and the country, he knows he is consecrated to Death. He faces it at every step of his stormy life. He goes forth to meet it fearlessly, when necessary, and can die without flinching, not like a Christian of old, but like a warrior accustomed to look death in the face.

He has no longer any religious feeling in his disposition. He is a wrestler, all bone and muscle, and has nothing in common with the dreamy idealist of the previous lustre. He is a mature man, and the unreal dreams of his youth have disappeared with years. He is a Socialist fatally convinced, but he understands that a Social Revolution requires long preparatory labor, which cannot be given until political liberty is acquired. Modest and resolute, therefore, he clings to the resolution to limit for the present his plans that he may extend them afterwards. He has no other object than to overthrow this abhorred despotism, and to give to his country, what all civilised nations possess, political liberty, to enable it to advance with a firm step towards its own redemption. The force of mind, the indomitable energy, and the spirit of sacrifice which his predecessor attained in the beauty of his dreams, he attains in the grandeur of his mission, in the strong passions which this marvellous, intoxicating, vertiginous struggle arouses in his heart.

What a spectacle! When had such a spectacle been seen before? Alone, obscure, poor, he undertook to be the defender of outraged humanity, of right trampled under foot, and he challenged to the death the most powerful Empire in the world, and for years and years confronted all its immense forces.

Proud as Satan rebelling against God, he opposed his own will to that of the man who alone, amid a nation of slaves, claimed the right of having a will. But how different is this terrestrial god from the old Jehovah of Moses! How he hides his trembling head under the daring blows of the Terrorist! True, he still stands erect, and the thunderbolts launched by his trembling hand often fail; but when they strike, they kill. But the Terrorist is immortal.

His limbs may fail him, but, as if by magic, they regain their vigour, and he stands erect, ready for battle after battle until he has laid low his enemy and liberated the country. And already he sees that enemy falter, become confused, cling desperately to the wildest means, which can only hasten his end.

It is this absorbing struggle, it is this imposing mission, it is this certainty of approaching victory, which gives him that cool and calculating enthusiasm, that almost superhuman energy, which astounds the world. It he is by nature a man capable of generous impulses, he will become a hero; if he is of stronger fibre, it will harden into iron; if of iron, it will become adamant.

He has a powerful and distinctive individuality. He is no longer, like his predecessor, all abnegation. He no longer possesses, he no longer strives after, that abstract moral beauty which made the propagandist resemble a being of another world; for his look is no longer directed inwardly, but is fixed upon the hated enemy. He is the type of individual force, intolerant of every yoke. He fights not only for the people, to render them the arbiters of their own destinies, not only for the whole nation stifling in this pestiferous atmosphere, but also for himself; for the dear ones whom he loves, whom he adores with all the enthusiasm which animates his soul; for his friends who languish in the horrid cells of the central prisons, and who stretch forth to him their skinny hands imploring aid. He fights for himself. He has sworn to be free and he will be free, in defiance of everything. He bends his haughty head before no idol. He had devoted his sturdy arms to the cause of the people. But he no longer deifies them. And if the people, ill-counselled, say to him, 'Be a slave,' he will exclaim, 'No;' and he will march onward, defying their imprecations and their fury, certain that justice will be rendered to him in his tomb.

Such is the Terrorist.

TERRORIST DEMANDS

After the death of Alexander II, the terrorists published their demands in an open letter to the new Tsar, Alexander III.

March 10, 1881.

Your Majesty,

Although the Executive Committee understands fully the grievous oppression that you must experience at this moment, it believes that it has no right

Source: Stepniak (S. Kravchinskii), *Nihilism as it is* (London, n.d.), 81–90.

to yield to the feeling of natural delicacy which would perhaps dictate the postponement of the following explanation to another time. There is something higher than the most legitimate human feeling, and that is duty to one's country—the duty for which a citizen must sacrifice himself and his own feelings, and even the feelings of others. In obedience to this all-powerful duty we have decided to address you at once, waiting for nothing, as will wait for nothing the historical process that threatens us with rivers of blood and the most terrible convulsions.

The tragedy enacted on the Ekaterinski Canal was not a mere casualty, nor was it unexpected. After all that had happened in the course of the previous decade it was absolutely inevitable, and in that fact consists its deep significance for a man who has been placed by fate at the head of Governmental authority. Such occurrences can be explained as the results of individual malignity, or even of the evil disposition of 'gangs' only by one who is wholly incapable of analysing the life of a nation. For then whole years, notwithstanding the strictest persecution, notwithstanding the sacrifice by the late Emperor's Government of liberty, even its own dignity; notwithstanding the absolute sacrifice of everything in the attempt to suppress the revolutionary movement, that movement has obstinately extended, attracting to itself the best elements of the country, the most energetic and self-sacrificing people of Russia, and the revolutionists have carried on for three years a desperate warfare with the administration.

You are aware, your Majesty, that the government of the late Government could not be accused of a lack of energy. It hanged the innocent and guilty and filled prisons and remote provinces with exiles. Tens of so-called 'leaders' were captured and hanged, and died with the courage and tranquility of martyrs; but the movement did not cease—on the contrary, it grew and strengthened. The revolutionary movement, your Majesty, is not dependent upon any particular individuals. It is a process of the social organism, and the scaffolds raised for its more energetic exponents are as powerless to save the outgrown order of things as the cross that was erected for the Redeemer was powerless to save the ancient world from the triumph of Christianity. The Government, of course, may yet capture and harry an immense number of individuals, it may break up a great number of separate revolutionary groups, it may even destroy the most important of existing revolutionary organisations; but all this will not change in the slightest degree the condition of affairs. Revolutionists are the creation of circumstances of the general discontent of the people—of the striving of Russia after a new social framework. It is impossible to exterminate a whole people—it is impossible, by means of repression, to stifle its discontent. Discontent only grows the more when it is repressed. For this reason the places of slain revolutionists are constantly taken by new individuals, who come forth from among the people in ever-increasing numbers, and who are still more embittered, still more energetic. These persons, in order to carry on the conflict, form an association in the light of the experience of their predecessors, and the revolutionary organisation thus grows stronger numerically and in quality with the lapse of time. This we actually see from the history of the last ten years. Of what use was it to destroy the Dolgushinzy, the Chaikovzy, and the workers of 1874? Their places were taken by much more resolute democrats. Then the awful repressive measures of the Government called upon the stage the terrorists of 1878 and 1879. In vain the Government put to death the Kovalskys, the Dubrovins, the Ossinskys, and the Lisogubs. In vain it destroyed dozens of revolutionary circles. From among those incomplete organisations, by virtue of natural selection, arose only stronger forms, until at last there has appeared an Executive Committee, with which the Government has not yet been able successfully to deal.

A dispassionate glance at the grevious decade through which we have just passed will enable us to forecast accurately the future progress of the revolutionary movement, provided the policy of the Government does not change. The movement will continue to grow and extend, deeds of terrorist nature will increase in frequency and intensity, and the revolutionary organisation will constantly set forth in the places of destroyed groups stronger and more perfect forms. Meanwhile the number of the discontented in the country will grow larger and larger; confidence in the Government on the part of the people will decline, and the idea of revolution, of its possibility and inevitability, will establish itself in Russia more and more firmly. A terrible explosion, a bloody hurly-burly, a revolutionary earthquake throughout Russia will complete the destruction of the old order of things. Upon what depends this terrible prospect? Yes, your Majesty, "terrible and lamentable"! Do not take this for a mere phrase. We understand better than any one else can how lamentable is the waste of so much talent and energy, the loss in bloody skirmishes, and in the work of destruction of so much strength, that under other conditions might have been expended in creative labour and in the development of the intelligence, the welfare, and civil life of the Russian people. Whence proceeds this lamentable necessity for bloody conflict? It arises, your Majesty, from the lack in Russia of a real Government in the true sense of that word. A Government, in the very nature of things, should only give outward form to the aspirations of the people and effect to the people's will. But with us—excuse the expression—the Government has degenerated into a mere camarilla, and deserves the name of a 'usurping gang' much more than does the Executive Committee.

Whatever may be the *intentions* of the Tzar, the *actions* of the Government have nothing in common with the popular welfare or the popular aspirations. The Imperial Government subjected the people to serfdom, put the masses into the power of the nobility, and is now openly creating the most injurious class of speculators and jobbers. All of its reforms result merely in a more perfect enslavement and a more complete exploiting of the people. It has brought Russia to such a pass that at the present time the masses of the people are in a state of pauperism and ruin, are subjected to the most humiliating surveillance, even at their own domestic hearths, and are powerless to regulate their own communal and social affairs. The protection of the law and of the Government is enjoyed only by the extortionists and the exploiters, and the most exasperating robbery goes unpunished. But, on the other hand, what a terrible fate awaits the man who seriously considers the general good! You know very well, your Majesty, that it is not only socialists who are exiled and prosecuted. Can it be possible that the *Government* is the guardian of such "order"? Is it not rather probable that this is the work of a "gang," the evidence of a complete usurpation?

These are the reasons why the Russian Government exerts no moral influence and has no support among the people. These are the reasons why Russia brings forth so many revolutionists. These are the reasons why even such a deed as Tzaricide excites in the minds of a majority of the people only gladness and sympathy. Yes, your Majesty! do not be deceived by the reports of flatterers and sycophants—Tzaricide in Russia is popular.

From such a state of affairs there can be only two exits: either a revolution, absolutely inevitable and not to be averted by any punishments, or a voluntary turning of the Supreme Power to the people. In the interest of our native land, in the hope of preventing the useless waste of energy, in the hope of averting the terrible miseries that always accompany revolution, the Executive Committee approaches your Majesty with the advice to take the second course. Be assured, so soon as the Supreme Power ceases to rule arbitrarily, so soon as it firmly resolves to accede to the demands of the people's conscience and consciousness, you may, without fear, discharge the spies that disgrace the administration, send your guards back to their barracks, and burn the scaffolds that are demoralising the people. The Executive Committee will voluntarily terminate its own existence, and the organisation formed about it will disperse, in order that their members may devote themselves to the work of culture among the people of their native land.

We address your Majesty as those who have discarded all prejudices and who have suppressed the distrust created by the actions of the Government throughout the century. We forget that you are the representative of the authority that has so often deceived and that has so injured the people. We address you as a citizen and as an honest man. We hope that the feeling of personal exasperation will not extinguish in your mind your consciousness of your duties and your desire to know the truth. *We* also might feel exasperation. You have lost your father. We have lost not only our fathers, but our brothers, our wives, our children, and our dearest friends. But we are ready to suppress personal feeling, if it be demanded by the welfare of Russia. We expect the same from you.

We set no conditions for you; do not let our propositions irritate you. The conditions that are pre-requisite to a change from revolutionary activity to peaceful labour are created not by us, but by history. These conditions in our opinion are two:—

1. A general amnesty to cover all past political crimes; for the reason that they were not crimes, but fulfillments of civil duties.
2. The summoning of representatives of the whole Russian people to examine the existing framework of social and Governmental life, and to remodel it in accordance with the people's wishes.

We regard it as necessary, however, to remind you that the legalisation of the Supreme Power by the representatives of the people, can be valid only in case the elections are perfectly free. For this reason such elections must be held under the following conditions:—

1. Delegates are to be sent from all classes without distinction, and in number are to be proportionate to the number of inhabitants.
2. There shall be no limitations either for voters or delegates.
3. The canvass and the elections shall be absolutely unrestricted, and therefore the Government, pending the organisation of the National Assembly, shall authorise, in the form of temporary measures—
   a) Complete freedom of the press.
   b) Complete freedom of speech.
   c) Complete freedom of public meeting.
   d) Complete freedom of election programmes.

This is the only way in which Russia can return to the path of normal and peaceful development.

We declare solemnly, before the people of our native land and before the whole world, that our party will submit unconditionally to the decisions of a National Assembly elected in the manner above indicated, and that we will not allow ourselves in the future to offer violent resistance to any Government that the National Assembly may sanction.

And now, your Majesty, decide! Before you are two courses, and you are to make your choice between them. We can only trust that your intelligence and conscience may suggest to you the only decision that is compatible with the welfare of Russia, with your own dignity, and with your duty to your native land.

The Executive Committee.

THE LENINIST PARTY

In the long run, terrorist activity could anger and torment the Tsarist government, but it could not fundamentally change that government. It remained for the revolutionaries to develop new theories, new concepts of organization. By the beginning of the 20th century, Marxism had provided the most popular world outlook for the revolutionaries. Among the adepts of this philosophy, V. I. Lenin distinguished himself by his conception of party organization.

It was originally intended to hold the congress in Brussels, and in fact the first sittings were held there. Koltsov, an old Plekhanovite, lived in Brussels at the time, and he undertook to see to all the arrangements. As it turned out, however, it was not so easy to arrange the congress there. All the delegates were to have reported to Koltsov, but after four or five Russians had called on him his landlady told him that she would not stand any more of this coming and going, and if one more person called he would have to move out at once. Koltsov's wife after that stood on the street corner all day long, intercepting the delegates and directing them to the socialist hotel Coq d'Or, as I believe it was called.

The delegates overran the whole hotel, and Gusev, after a drop of brandy, sang operatic arias in the evening in such a powerful voice that crowds collected at the windows outside. (Vladimir Ilyich liked Gusev's singing, especially the song *We Were Wedded Out of Church*.)

We overdid the secrecy precautions, though. The Belgian Party thought it would be safer to hold the congress in a vast flour warehouse. Our intrusion there only succeeded in astonishing the rats and the policemen. The word went round that Russian revolutionaries had got together to plot in secret.

The congress was attended by forty-three delegates with a deciding vote and fourteen with a deliberative vote. In comparison with present-day congresses, where the numerous delegates represent hundreds of thousands of Party members, this congress would seem a small one, but at that time we thought it big. The First Congress held in 1898 was attended by only nine persons. Everyone felt that considerable progress had been made in those five years. Most important of all, the organizations these delegates came from were no longer semi-mythical, they definitely existed and were already in

Source: N. K. Krupskaya, *Reminiscences of Lenin* (Moscow, 1959), 88–97.

touch with the working-class movement, which was beginning to spread ever wider.

How Vladimir Ilyich had dreamt of such a congress! He always, as long as he lived, attached tremendous importance to Party congresses. He held the Party congress to be the highest authority, where all things personal had to be cast aside, where nothing was to be concealed, and everything was to be open and above board. He always took great pains in preparing for Party congresses, and was particularly careful in thinking out his speeches.

Plekhanov looked forward to the congress just as eagerly as Vladimir Ilyich. He opened it. The big window of the flour warehouse near the improvised platform was covered with some red cloth. Everyone was excited. Plekhanov's speech, uttered with genuine deep feeling, sounded very solemn. And no wonder! The long years of emigrant life seemed to be a thing of the past. He was opening the Congress of the Russian Social-Democratic Labour Party.

Strictly speaking, the Second Congress was an inaugural congress. Fundamental questions of theory were raised there, and the foundations of Party ideology were laid. At the First Congress only the Party's designation and a manifesto on its formation had been adopted. Up to the time of the Second Congress the Party had had no programme. The editorial board of *Iskra* had drafted such a programme, and it had been under discussion for a long time. Every word, every sentence had been motivated, and weighed, and hotly debated. Correspondence on the programme had been carried on for months between the Munich and Swiss sections of the editorial board. Many practical workers regarded these disputes to be of a purely abstract nature, and did not think it mattered whether a "more-or-less" proviso was left standing in the programme or not.

Vladimir Ilyich and I were once reminded of a simile used by Lev Tolstoi. He was going along and saw from afar a man squatting and waving his arms about in a ridiculous way; a madman, he thought, but when he drew nearer, he saw it to be a man sharpening a knife on the kerb. The same thinking happens in theoretical disputes. From the outside it seems a sheer waste of time, but when you go into the matter more deeply you see that it is a momentous issue. It was like that with the programme.

When the delegates began to arrive in Geneva the chief question discussed with them in greatest detail was that of the programme. That question went through at the congress more smoothly than any other.

Another question of tremendous importance discussed at the Second Congress was that of the Bund. It had been resolved at the First Congress that the Bund constituted a section of the Party, albeit an autonomous one. During the five years that had elapsed since the First Congress the Party, practically speaking, had not existed as a united whole, and the Bund had led a separate existence. Now the Bund wanted to make good this separateness and to establish merely federative relations with the R.S.D.L.P. The motive behind this was that the Bund, reflecting as it did the mood of the artisans of the small Jewish towns, was much more interested in the economic than in the political struggle, and therefore sympathized much more with the "Economists" than with the *Iskra*-ists. The issue at stake was whether the country was to have a strong united workers' Party, rallying solidly around it the workers of all nationalities living on Russian territory, or whether it was to have several workers' parties constituted separately according to nationality. It was a question of achieving international solidarity within the country. The *Iskra* editorial board stood for international consolidation of the working class. The Bund stood for national separatism and merely friendly contractual relations between the national workers' parties of Russia.

The question of the Bund had also been discussed in detail with the delegates as they arrived, and was likewise decided on *Iskra* lines by an overwhelming majority.

The vast importance of the fundamental issues dealt with and decided at the Second Congress was later over-shadowed for many by the split. During the debates on these questions Vladimir Ilyich felt more than usually close to Plekhanov. The latter's speech to the effect that the thesis "the good of the revolution is the highest law" should be considered the basic democratic principle, and that even the idea of universal franchise should be regarded from the point of view of this principle, made a profound impression on Vladimir Ilyich. He recollected it fourteen years later, when the Bolsheviks were faced with the question of dismissing the Constituent Assembly.

Another speech of Plekhanov's that fell in with Vladimir Ilyich's ideas was that in which he spoke about the importance of popular education as being the "guarantee of the rights of the proletariat."

Plekhanov felt close to Lenin, too, at the congress. Replying to Akimov, an ardent supporter of the *Rabocheye Delo* group, who was all out to create dissension between Plekhanov and Lenin, Plekhanov said humorously: "Napoleon had a craze for making his marshals divorce their wives. Comrade Akimov reminds me of Napoleon in that respect—he wants to divorce me and Lenin at all costs. But I shall show more character than Napoleon's marshals—I shall not divorce Lenin and I hope he does not intend to divorce me." Vladimir Ilyich laughed and shook his head.

During the discussion of the first item on the agenda (the constitution of the congress) an unexpected incident occurred over the question of inviting a representative of the *Borba* (Struggle) group (Ryazanov, Nevzorov, Gurevich). The O.C. [Orangizing Committee] wanted to come forward with its own opinion. It was not a question of the *Borba* group at all; the O.C. was trying to impose a special discipline on its members in face of the congress.

The O.C. wanted to act as a group, which had previously decided among themselves how they were going to vote, and to speak at the congress as a group. Thus the supreme authority for a member of the congress would be the group and not the congress itself. Vladimir Ilyich was fairly boiling with indignation. He was not the only one to support Pavlovich (Krasikov), when the latter protested against these tactics; he was backed by Martov, too, and others. Although the O.C. was dismissed by the congress, the incident was significant and augured all kinds of complications. The incident, however, was temporarily pushed into the background by such momentous issues as the Bund's place within the Party and the Party's programme. On the question of the Bund, the *Iskra* editorial board, the O.C. and the local delegates were of one mind. Yegorov (Levin), representative of *Yuzhny Rabochy* and member of the O.C. also came out emphatically against the Bund. Plekhanov complimented him during the recess, saying that his speech ought to be "spread wide through all the communes." The Bund was utterly defeated. The thesis that national peculiarities must not interfere with the unity of Party work and the monolithic unity of the Social-Democratic movement was securely established.

Meanwhile we were compelled to move to London. The Brussels police made things difficult for the delegates, and when they deported Zemlyachka and someone else, we all got moving. In London the Takhtarevs did all they could to make congress arrangements. The London police raised no obstacles.

The discussion of the Bund question was continued. Then, while the question of the programme was in its committee stage, we passed to the fourth item of the agenda—the question of approving the central organ. *Iskra* was unanimously recognized as such, the *Rabocheye Delo* group alone being against. *Iskra* was hailed with enthusiasm. Even Popov (Rozanov), the representative of the O.C., said: "Here, at this congress, we see a united Party, created largely through the activity of *Iskra*." That was the tenth sitting. There were thirty-seven sittings in all. Clouds steadily began to gather. Three persons had to be elected to the Central Committee. No nucleus of a C.C. was yet available. One unquestionable candidature was Glebov (Noskov), who had proved himself to be an energetic organizer. Another would have been that of Clair (Krzhizhanovsky), had he been at the congress. But he was not. The voting for him and Kurz had to be done by proxy, which was extremely awkward. On the other hand, there were far too many "generals" at the congress who were candidates for the Central Committee. These were Jacques (Stein-Alexandrova), Fomin (Krokhmal), Stern (Kostya-Rosa Galberstadt), Popov (Rozanov) and Yegorov (Levin). All these were candidates for two seats on the C.C. trio. We all knew one another not only as Party workers, but in intimate personal life. It was all a tangle of personal

sympathies and antipathies. The atmosphere grew tenser as the time for
voting approached. Although the accusations of the Bund and *Rabocheye
Delo* about the foreign Centre wanting to control and dictate, etc., had met
with a solid rebuff at the outset, they had done their work by influencing the
Centre and the waverers, although they may not have been aware of it. Of
whose "control" were people afraid? Not of Martov's, Zasulich's, Starover's
and Axelrod's, of course. They were afraid of Lenin's and Plekhanov's control. But they knew that the questions of personnel and Russian work would
be decided by Lenin, and not by Plekhanov, who took no part in the practical
work.

The congress had endorsed the *Iskra* line, but the *Iskra* editorial board had
still to be elected.

Vladimir Ilyich moved that the editorial board of *Iskra* should consist of
three members. He had told Martov and Potresov about this proposal beforehand. Speaking with the delegates on their arrival, Martov had supported the
idea of three editors as being the most expedient. He realized then that the
three-man proposal was aimed chiefly against Plekhanov. When Vladimir
Ilyich handed Plekhanov his draft proposal for an editorial board of three,
Plekhanov had read it and put it in his pocket without saying a word. He
understood what it was about, and agreed to it. Once there was a Party,
practical work was necessary.

Martov mixed more with the members of the Organizing Committee than
anyone else on *Iskra*. It did not take long to persuade him that the three-man
idea was directed against him, and that if he joined it he would be betraying
Zasulich, Potresov and Axelrod. Axelrod and Zasulich were greatly upset.

In such an atmosphere, the dispute over the first paragraph of the Rules
assumed an extremely acrimonious character. Lenin and Martov disagreed
both politically and organizationally on the question of Paragraph I of the
Party Rules. They had often disagreed before, but such differences had then
been confined to narrow limits and had soon been sunk. Now they had come
out at the congress, and everyone who had had a grudge against *Iskra*, against
Plekhanov and Lenin, went out of his way to fan it up into a disagreement
on a fundamental issue. Lenin was attacked for his article *Where to Begin?*
and his pamphlet *What Is To Be Done?* and accused of being ambitious,
and so on. In his booklet *One Step Forward, Two Steps Back* he wrote:

I cannot help recalling in this connection a conversation I happened to have
at the congress with one of the 'Centre' delegates. 'How oppressive the atmosphere
is at our congress!' he had complained. 'This bitter fighting, this agitation one
against the other, this biting controversy, this uncomradely attitude . . .' 'What
a splendid thing our congress is!' I replied. 'A free and open struggle. Opinions
have been stated. The shades have been brought out. The groups have taken

shape. Hands have been raised. A decision has been taken. A stage has been passed. Forward! That's the stuff for me! That's life! That's not like the endless, tedious word-chopping of intellectuals which terminates not because the question has been settled, but because they are too tired to talk any more. . . .' The comrade of the 'Centre' had looked at me with a puzzled expression and shrugged his shoulders. We were speaking in different tongues. (*Works*, Vol. 7, p. 320, *Note*.)

Here, in this quotation we have the whole of Ilyich.

His nerves had been keyed up from the very beginning of the congress. The Belgian woman worker with whom we lodged in Brussels was very upset at Vladimir Ilyich not eating the lovely radishes and Dutch cheese which she served up for breakfast every morning. He was too worried to be able to eat anything. In London he worried so much that he stopped sleeping altogether.

Vehement though he was in the debates, Vladimir Ilyich was absolutely impartial as chairman and never treated an opponent unfairly. Not so Plekhanov. When he was in the chair he liked to flash his wit and tease his opponent.

Although there were no differences among the overwhelming majority of the delegates on the question of the Bund's place in the Party, on the question of the programme, and the acceptance of the *Iskra* line as their banner, a definite rift made itself felt half-way through the congress, which deepened towards the end. Strictly speaking, no serious differences standing in the way of joint work or making such work impossible had yet come to light at the congress. They existed in a latent form, however, potentially, so to speak. Yet the congress was clearly divided. Many were inclined to blame Plekhanov's tactlessness, Lenin's "vehemence" and "ambition," Pavlovich's pinpricks, and the unfair treatment of Zasulich and Axelrod—and they sided with those who had a grievance. They missed the substance through looking at personalities. Trotsky was one of them. He became a fierce opponent of Lenin. And the substance was this—that the comrades grouped around Lenin were far more seriously committed to principles, which they wanted to see applied at all cost and pervading all the practical work. The other group had more of the man-in-the-street mentality, were given to compromise and concessions in principle, and had more regard for persons.

The struggle during the elections was very sharp. One or two scenes before the voting started are still fresh in my memory. Axelrod accused Bauman (Sorokin) of an alleged lack of moral sense, and brought up some gossip about an incident supposed to have taken place in Siberian exile. Bauman said nothing, but there were tears in his eyes.

Another scene. Deutsch was angrily telling off Glebov (Noskov), who looked up with flashing eyes and said with annoyance: "I'd keep my mouth shut if I were you, old boy!"

The congress ended. Glebov, Clair and Kurz were elected to the Central

Committee, twenty out of the forty-four votes being abstentions. Plekhanov, Lenin and Martov were elected to the Central Organ. Martov refused to work on the editorial board. The split was obvious.

⊏━━━⊐

TSARIST FOREIGN POLICY

Russia's crisis found expression both in internal and in external events. An ignominious showing in war with Japan, together with revolutionary developments at home in 1905, forced the Tsarist government grudgingly to make domestic political concessions, but the crisis continued. The following selection, by a Soviet historian, seeks to explain in Marxist terms the interrelationships of domestic and foreign policy after 1905.

An analysis of the struggle in Russia on questions of foreign policy leads to the following conclusions.

The same classes clashed in this area as in the area of domestic politics. But because of the characteristics of foreign policy, the alignment of class forces in questions connected with this was rather different.

The main characteristic of foreign policy in this regard was that the interests of both ruling classes basically coincided here.

Both the landowners and the bourgeoisie were alike interested in the conduct of an imperialist foreign policy which would strengthen their position in the international arena in the struggle for the partition and repartition of the world as well as at home in the struggle against the revolutionary movement. So long as Tsarism conducted just such a foreign policy it found support in both counter-revolutionary camps—both the conservative, Black Hundred camp and the liberal, bourgeois camp.

There were no essential differences between them here; on all questions of principle in foreign policy the liberals, as a rule, came out on the side of the Black Hundreds against the revolutionary, democratic camp led by the Bolsheviks.

The differences between the bourgeois and landlord groupings came only in questions of the concrete directions of the imperialist foreign policy of Tsarism. These differences were determined by the characteristics of the international and domestic situation of Russia in the epoch of imperialism.

The chief characteristics of Russia's international situation at that time

Source: I. V. Bestuzhev, *Bor'ba v Rossii po voprosam vneshnei politiki 1906–1910* (Moscow, 1961), 382–88.

stemmed from the growth of Russo-German and Russo-Austrian contradictions, from the retreat of Russo-English and Russo-Japanese contradictions into the background, and from the decline of Tsarist Russia's independent role as a great power in the world arena.

The chief characteristics of Russia's domestic situation stemmed from the possibility, despite the temporary victory of the reaction, of a new surge of the revolutionary movement, from the continuing process of converting Russia into a bourgeois monarchy, and from the inability of the Russian army, after the events of 1904–1907, of conducting a large-scale war.

Under these conditions almost all the bourgeois and landowning groupings of Russia—from the Kadets to the moderate right—favored a rapprochement with England and France against Germany and Austria-Hungary.

By relying on England and France, the Russian bourgeoisie reckoned on weakening Germany, the bourgeoisie of which was its strongest competitor in the national market.

In addition, with the aid of England and France the Russian bourgeoisie planned to carry out further bourgeois reforms and thereby avert the danger of a new revolution.

By relying on England and France, the majority of Russian landowners hoped to force Germany to lower tariffs on the import of agricultural products. Germany was Russia's chief market in this respect.

In addition, this group of Russian landowners hoped by means of a rapprochement with England to obtain more favorable terms for the export of Russian agricultural products to that country.

Finally, by relying on England and France, the great mass of Russian landowners and bourgeoisie hoped to end the threat posed to Russia's position as a great power by German imperialism's growth in power and aggressiveness.

From this point of view, the overwhelming majority of Russian landowners and bourgeoisie considered it necessary above all to concentrate Russia's forces in the struggle with German expansion in the Near and Middle East, in order to protect former markets and to gain new ones for raw materials and for the sale of industrial products, and also in order to prevent Germany from taking the Black Sea straits—the main maritime artery of the Russian grain trade, the guarantee of political influence in the Near East, and the strategic key to the whole Russian Black Sea coast.

The demand of the greater part of the Russian bourgeoisie and landowners to concentrate Russia's forces in the struggle with Germany led logically to the demand to protect the rear in the Near and Middle East through an agreement with England and Japan.

Hence came the calls to end the agreement with Austria-Hungary on cooperation in Balkan politics, an agreement which had lost all significance, and to oppose Austro-German expansion by means of a union of Balkan states under the aegis of Russia.

Despite the fact that a significant number of Russian landlords were among the supporters of a rapprochement with England and France, this tendency among the ruling classes of Russia, as was shown above, had basically a bourgeois character. As for participation by landowners in this bourgeois tendency, this testifies to the contemporaneous "bourgeoisification" of the land-owning class in Russia. It is known that an ever greater part of Russian landowners were converting their estates to capitalist ways and were economically merging with the bourgeoisie. Hence the development of a solidarity of both ruling classes in the area of foreign policy.

But the same characteristics of the international and internal situation of Russia led a part of the ruling classes of Russia to favor a rapprochement with Germany and Austria-Hungary against England and France. These were bascially the extreme right-wing landowning circles, especially closely linked with the German market, less affected by Russo-German economic contradictions, and more actively opposing bourgeois "constitutionalism."

In relying on Germany, this part of Russian landowners reckoned on avoiding an open conflict with her, a conflict which threatened Russia with military disaster and an inevitable recurrence of revolutionary outbursts.

In addition, in the event of a new revolution in Russia this part of Russian landowners expected the most effective help from the Kaiser's Germany, even armed intervention.

Finally, the orientation toward Germany attracted this part of Russian landowners because, in contrast to the orientation toward England and France, it required no such bourgeois reforms as the Anglo-French creditors sought in order to guarantee the faithfulness of Tsarism, which itself had traditional, dynastic ties with Germany.

From this point of view, the extreme right-wing landlord circles considered it necessary to reconcile themselves for a time with German expansion in the East, to gain time for a final "pacification" of the country, and at the same time, relying on Germany, to carry out a "small victorious war" in order to bolster the prestige of the autocracy both at home and abroad—a war somewhere in the Middle or Far East against England or Japan.

Among the partisans of a rapprochement with Germany was also a part of the Russian bourgeoisie who had special ties with German capital. But they were so insignificant in comparison with the great mass of the bourgeoisie that they could not alter the essentially feudal character of this particular tendency.

The evidence of this tendency testifies to the fact that the process of "bourgeoisification" of the landowning class in Russia was far from complete and that a part of Russian landowners were still such advocates of serf-dom for whom the strengthening of dynastic ties, for purposes of not only the struggle against revolution but also of opposing bourgeois reforms, was incomparably more important than all other considerations.

The struggle among the bourgeois and the landowning groups in questions of foreign policy was not only limited to the problem of the general foreign political orientation of the country.

It had many aspects, including such important ones as the choice between an agreement with Japan and the formation of a Russo-American coalition for the containment of Japanese expansion in the Far East, the choice between an agreement with Austria-Hungary and the formation of a union of Balkan states (with or without Turkey) for the containment of Austro-German expansion in the Near East, etc. But at the basis of this struggle lay the conflict between the pro-English and the pro-German (between bourgeois and feudal) tendencies in the ruling classes of Russia.

The support of the basic mass of Russian landowners and bourgeoisie for the pro-English tendency of itself decided the outcome of the struggle over foreign policy in its favor. Nevertheless, in the conditions of Russia of that day, the positions of the comparatively small group of the extreme right were so strong that a lively and extended struggle was necessary before the pro-German tendency suffered a decisive defeat.

Tsarism, forced after the first Russian revolution to vacillate between the feudal landowners and the bourgeoisie, sought for a long time to reconcile the demands of both tendencies, and it thereby enhanced the chances of success for the partisans of a rapprochement with Germany.

The fear of military disaster and the inevitable repetition of revolution in the event of an open Russo-German conflict, the illusory hope to remain aside from the impending clash between England and Germany, all stimulated the "neutralist" tendencies of the Tsarist government.

As a result, through the entire period 1906–1910, at the basis of the Tsarist government's foreign policy was an unreal plan of combining Russo-English and Russo-Japanese agreements with identical Russo-German and Russo-Austrian agreements.

Only the further sharpening of Russo-German contradictions in connection with Austro-German expansion in the Balkans, the increased dependence of Tsarism on its Anglo-French creditors, and the influence of the Russian imperialist bourgeoisie which demanded a decisive opposition to German expansion finally forced the Tsarist government to give up its efforts to reach agreement with Germany and Austria-Hungary and to decide definitely to participate in the Anglo-French coalition against Germany.

The position of the pro-German tendency in Russia was strengthened by the fact that the control over the country's foreign policy, thanks to the direct subordination of the Ministry of Foreign Affairs to the Tsar, was in fact in the hands of a camarilla, the majority of which favored a rapprochement with Germany.

It is therefore not surprising that the pro-English bourgeois and landowning groups opened a struggle to transfer the control of foreign policy, at least to some degree, to the hands of the official government which considered the interests of these groups more carefully. At first the liberal bourgeoisie sought to establish even the responsibility of the Minister of Foreign Affairs to the Duma, but after the reaction set in, this was given up. There remained only the demand to subordinate the Minister of Foreign Affairs to the Chairman of the Council of Ministers and to permit the Duma to discuss questions of foreign policy in order to force the government to listen more carefully to the voice of bourgeois-landowning public opinion.

In the end, the real conduct of foreign policy was in the hands of the Chairman of the Council of Ministers. There was a reform of the Ministry of Foreign Affairs and those diplomats were removed who had especially opposed the rapprochement with England. The government considered it expedient not only to permit the discussion of questions of foreign policy in the Duma but also to consult regularly on such questions with representatives of the great bourgeoisie of Russia. All this greatly strengthened the pro-English tendency among the ruling circles of Russia.

But even with this, the influence of the camarilla (and consequently the pro-German tendency) on the determination of foreign policy remained so strong that the struggle over the foreign political orientataion of the country continued, with varying results, through the whole period of 1906–1910.

At first the pro-English tendency won notable victories: the reorganization of the Ministry of Foreign Affairs, the discussion of questions of foreign policy in the Duma, the transfer of basic questions of foreign policy into the sphere of competence of the Council of Ministers, the concentration of the real conduct of foreign policy in the hands of the head of the government, agreements with England and Japan, and the abandonment of the contemplated agreements with Germany and Austria-Hungary.

Especially great changes are to be seen in this regard during the Bosnian crisis, when the autocracy, in the face of a serious diplomatic failure, had to flirt with bourgeois-landowner opinion, consult regularly with the leaders of the bourgeoisie, and consider their voice in the direction of foreign policy.

Nevertheless when the international position of Tsarism had somewhat stabilized, it sought to take back the "excessive"—in the opinion of the camarilla—concessions to the liberal bourgeoisie. The consultations of the government with the leaders of the bourgeoisie were more rare, the discussion of questions of foreign policy in the Duma in fact ceased, the influence of the pro-German tendency on the determination of foreign policy was strengthened, and the question of a far-reaching agreement with Germany again entered the order of the day.

The relationship of forces in the ruling classes was such that the pro-English tendency finally won.

The efforts for a rapprochement with Germany came to naught and the course of rapprochement with England was finally established. But this struggle was completed only in a different domestic situation, that of the new revolutionary wave of 1911–1914.

CHAPTER 8

World War and Revolution

THE FRANCO-RUSSIAN MILITARY AGREEMENT

World War I brought the Tsarist regime crashing down. Historians may still debate whether Tsarist Russia in 1914 had any real hope of peaceful evolution into a parliamentary system of government, but the fabric of the Tsarist empire was obviously too weak to resist the strains of 20th century total war. An earlier reading spoke of Russia's wars of the 19th century as being popular. The First World War demanded greater popular support than any previous war.

Ironically, Russia's involvement in the conflict can be traced back to Russia's allying itself with republican France against the German Empire. In 1892 the two powers signed a secret military agreement which the French government did not dare to submit as a treaty to its own parliament.

August 17, 1892

France and Russia, motivated by an equal desire to keep the peace and having no aim but to prepare for the necessities of a defensive war provoked by an attack of the forces of the Triple Alliance against one or the other, have agreed on the following provisions:

1. If France is attacked by Germany or by Italy supported by Germany, Russia will employ all its available forces to fight against Germany.

If Russia is attacked by Germany, or by Austria supported by Germany, France will employ all its available forces to fight against Germany.

2. In case the forces of the Triple Alliance, or of one of the Powers which are a part of it, mobilize, France and Russia, at the first notice of this event and without the necessity of previous consultation, will immediately and simultaneously mobilize all their forces and will send them as quickly as possible to their frontiers.

Source: Great Britain, Foreign Office, *British and Foreign State Papers*, CXXI, 1079–80.

3. The available forces which should be employed against Germany are: by France 1,300,000 men and by Russia from 700,000 to 800,000 men.

These forces will basically be used, with all care, to force Germany to fight simultaneously both in the east and in the west.

4. The General Staffs of the armies of the two countries will confer constantly to prepare and facilitate the execution of the measures provided herein. They will communicate to each other, in time of peace, all information relative to the armies of the Triple Alliance which they might have or might learn.

The ways and means of communication in time of war will be studied and provided in advance.

5. Neither France nor Russia will conclude a separate peace.

6. The present convention will have the same duration as the Triple Alliance.

7. All the provisions listed herein are to be kept strictly secret.

Obrutschew,
Aide de Camp general,
Chef de l'etat major general.

Boisdeffre,
General de Division,
Conseiller d'Etat,
Sous-Chef d'Etat-major de l'Armee.

⊏══════⊐

THE SOCIALIST CRISIS

The outbreak of World War I evoked a crisis in European Socialist thought. In previous years, the Socialists of the various countries of Europe had loudly proclaimed their solidarity and opposition to war. In 1914, however, in one belligerent country after another, most Socialists rallied to the flag, and their parliamentary delegations voted in favor of the necessary war credits. Lenin, who arrived in Switzerland in September 1914, soon emerged as a leader of anti-war sentiment, not because of pacifist sentiments but rather with his demands that the war be converted into a civil war. He found himself now even opposed to his old mentor Georgii Plekhanov.

Ilyich was afraid he would not be admitted to Plekhanov's lecture and say what he had to say—the Mensheviks might not let in so many Bolsheviks.

Source: N. K. Krupskaya, *Reminiscences of Lenin* (Moscow, 1959), 287–90.

I can imagine how reluctant he was to see people and carry on small talk with them, and I can understand the naive ruses he devised to shake them off. I can clearly see him amid the dinner-table bustle at the Movshovichs', so withdrawn, absorbed and agitated that he could not swallow a bite. One can understand the rather forced humour of the remark uttered in an undertone to those sitting next to him about Plekhanov's opening speech, in which the latter had declared that he had not been prepared to address such a large audience. "The slyboots," Ilyich muttered, and gave himself up entirely to hearing what Plekhanov had to say. The first part of the lecture in which Plekhanov attacked the Germans had his approval, and he applauded it. In the second part, however, Plekhanov set forth his "defence-of-the-country" views. There was no room for doubt any more. Ilyich asked for the floor—he was the only one to do so. He went up to the speaker's table with a pot of beer in his hand. He spoke clamly, and only the pallor of his face betrayed his agitation. He said in effect that the war was not an accidental occurrence, that the way for it had been paved by the whole nature of the development of bourgeois society. The international congresses at Stuttgart, Copenhagen and Basle had defined what the attitude of the Socialists should be towards the impending war. Only by combatting the chauvinist intoxication in their countries would the Social-Democrats be fulfilling their duty. The war, which had just begun, ought to be converted into a decisive fight against the ruling classes on the part of the proletariat.

Ilyich had only ten minutes. He could only deal with the bare essentials. Plekhanov retorted with his usual display of wit. The Mensheviks, who were an overwhelming majority, wildly applauded him. The impression was that Plekhanov had won the day.

Three days later, on October 14, in the same hall where Plekhanov had spoken—the Maison du Peuple—Ilyich was to deliver his own lecture. The hall was packed. The lecture was a great success. Ilyich was in a buoyant fighting mood. He elaborated his views on the war, which he branded as an imperialist war. He pointed out in his speech that a leaflet against the war had already been issued in Russia by the Central Committee and that similar leaflets had been issued by the Caucasian organization and other groups. He pointed out that the best socialist newspaper in Europe at the moment was *Golos* (*Voice*), in which Martov was writing. "The more often and seriously I have disagreed with Martov," he said, "the more definitely must I now say that this writer is doing just what a Social-Democrat should do. He is criticizing his government, denouncing the bourgeoisie of his own country, railing against its ministers."

In private conversation Ilyich often remarked what a good thing it would be if Martov came over to our side altogether. But he doubted whether Martov would stick to his present position for long. He knew how prone Martov was to yield to outside influences. "He writes like that while he is alone," Ilyich added. Ilyich's lecture was a tremendous success. He repeated the same lecture—"The Proletariat and the War"—in Geneva at a later date.

Ilyich returned from his lecture trip to find a letter of Shlyapnikov's from Stockholm informing him about the work in Russia, about Vandervelde's telegram to the Duma group and the replies of the Menshevik and Bolshevik deputies. When war was declared Émile Vandervelde, Belgian representative on the International Socialist Bureau, accepted a ministerial post in the Belgian Government. He had been in Russia shortly before the war and seen the struggle which the Russian workers were waging against the autocracy, but had failed to grasp its full import. Vandervelde had sent telegrams to both sections of the Social-Democratic group of the Duma. He called on the group to help the Russian Government conduct a determined war against Germany on the side of the Entente.

The Menshevik deputies, who, for the moment, had refused to vote for war credits, began to vacillate when they learned what position the majority of the Socialist parties had taken up. Their answer to Vandervelde, therefore, showed a complete change of front. They declared in it that they would not oppose the war. The Bolshevik group sent a reply emphatically rejecting any suggestion of supporting the war and discontinuing the struggle against the tsarist government. Much was left unsaid in this reply, but the main line was correct. It showed how important it was to maintain contact with Russia, and Ilyich strongly insisted that Shlyapnikov should remain in Stockholm and establish still closer contact with the Duma group and the Russians at large. This could best be arranged through Stockholm.

As soon as Ilyich arrived in Berne from Cracow, he wrote to Karpinsky, enquiring whether it was possible to have a leaflet printed in Geneva. The theses were adopted in Berne soon after our arrival, and a month later it was decided to recast and publish them in the form of a manifesto. Ilyich got in touch with Karpinsky again concerning its publication. He sent him letters by trusted messengers, avoiding the post and maintaining strict secrecy. It was not clear at the time what attitude the Swiss Government would adopt towards anti-militarist propaganda.

The day after receiving Shlyapnikov's first letter, Vladimir Ilyich wrote to Karpinsky:

Dear K. Just when I happened to be in Geneva we received *gratifying* news from Russia. The text of the Russian Social-Democrats' reply to Vandervelde arrived too. We have therefore decided, instead of a separate manifesto, to issue a paper *Sotsial-Demokrat (The Social-Democrat)*, the Central Organ. . . . By Monday we shall send you some slight corrections to the manifesto and a *different* signature (for after having got in touch with Russia we are coming out *more officially*). (*Works*, Vol. 35, p. 119.)

Ilyich went on a lecture tour again at the end of October, first to Montreux, then to Zurich. Trotsky spoke at the lecture in Zurich, protesting against Ilyich calling Kautsky a "traitor." Ilyich deliberately put the case very strongly in order to make it quite clear what line people were taking. The fight with the defencists was in full swing.

The struggle was not an internal Party affair that concerned Russian matters alone. It was an international affair.

"The Second International is dead, vanquished by opportunism," Vladimir Ilyich maintained. Forces had to be rallied for a new International, the Third, purged of opportunism.

LENIN AND ZIMMERWALD

Lenin sought to put his ideas into action when international socialists gathered at Zimmerwald, in Switzerland, in September 1915.

In Switzerland Robert Grimm called a preliminary conference for July 11 at Bern to discuss the preparations for the international conference of Left-wingers. The meeting was attended by seven persons—Grimm, Zinoviev, P. B. Axelrod, Warski, Valetsky, Balabanova and Morgari. As a matter of fact, apart from Zinoviev, there were no real Left-wingers at that preliminary conference, and one could gather from the drift of their talk that none of its participants was seriously interested in convening a conference of the Lefts.

Vladimir Ilyich was worried, and sent letters out in all directions—to Zinoviev, Radek, Bèrzinš, Kollontai and the Lausanne comrades—to make sure that places were secured for genuine Lefts at the forthcoming conference, and to ensure the greatest possible unity among them. By the middle of August the Bolsheviks had drawn up: 1) a manifesto; 2) draft resolutions; 3) a draft declaration, which were forwarded to comrades of the extreme Left for consideration. By October Lenin's and Zinoviev's pamphlet *Socialism and War* had been translated into German.

The conference was held in Zimmerwald on September 5–8. Delegates were there from eleven countries (thirty-eight delegates in all). What was known as the Zimmerwald Left group consisted of only nine people (Lenin, Zinoviev, Bèrzinš, Höglund, Nerman, Radek, Borchardt and Platten; after the conference Roland-Holst joined them). Other Russian delegates at the conference were Trotsky, Axelrod, Martov, Natanson, Chernov and a Bundist. Trotsky did not join the Left Zimmerwaldists.

Source: *Ibid.*, 308–11.

Vladimir Ilyich left for the conference before it was due to open, and at a private meeting on the 4th made a report on the character of the war and the tactics to be applied by the international conference. The dispute centered around the question of the manifesto. The Lefts submitted their draft manifesto and resolution on the war and the tasks of the Social-Democrats. The majority rejected the draft of the Lefts and adopted a much vaguer and less militant manifesto. The Lefts signed the general manifesto. The following appraisal of the Zimmerwald Conference was given by Vladimir Ilyich in his article "The First Step":

Should our Central Committee have signed a manifesto that suffered from inconsistency and timidity? We think we should. Our disagreement, the disagreement not only of our Central Committee but of the whole Left, *international*, *revolutionary-Marxist* part of the conference is openly expressed in a special resolution, and in a special draft manifesto, and in a special declaration on the motives of voting for a compromise manifesto. We did not conceal one iota of our views, slogans and tactics. The German edition of our pamphlet *Socialism and War* was distributed at the conference. We have promulgated, are promulgating and shall promulgate our views to no less an extent than the manifesto will be promulgated. That this manifesto is a *step forward* towards a real struggle against opportunism, towards breaking and splitting with it, is a fact. It would be sectarianism to refuse to take this step *together* with the German, French, Swedish, Norwegian and Swiss minority, when we retain complete freedom and the full possibility to criticize inconsistency and achieve something greater. (*Works*, Vol. 21, pp. 353–54.)

At the Zimmerwald Conference the Lefts organized a bureau of their own and in general formed a distinct group.

Although Ilyich had written before the Zimmerwald Conference that the Kautskyites ought to have had our draft resolution presented to them: "The Dutch plus ourselves plus the Left Germans plus nought—that does not matter, it will not be Nought afterwards, but All," the rate of progress was nevertheless very slow indeed, and Ilyich could not reconcile himself to it. In fact, his article "The First Step" begins by emphasizing the slow rate of development of the revolutionary movement. "The development of the international socialist movement is making slow progress in the epoch of extremely acute crisis caused by the war." (*Ibid.*, p. 350.) It was therefore in a pretty irritable frame of mind that Ilyich returned from the Zimmerwald Conference.

The day after Ilyich's return we climbed the Rothorn. We climbed with "glorious zest," but when we got to the top Ilyich suddenly lay down on the ground in a rather uncomfortable position, and fell asleep almost right in the snow. Clouds gathered, then broke, and a wonderful view of the Alps opened before us, but Ilyich slept like the dead, without stirring. He slept for over an hour. Zimmerwald must have taken it out of him pretty badly.

LENIN ON IMPERIALISM

As part of his anti-war campaign, Lenin produced one of his most famous works, Imperialism: The Highest Stage of Capitalism, *which purported to discredit both defensism and pacifism on the grounds that capitalist governments by their very nature could not remain at peace with each other.*

For the old capitalism, with its completely free competition, the export of *goods* was typical. For the modern capitalism, with its rule of monopolies, the export of *capital* has become typical. . . .

So long as capitalism remains capitalism, surplus capital will not be used to raise the standard of living of the masses in a given country, for this would mean a decrease in profits for the capitalists. Rather, it will be used to raise profits by the export of capital abroad, to the backward countries. In these backward countries, profits are usually high, since there is little capital, the price of land is relatively low, wages are low, and raw materials are cheap. The possibility of exporting capital comes from the fact that a number of backward countries have already been drawn into the purview of international capitalism: main rail lines have been built or are being begun, the basic conditions for the development of industry have been assured, etc. The necessity to export capital comes from the "overripening" of capitalism in certain countries where capital lacks possibilities for "profitable" investment (because of backwardness of agriculture and mass poverty). . . .

The countries exporting capital have divided the world in the figurative sense of the word. But finance capital has also led to an *actual* division of the world.

THE DIVISION OF THE WORLD BETWEEN CAPITALIST COMBINES

Monopolistic combinations of capitalists—cartels, syndicates, trusts—divide among themselves first the internal market, more or less seizing control of production in a given country. But the internal market, under capitalism, is of necessity connected with the external market. Capitalism long ago created a world market. And as the export of capital increased, and as foreign and colonial relations were extended, together with the "spheres of influence" of the largest monopolistic combinations, things "naturally" led to a global agreement between them, to the formation of international cartels.

Source: V. I. Lenin, *Sochineniia*, 4th ed., XX (Moscow, 1948), 173–290 (excerpts).

This is a new stage in the world concentration of capital and production, incomparably higher than the previous ones. . . .

Certain bourgeois writers . . . have expressed the opinion that international cartels, being one of the most striking expressions of the internationalization of capital, offer us hope of peace between nations under capitalism. This opinion is theoretically absurd, and in practice it is a sophism and a dishonest defense of the worst opportunism. . . . The capitalists divide up the world not because of some personal wickedness but because the degree of concentration which has been achieved forces them to take this course in order to obtain profits. And they divide it in proportion to "capital", to "strength"—no other division is possible in the system of commodity production and capitalism. But strength varies according to economic and political development; in order to understand what is taking place it is necessary to know what questions are being resolved by changes in strength. Whether these changes are "purely" economic or *non*-economic (e.g., military) is a secondary question which can in no way alter the fundamental view of the modern epoch of capitalism. To replace the question of the *content* of the struggle and agreements between the capitalist combinations with the question of the form of the struggle and agreements (today peaceful, tomorrow not, the day after again not peaceful) is to descend to the role of a sophist.

The epoch of modern capitalism shows us that definite relations are being established between capitalist groups, relations *based* on the economic division of the world, and together with this, definite relations are being established between political groups, states, on the basis of the territorial division of the world, the struggle for colonies, and the "struggle for economic territory."

IMPERIALISM IS A PARTICULAR STAGE OF CAPITALISM

If it were necessary to give the briefest possible definition of imperialism, it would be necessary to say that imperialism is the monopoly stage of capitalism. Such a definition would include the most important feature: on the one hand, finance capital is bank capital of the monopolistically few largest banks, merged with the capital of the monopolistic combinations of industrialists; and on the other hand, the division of the world is a transition from a colonial policy which had spread unopposed to regions unoccupied by any capitalist power, to a colonial policy of monopolistic possession of the territories of the world, carried out to its extreme.

But too brief definitions, although useful since they summarize the main points, are nevertheless inadequate if one must determine the most essential features of the phenomenon in question. Therefore, not forgetting the conditional and relative value of all definitions, which can never include all the aspects of the phenomenon in its full development, we must give a definition of imperialism which would include the five following basic features: 1) the concentration of production and capital, developed to such a degree that it creates monopolies which play a decisive role in economic life; 2) the merging of bank capital with industrial capital, and the creation, on the basis of this "finance capital," of a financial oligarchy; 3) the export of capital, as distinct from the export of goods, acquires particularly important meaning; 4) the formation of international monopolistic combinations of capitalists, which divide up the world: and 5) the completion of the territorial division of the world by the largest capitalist powers. . . .

THE CRITIQUE OF IMPERIALISM

It is a fundamental question in the critique of imperialism whether it is possible to change the bases of imperialism by reforms, whether we must go forward to a further sharpening and deepening of the antagonisms which it engenders or whether we can reduce them. . . . The break with Marxism by Kautsky and the broad international tendency of Kautskyism consists just in the fact that Kautsky not only did not care but actually could not take a stand against this petty bourgeois, reformist opposition, which is basically economically reactionary, and on the contrary he practically joined it. . . .

Kautsky broke with Marxism by defending, in the period of finance capital, the "reactionary ideal" of "peaceful democracy," "the simple action of economic factors,"—for this ideal *objectively* pulls back, from monopolistic capitalism to non-monopolistic, and it is a reformist deception. . . . .

Kautsky's theoretical critique of imperialism has nothing in common with Marxism and therefore serves only as a preamble to propaganda for peace and unification with the opportunists and social-chauvinists. This critique avoids and obscures precisely the deepest and most essential contradictions of imperialism: the contradiction between monopolies and free competition existing side by side, the contradiction between gigantic "operations" (and gigantic profits) of finance capital and "honest" trade in a free market, the contradiction between cartels and trusts on the one hand and non-cartelized industry on the other, etc. . . .

Under capitalism there can be no other conceivable basis for the division of spheres of influence, colonies, interests, etc., than a calculation of the *strength* of the participants in the division, their general economic, financial, military strength, etc. And the strength of the participants of the division changes unevenly, for there can be no *equal* development of individual enterprises, trusts, branches of industry, or countries under capitalism. A half century ago Germany was a pitiful nonentity if one compares it with the capitalist power of England at that time; similarly Japan with Russia. Is it "conceivable" that in ten or twenty years there will be no changes in the relative strength of the imperialist powers? Absolutely not.

Therefore "inter-imperialist" or "ultra-imperialist" alliances, whatever form they might take . . . in capitalist conditions (and not in the banal fantasies of English priests or of the German "Marxist" Kautsky) inevitably are only "breathing spaces" between wars. Peaceful alliances prepared wars and in turn grow out of wars, the one conditioning the other, the alternating forms of peaceful and nonpeaceful struggle arising from *one and the same* soil of imperialist connections and the interrelationship between world economics and world politics.

THE CRISIS OF TSARIST GOVERNMENT

In Russia itself, the government had first enjoyed an unprecedented wave of popular sympathy in the war against Germany, but as the strains and demands of war became greater, the Tsarist regime disintegrated. No single speech better represents the dilemma of Russia's war effort than Paul Miliukov's impassioned oration to the Russian Duma in November, 1916. Miliukov's insistence on intensifying the war effort, moreover, was a harbinger of the crisis which he himself was to face as Foreign Minister in 1917.

Members of the Duma:

I come to this platform today with heavy heart. You will remember the situation when the Duma last met over a year ago, on July 19, 1915. The Duma was concerned with our military failures; it attributed these to a shortage of military supplies, and it blamed War Minister Sukhomlinov for this. You will remember that at that moment, under the influence of the terrible danger which had become obvious to all, the country demanded unity of national forces and the creation of a ministry with persons in whom it could place its trust. And you will remember that then, from this platform, even Minister Goremykin admitted that "the progress of the war demands a tremendous, extraordinary amount of spirit and strength." You will remember that the government then made concessions. The ministers hated by society were removed. Sukhomlinov, whom the country considered a traitor (*Voices from the left:* "And he is"), was removed, and, in response to the demand of the people's representatives, Polivanov, on July 28, you will remember, told us, amid general applause, that a commission of inquiry had been set up and that a beginning had been made toward bringing the former War Minister to justice. And, gentlemen, the public's efforts were not vain. Our

Source: *Rech'*, No. 330, November 30, 1916.

army received what it needed. And our country entered the second year of war with the same enthusiasm with which it had the first.

What a difference today, gentlemen, in the twenty-seventh month of war! A difference which I especially note, having spent a few months abroad. New difficulties stand before us, and these difficulties are no less complex, no less serious, no less profound, than those which we faced in the spring of last year. The government needed heroic measures to combat the general dislocation of the national economy.

We ourselves are the same as before. We are the same in this, the twenty-seventh month of the war, as we were in the tenth and as we were in the first. As before, we seek a complete victory; as before we are ready to make all necessary sacrifices, and as before we want to preserve national unity. But I will say openly: there is a difference in our position. We have lost hope that this government can lead us to victory (*Voices:* "True."), since none of our efforts to correct or improve this government have been successful. All the Allied governments have summoned to power the best men from all parties. They won trust, they gathered together all the elements of organization, which are more developed in other countries than in ours. What has our government done? Our declaration has told the story. From the time a majority appeared in the Duma, a majority previously nonexistent and now ready to express confidence in a worthy cabinet, from that time almost all cabinet members who could expect such confidence have been systematically forced, one after another, to leave the cabinet. And if we said earlier that our government lacked the knowledge, the talent necessary for the present moment, then, gentlemen, that government has now descended to even a lower level than that upon which it stood in normal times of Russian life. (*Voices from the left:* "True! correct!") And the gulf between it and us has broadened and become unbridgeable. (*Voices from the left:* "True!") Gentlemen, a year ago Sukhomlinov was put under investigation. The hated ministers were removed. Now their number has grown by one. (*Voices from the left:* "True." *Voice from the right:* "Protopopov?") We did not then appeal to the reason and understanding of the government but rather to its patriotism and its conscience. Can we do that now? (*Voices from the left:* "Of course not!")

A German document was published in the French Yellow Book laying down rules for disorganizing an enemy country, how to stir up trouble and disorder in it. Gentlemen, if our government had wanted to take up this task systematically and if the Germans had wanted to employ their own means for this, be it influence or bribery, then they could have done nothing better than what the Russian government has actually done. (*Voices from the left:* "Correct." *Rodichev:* "Unfortunately, that is true.") And you gentlemen, now have the consequences. On June 13, 1915, from this platform, I warned that "the poisonous seed of suspicion is already yielding abundant fruit," that "from one end of Russia to the other, dark rumors of treason and treachery are spreading." I am citing my own words. I then pointed out that "these rumors reach high and spare no one." But, gentlemen, this warning, just as others, was not heeded. As a result, in the declaration of the twenty-eight chairmen of provincial boards, meeting in Moscow last October 29, you find the following statement: "Painful, terrible suspicion, the vilest rumors of treachery and treason, of dark forces working to aid Germany and striving, through disruption of our national unity and sowing distrust, to prepare the ground for a disgraceful peace, have now passed on to an open conviction that an enemy hand is secretly influencing the direction of our governmental affairs. It is natural that on this ground should arise rumors that government circles see no use in further struggle, that they recognize the timeliness of ending the war and the necessity of concluding a separate peace." Gentlemen, I wouldn't want to dwell on superfluous, perhaps exaggerated suspicions with which the excited feelings of a Russian patriot might react to what has happened. But how can you reject the possibility of such suspicions, when a handful of sinister personalities direct the most important governmental matters in their own personal and base interests. (*Applause from the left and cries:* "True!")

I have in my hands a copy of the *Berliner Tageblatt* for September 16, 1916, and in it is an article entitled "Manuilov, Sturmer." The news in this article is a bit outdated, partly not correct. The German author naively believes that Sturmer arrested Manasevich-Manuilov, his own personal secretary. Gentlemen, you all know that this is not so, that the men who arrested Manasevich-Manuilov without consulting Sturmer were as a result removed from the cabinet. No, gentlemen, Manasevich-Manuilov knew too much to be arrested. Sturmer did not arrest Manasevich-Manuilov. Sturmer freed Manasevich-Manuilov. (*Applause from the left and voices:* "True." *Rodichev:* "Unfortunately, that is the truth.") You may ask, who is Manasevich-Manuilov? Why is he interesting? I will tell you, gentlemen, Manasevich-Manuilov was a former official of the Russian secret police in Paris, known as "Mask" of *Novoe Vremia*, who supplied this newspaper with piquant details from the life of the revolutionary underground. But what is more interesting to us, he is also the executor of special, secret tasks. Of these tasks, one may be of interest to us here. A few years ago, Manasevich-Manuilov sought to carry out a mission for the German Ambassador Pourtales, who provided a large sum, said to be 800,000 rubles, for bribing the *Novoe Vremia*. I am happy to relate that a member of the *Novoe Vremia* staff threw Manasevich-Manuilov out of his apartment. It cost Pourtales no small effort to hush up this unpleasant matter. But this, gentlemen, is the kind of mission which, not so long ago, employed the private secretary of Foreign Minister Sturmer. (*From the left prolonged noise and voices:* "Shame!")

Chairman: Please come to order.

Miliukov: Why was this man arrested? This has long been known, and I will be telling you nothing new if I repeat what you know. He was arrested for accepting a bribe. And why was he released? This too is no secret. (*Noise. Rodichev:* "Everyone knows." *Noise. Voices:* "Listen! Quiet!")

Chairman: I ask the Duma deputies for quiet.

Miliukov: Manuilov, Sturmer—the article mentioned two more names: Prince Andronnikov and Metropolitan Pitirim. (*Noise from the left.*) Allow me to dwell in greater detail upon the appointment of Sturmer as Minister of Foreign Affairs. I was abroad at this time; for me it is mixed with impressions of my travels abroad. I will simply relate to you what I learned while underway, and you may draw your own conclusions. I had scarcely crossed the frontier, a few days after Sazonov's retirement, when first Swedish and then German and Austrian newspapers carried articles on German reactions to Sturmer's appointment. This is what they said—I read excerpts without commentary. *Berliner Tageblatt:* "The personality of Sazonov gave the Allies a guarantee of stability in the foreign policy of the last five years. In foreign policy Sturmer is a blank sheet of paper. Undoubtedly he belongs to circles which look upon the war with Germany without great enthusiasm." *Kolnische Zeitung:* "We Germans have no basis to regret this newest change in the Russian government. Sturmer will not oppose the wishes in Russia for peace." *Neues Wiener Tageblatt:* "Although it is not now the time of diplomats, nevertheless it is a relief that the man retires upon whom rests the blame for the beginning of the war." *Reidispost:* "In every way, Sturmer will be more independent in his relations with Downing Street." Especially interesting is the lead article in *Neue Freie Presse* of July 25. Listen: "However Russified old Sturmer may be (*Laughter*), Prime Minister Sturmer is free of the illusions which led to war. He did not promise"—note gentlemen, "he did not promise never to make peace without Constantinople and the Straits. In Sturmer's person is a weapon which may be used as wished. Thanks to the policy of weakening the Duma, Sturmer has become a person who satisfies the secret wishes of the right, which never did want an alliance with England. He will not insist, as did Sazonov, that it is necessary to purge the Prussian military caste."

Whence comes the German and Austrian newspapers' conviction that Sturmer, carrying out the wishes of the right, will act against England and against the continuation of the war? From news in the Russian press. At just the same time the Moscow press carried a memorandum by the extreme right—again, gentlemen, the extreme right, always the extreme right (*Zamyslovski:* "And always it is a lie.")—a memorandum sent to headquarters in July before Sturmer's second trip. In this memorandum, it is stated that although it is necessary to fight on to final victory, still the war must be ended in due time. Otherwise, the fruits of victory will be lost in a revolution. (*Zamyslovski:* "The signatures! The signatures!") This is an old theme of our Germanophile, but it develops in a number of new attacks. (*Zamyslovski:* "The signatures! Read the signatures!")

Chairman: Deputy Zamyslovski please do not speak from your seat.

Miliukov: I cite the Moscow press. (*Zamyslovski:* "Slanderer, read the signatures! Do not slander!")

Chairman: Deputy Zamyslovski, I ask you kindly not to speak from your seat. (*Zamyslovski:* "Give us the signatures, slanderer.")

Chairman: Deputy Zamyslovski, I call you to order. (*Vyshevski:* "We demand the signatures, let us have no slander!") Deputy Vyshevski, I call you to order.

Miliukov: I have told you my source—Moscow newspapers, excerpts of which were published in foreign newspapers. I am passing on the impressions which determined the opinion of the foreign men about Sturmer's appointment. I say that foreign opinion was influenced by the reprinting of reports from Moscow newspapers, such as the memorandum sent to headquarters by the extreme right which contained the view that the war should be ended quickly. Otherwise there would be trouble for there would be a revolution. (*Zamyslovski:* "Slanderer! That is what you are!" *Markov:* "He only reported a known falsehood!" *Voice from the left:* "Are these statements from the seats to be permitted, Mr. Chairman?")

Chairman: I repeat, Deputy Zamyslovski, I call you to order.

Miliukov: I am not offended by Mr. Zamyslovski's expression. (*Voices from the left:* "Bravo!") I repeat that the old theme is now unfolding with new details. Who is planning revolution? This is who: apparently the city and rural unions, the military-industrial committee, the congresses of liberal organizations. These are the most indisputable signs of impending revolution. "The left parties," asserts the memorandum, "want to extend the war so as in the meantime to organize and prepare revolution." Gentlemen, you know that besides this memorandum, there are many other memoranda which develop the same thought. There is an act of indictment against city and rural organizations. There are many other acts of indictment, known to all. And so, gentlemen, this *idée fixe*—the revolution threatening on the left— this *idée fixe* the craze for which is obligatory for any new member of the cabinet (*Voices from the left:* "That is correct.")—everything is sacrificed to this *idée fixe:* the great national spirit, the war effort, the embryo of Russian freedom and even the stability of relations with our allies.

Of this last condition I was especially convinced when I continued my travel to London and Paris. There I found the first impression of Sazonov's retirement. I must tell you that this was an impression of some sort of vandalism. Just think, gentlemen, the bases of the present international situation date back to 1907. Gradually, slowly, as is always so, old suspicions, old prejudices, were eliminated, mutual trust was established and conviction grew in the stability of future relations. And, gentlemen, only on the grounds of this conviction in the stability of our relations, that they will continue so after the war, only on these grounds can the readiness develop to waive old views to the benefit of Russian national interests. Only on the basis of full trust in each other could that agreement be signed about which I spoke, the agreement on Constantinople and the Straits. The Allies displayed amazing resilience in the struggle and a readiness to endure sacrifice. In this they disappointed the expectations of our enemies, and they surpassed our own. And so it seemed that Russia was about to reap the fruits of its own labor and the fruits of two ministers of foreign affairs, at just the time of an extraordinary, rare, perhaps unique political situation, the beginning of which was marked by the activity of King Edward VII. And so, gentlemen, just at this moment, instead of experienced leaders enjoying personal confidence— and this is capital which is difficult to accumulate—"the blank sheet of paper" appears, an unknown person unfamiliar with the alphabet of diplomacy (*Voices from the left:* "Correct"), ready to serve any dubious influences.

Gentlemen, you will understand the consequences of this change. When Sazonov directed the ministry, people in England and France knew that when our ambassadors spoke, they spoke in the name of our government. What trust can there be in our ambassadors when Sturmer stands behind them? Naturally, gentlemen, the work of decades cannot be destroyed in one minute by the caprice of one individual. In this respect the Allied press, and ours too, was correct when it declared that Russian policy had not changed with the change in personality. But there are shades to the delicate work of diplomacy. There is lace work, and there is clumsy sewing. Lace work is possible only in a special situation, in especially favorable circumstances. Gentlemen, I saw the destruction of these most fine, most delicate fibers of the international fabric. I saw this destruction. It happened before my eyes in London and in Paris. That is what Mr. Sturmer has done, and perhaps it was not in vain that he did not promise the acquisition of Constantinople and the Straits. I asked myself, "By what recipe is this being done?"

I traveled on, to Switzerland, to relax, not to engage in politics. But there too those dark shadows followed me. On the shores of Lake Geneva, in Bern, I could not escape Mr. Sturmer's former department, the Ministry of Internal Affairs and the police department. Of course Switzerland is a place where all sorts of propaganda cross, where it is especially convenient to observe the machinations of our enemies, and it is understandable that the system of "special missions" should be especially well developed there. But among these are missions of a special sort, which call to themselves our at-

tention. People came to me and said, "Please ask in Petrograd what the no-
torious Rataev is doing here." "Ask why this unknown official Lebedev,
whom I do not know, has come here?" "Ask why these officials of the police
department are continuous visitors at salons of Russian ladies known for
their Germanophilism." It appears, gentlemen, that Mme. Vasilchikova has
her heirs and successors. I will not name the lady, who changed from a sympathy for an Austrian prince to a sympathy for a German baron, whose
salon on the Via Curia in Florence, and later in Montreux in Switzerland,
was known for the open Germanophilism of its mistress. Now this woman
has moved from Montreux here, to Petrograd. The newspapers mention her
name on solemn occasions. Upon my return through Paris I found still fresh
traces of her visit there. The Parisians were scandalized by this lady's German sympathies and, I must add with distress, by her relations with the Russian embassy, for which, however, our ambassador is not to blame. This is
the same woman who began Mr. Sturmer's diplomatic career, attempting a
few years ago to gain for him the post of ambassador to one of the secondary
states of Europe. I must say that these proposals were then found ridiculous
and they met with no success (Laughter).

What do I want to say with this? Gentlemen, I do not assert that I have
definitely found a channel of communications. But this is one of the links in
a whole fabric which ties very closely together known social circles. In order
to expose the ways and means of that propaganda about which Sir George
Buchanan recently spoke openly to us, we need a judicial investigation such
as was conducted against Sukhomlinov. When we indicted Sukhomlinov,
we did not have the facts which the investigation uncovered. We had just
what we have today—the instinctive voice of the entire country and its sub-
jective conviction (Applause). Gentlemen, perhaps I would not have decided to speak about each of my impressions, had there been no general picture, and in particular if there had been no confirmation such as that which
I received travelling from Paris to London (Cries from the left: "Aha!").
In Switzerland and Paris I posed myself a question: is there not, behind our
official diplomacy, some other diplomacy? Here I had to ask questions of
a different sort. Please excuse me if, in reporting such an important matter, I
cannot name my source. But if my information is true, Mr. Sturmer will
probably find traces of it in his archives (Rodichev: "He will destroy them").
I will pass over the Stockholm affair, which, as is known, predated the appointment of the present Minister of Internal Affairs and which made a painful impression upon our allies. I can speak about this impression, for I witnessed it. I would like to think that this was merely an event of the sort which
is well known among old acquaintances of Alexander Dmitrievich Protopopov—his inability to calculate the consequences of his own acts. (Voice
from the left: "A fine qualification for a minister!" Voice from the right:

"Your leader!") Fortunately, in Stockholm, he was no longer a member of the delegation since the delegation did not then exist. It was returning to Russia in groups. What Alexander Dmitrievich Protopopov did in Stockholm, he did in our absence. (*Markov:* "You did the same thing in Italy!"). Nevertheless, gentlemen, not having any personal suspicion, I cannot say just what role this affair played in that entrance hall, through which Alexander Dmitrievich Protopopov followed others on the way to a minister's chair (*Noise and voices from the left:* "Marvelous!"). Certainly they love that sort of thing there (*Voices from the right:* "What entrance?"). I will name these people for you: Manasevich-Manuilov, Pitirim, Sturmer. This is the party, whose triumph, in the words of the *Neue Freie Presse*, was the appointment of Sturmer. In any case, I have reasons to think that the proposals made by the German Counsellor Warburg to Alexander Dmitrievich Protopopov, were repeated. That is why I was in no way surprised when I heard from the lips of the British Ambassador the grave indictment that this same circle of persons wished to prepare the way for a separate peace.

Perhaps I am spending too much time on Mr. Sturmer? (*Voices:* "No, no!") But, gentlemen, it is upon him that the feelings and attitudes, of which I spoke earlier, have mainly concentrated. I think that these feelings and attitudes have prevented him from occupying this chair. He heard how we greeted his advent. We will hope that he will not return again. (*Applause from the left, noise and voices:* "Bravo!")

Yes, gentlemen, there is a great difference between that meeting of ours under Goremykin on July 15, 1915 or even in February 1916, and today's meeting. Those meetings are as different as the situation of our country. We could then speak of the country's organization through legislation of the Duma. Had we then been given the opportunity to enact the laws which we proposed and prepared, including the law on volosts, then Russia today would not stand so impotently before the question of the organization of food supplies. This was then. But now gentlemen, the question of legislation has receded. Now we see and we know that with this government we cannot legislate, just as we cannot lead Russia to victory with it. (*Voices from the left:* "True"). Previously we attempted to show that it was impossible to enter into battle with all the vital forces of the country, to conduct war within the country, if you are conducting war at the front. It is necessary to exploit the popular spirit for the achievement of national aims. Otherwise, only deadly oppression is possible, and this will only heighten the danger which the oppression seeks to avert. It now seems, gentlemen, that everyone is convinced that it is useless to go to them with arguments, useless because fear of the people, fear of their own country, is blinding their eyes and since their basic task has become that of ending the war as quickly as possible, even in a stalemate, just to be freed as quickly as possible of the necessity of seeking popular support (*Voices from the left:* "True!"). On February 23, 1916, I ended my speech with the assertion that we would no longer appeal to the "political wisdom of the government," and that I expect no answer to troubled questions from the present makeup of the cabinet. At that time, to some, my words appeared to be superfluous, pessimistic. But now we go further, and perhaps these words will be more clear, more bright. We say to this government, just as the declaration of the Bloc declared: we shall fight you; we shall fight with all legal means until you resign. (*Voices from the left:* "Correct! True!")

It is said that a member of the council of ministers—and Deputy Chkheidze heard this—upon hearing that now the State Duma was preparing to discuss treason, excitedly exclaimed, "Maybe I am a fool, but I am not a traitor" (*Laughter*). Gentlemen, the predecessor of this minister was undoubtedly a wise minister, just as the predecessor of the Foreign Minister was an honest minister. But they are no longer in the cabinet. And, as a practical question, gentlemen, isn't it all the same whether in a given case we have to deal with stupidity or with treason? When the Duma insists, ever more firmly, that the land must be organized for a successful struggle, and the government continues to assert that to organize the country means to organize revolution, and it deliberately prefers chaos and disorganization—what is this: stupidity? —or treason? (*Voice from the left:* "This is treason." *Adzhemov:* "Stupidity!" *Laughter*). And what's more, gentlemen, when in the midst of this general discontent and anxiety, the authorities calculatingly engage in stirring up popular outbreaks, that is they deliberately arouse unrest and outbreaks by means of provocations, is this being done consciously—or unconsciously? One cannot, therefore, blame the population if it comes to conclusions such as those, which I read here in the words of the chairmen of the provincial boards.

You must understand also why we have no other task than that which I have already outlined: to bring about the retirement of this government. You ask, how can we begin such a struggle in time of war? But gentlemen, they are only dangerous in time of war. They are dangerous to the war, and it is just for this reason, in time of war and in the name of the war, in the name of that very thing which brought us to unite, that we now struggle with them (*Voices from the left:* "Bravo!" *Applause*). Gentlemen, you understand that I could have no other theme today than this one. I cannot copy Deputy Chkheidze and take up our internal polemics. Today is not the time for that, and I shall make no reply to his references and attacks on me. The contents of the declaration read here will speak for me. We have many, very many different reasons to be dissatisfied with the government. If we have time, we will speak about them. But all the private reasons add up to this one general reason: the incompetence of the present makeup of the govern-

ment (*Voices from the left:* "Correct!"). This is the main evil, the victory
over which will be tantamount to winning the entire campaign (*Voices from
the left:* "True!"). And therefore, gentlemen, in the name of millions of
victims and of the streams of shed blood, in the name of the realization of
our national interest—which Sturmer does not promise us—in the name
of our responsibility before the people who sent us here, we will fight until
we achieve true responsibility in government as defined in three points of
our general declaration: a complete understanding by the members of the
cabinet of the most pressing tasks of the moment, their agreement and readiness to carry out the program of the majority of the State Duma, and their
obligation, not only in fulfilling this program but in all their work, to seek
the support of the majority of the State Duma. A cabinet which does not
satisfy these terms cannot have the confidence of the State Duma, and it must
resign. (*Voices:* "Bravo!" *Loud and prolonged applause from the left, the
center, and the left part of the right.*)

THE FEBRUARY REVOLUTION

*In February and March of 1917, the Tsarist regime was not overthrown;
it collapsed. In its stead arose a dual authority: a provisional government
organized by Duma liberals under the leadership of Miliukov, and a soviet
(council) of workers' deputies, made up of Socialists. The Socialists refused
the responsibilities of government, and the Provisional Government found
itself reigning but not ruling. Over all hung the heavy shadow of war. Miliukov sought to prosecute the war more vigorously, but the country was not
behind him. The Socialists found themselves then drawn into the Provisional
Government, but they too could find no answer to the problem of pursuing
internal reform while continuing to conduct a war which they did not know
how to end. In the fall of 1917, the Bolsheviks, Lenin's party, overthrew the
Provisional Government, which had proven unable to live up to the bold
promises of its first proclamation.*

Citizens!
The Provisional Committee of the members of the State Duma, with the
aid and sympathy of the troops and population of the capital, has triumphed
over the dark forces of the Old Regime to such an extent that it can now
proceed to organize a more stable executive power. Toward this end the

Source: *Izvestia*, No. 4, March 3, 1917.

Provisional Committee of the State Duma has appointed as ministers of the first public cabinet the following men whose past public and political life assures them the confidence of the country:

Chairman of the Council of Ministers and Minister of Internal Affairs, Prince G. E. Lvov.

Minister of Foreign Affairs, P. N. Miliukov.

Minister of War and Marine, A. I. Guchkov.

Minister of Finance, M. I. Tereshchenko.

Minister of Transportation, N. V. Nebrasov.

Minister of Commerce and Industry, A. I. Konovalov.

Minister of Education, A. A. Manuilov.

Over-Procurator of the Holy Synod, Vl. Lvov.

Minister of Justice, A. F. Kerensky.

In its immediate work the Cabinet will be guided by the following principles:

1. An immediate general amnesty in all political and religious cases, including terrorist acts, military revolts, agrarian offenses, etc.

2. Freedom of speech and press; freedom to form labor unions, to assemble, to strike. These political liberties should be extended to the army in so far as war conditions permit.

3. The abolition of all class, religious and national restrictions.

4. Immediate preparation for the calling of a Constituent Assembly— elected by universal, equal, direct and secret ballot—which shall determine the form of government and draw up a constitution.

5. The replacement of the police by a popular militia, with elected officers and subject to the organs of local self-government.

6. Elections to the organs of local self-government based on universal, direct, equal, and secret suffrage.

7. Military units which have taken part in the revolutionary movement shall not be disarmed or removed from Petrograd.

8. While strict military discipline is to be maintained in the lines and in the fulfillment of military service, soldiers shall have the same public rights granted to other citizens. The Provisional Government considers it necessary to add that it has no intention of using the war conditions to delay the realization of the above-mentioned reforms and measures.

President of the Duma, M. Rodzianko

President of the Council of Ministers, G. E. Lvov